*A Gestalt Institute
of Cleveland
publication*

THE COLLECTIVE SILENCE

THE COLLECTIVE SILENCE

*German Identity
and the Legacy of Shame*

EDITED BY

BARBARA HEIMANNSBERG

AND

CHRISTOPH J. SCHMIDT

Translated by

CYNTHIA OUDEJANS HARRIS

and

GORDON WHEELER

Jossey-Bass Publishers · San Francisco

This book was originally published as *Kollektive Schweigen* © 1988 Roland Asanger Verlag. Revised German edition © 1992 Edition Humanistische Psychologie.

 A Gestalt Institute of Cleveland publication

Substantial discounts on bulk quantities of Jossey-Bass books are available to corporations, professional associations, and other organizations. For details and discount information, contact the special sales department at Jossey-Bass Inc., Publishers. (415) 433-1740; Fax (415) 433-0499.

For sales outside the United States, contact Maxwell Macmillan International Publishing Group, 866 Third Avenue, New York, New York 10022.

Manufactured in the United States of America

The paper used in this book is acid-free and meets the guidelines for permanence and durability of the Committee on Production Guidelines for Book Longevity of the Council on Library Resources.

Library of Congress Cataloging-in-Publication Data

Kollektive Schweigen. English.
    The collective silence : German identity and the legacy of shame / Barbara Heimannsberg, Christoph J. Schmidt [editors] ; Cynthia Oudejans Harris, Gordon Wheeler [translators].
       p. cm. — (The Jossey-Bass social and behavioral science series)
    Includes bibliographical references and index.
    ISBN 1-55542-556-9 (acid-free paper)
    1. National socialism—Psychological aspects. 2. Children—Germany—History—20th century. 3. Children—Germany—Psychology. I. Heimannsberg, Barbara. II. Schmidt, Christoph J. III. Title. IV. Series.
DD256.5.K61613   1993
155.8'943—dc20   93–14265
                                                      CIP

FIRST EDITION
HB Printing   10 9 8 7 6 5 4 3 2 1   *Code 9395*

The Jossey-Bass
Social and Behavioral Science Series

CONTENTS

ACKNOWLEDGMENTS AND NOTE

We, the editors and translators of this book, chose to dedicate our translation to five of our German friends, three of whom are no longer living. All were profoundly anti-Nazi during the Hitler era. Two paid very dearly for their resistance to Hitler. Nazism caused them all great suffering. After the war they bore witness to us of the richness of German life as well as of the German language.

We are grateful to each other for the experience of working together, arguing, laughing, weeping. Our deepening intimacy with the material itself has become the ground of our own more profound encounter with these stories and the times of which they tell.

We are thankful to Edwin C. Nevis and James Kepner of the Gestalt Institute of Cleveland for their support throughout. We are grateful to Gardner Spungin of Gardner Press, who first brought this book to our attention, as well as to Rebecca McGovern of Jossey-Bass, who saw it through to completion. The German editors, Barbara Heimannsberg and Christoph J. Schmidt, who conceived this book and brought it to fruition, have continued to give us generous assistance.

Most important, we thank Leo Oudejans Harris, who read, commented, supported, and cooked while we were at work.

Our deepest thanks go to the original authors of these eleven chapters and to their clients/patients. Their courage and imagination gave us this book, which we can now share with you.

And a note on gender: in German as in English only the feminine case has a set of pronouns clearly its own, while by convention the masculine does multiple duty, covering collective and impersonal as well as masculine references. Obviously this convention is inadequate, confusing, and destructive to all sides. Unfortunately, no completely satisfactory alternative has yet emerged in English or German. In general, and with apologies to all concerned, we have tended to preserve the usage favored by each individual author in the essays which follow, improving on that usage where we could do so without sacrificing the clarity of the material.

— *Cynthia Oudejans Harris and Gordon Wheeler*

TRANSLATOR'S INTRODUCTION

What can we say, finally, to the Nazi Holocaust? A million children deliberately murdered, a great human culture swept from the face of the earth, and all of it in the context of a global war which took the lives of over fifty million human beings. What words can help us come to terms with numbers so unimaginable, suffering and horror on so sickening and so immense a scale? The face of absolute evil is a hideously grinning Medusa's head, which always threatens to turn our hearts and our tongues to stone. How then can we even approach the Holocaust, if the very sight is unbearable, and language itself is inadequate to hold the full weight of horror or to give form to our anguished wish that reality not be so?

Our bewilderment becomes worse, if that is possible, when we consider that the Judeocide itself was a significant military *diversion* from the overall Nazi war effort: SS "pacification" troops eventually amounted to a separate army of over half a million men, while Speer, crying out for supply trains for the front, was continually overridden by Himmler, the architect of the death camps. We want desperately to believe that evil in the world is only a kind of shortsightedness, a sort of ordinary selfishness run amok, and thus still open to rational influence, at least. But the Holocaust is plainly evil for its own sake, insane and not directed by any rational purpose, however heartlessly conceived. What words can capture the chill at the heart that comes with this realization or the paralyzing sense of a hidden flaw in human nature itself, which leave us mistrustful of our own thoughts and actions?

For the Holocaust also collapses the *projective theory of evil,* which Jung (himself shamefully late to see the true face of Nazism) identified as the central problem of our time. This was the comforting belief—itself based on denial of countless other atrocities—that evil was something that happened only in distant places, among faraway peoples unlike ourselves, without the enlightenment and benefits of Western Civilization (a term which, since the Holocaust, is impossible to use without irony). But the Judeocide happened right here, in our own neighborhood so to speak, among our own extended family of nations. When you add to this the fact that the liberation of the camps corresponded, generally by a matter of weeks, with the use of atomic weapons on the civilian population of Japan, then our prospects seem bleak indeed. If our capacity for evil is boundless and unrestrained, either by "civilization" or by some inherent human limit, and if our means of destruction are now limitless as well, then the grounds for hope seem vanishingly narrow. Our responsibility now, in the words of the biologist George Wald, is to life itself—life on the planet, and very possibly the only intelligent life in the universe. Unfortunately that responsibility does not seem to be in very reassuring hands. Small wonder then if we return over and over again to the silent sphynx of the mass graves of the Holocaust, still hoping for an answer to its riddle, or else oscillate wildly between obsession and agnosia, or again clutch at the straws of facile generalizations like national character, economic determinism, even fantasies of outright denial. The twin specters of Auschwitz and Hiroshima haunt the portals of the postwar world— our world—with Dante's warning, "Abandon hope all ye who enter here," written in flames over the gate.

Is there hope? How do we even approach the Holocaust, enter into some kind of new relationship to evil, as Jung said we must (since without any relationship, surely no change is possible), when that very approach threatens to turn the staunchest seeker to stone? Is there a way, or must we remain forever frozen with one arm upraised (whether to strike a blow or ward off the sight), like those statues which littered the ground around the Medusa's lair in the old tale?

I believe there is hope, and I believe it lies in another one of our most basic and defining human qualities, as deeply part of us as good and evil, hope and fear themselves. This is our uniquely human capacity and irrepressible human need to *tell our stories,* which shape and give meaning to our lives. The human being after all is the storytelling animal. We know ourselves and each other by the stories we hear and tell, orienting and connecting us, one to another, self to self, past to future, and future to past. Our stories are the link across the gulfs of time and individuality. Indeed, human trauma may be defined as the *blow which interrupts the story,* whether personal or collective, breaking the continuity of time and human relations, and thus blocking the ongoing formation of a meaningful whole. If a given injury can be encompassed within the frame of a meaningful story line, then we speak of stress or challenge or even tragedy, but not of breakdown or trauma. The person (or community) can nevertheless go on, and the resolution of the loss enters into the structure of identity, the ongoing creation of a personal or collective myth, in the best sense. This after all is the difference between character and pathology.

By this reckoning, the patient enters psychotherapy because of a loss or injury for which she has no words, which leaves her with a story that makes no sense, is unbearable to look at, has no role for her in it, or perhaps is repeated endlessly up to a certain point and then always breaks off. In psychotherapy she may learn to tell her life story in a different way—or perhaps to tell it for the first time, since she may not have had a listener before, and without a listener there is no meaningful speech. This is why psychotherapy always takes place interpersonally, as a dialogue between people, no matter what the stated program of the particular school of therapy may be. When the patient can tell the story in a way that makes sense to herself *and* to another person, then she is ready to leave therapy and get on with creating the story by living it, again or for the first time.

On the collective level, certainly the Nazi Holocaust is the example *par excellence* of such a break, and we return to it again and again as to an oracle, waiting for some answer, however Delphic, that will enable us to pick up the thread and go on. Our means of return are the stories that are given to us, and which we alternately treasure or hide away shamefully, embrace or shrink from, all depending on whether or not we feel an empathic echo, a community of other listeners (and tellers) who can help us bear the stories as they come. In the old myth, the goddess gives the hero, Perseus, a polished shield, which he can use as a mirror so as to approach the Medusa by indirection, and thus come close enough to grapple with the monster without being withered by its direct hypnotic stare. For us, each individual story, informed with its particular detail and feelings, is a mirror we can hold up to unspeakable horror, and yet find words. Seeing, after all, is private (and thus unbearable); telling is collective by definition, and somewhere in that shared participation lies the key to our survival.

First came the stories of the victims—Anne Frank, Primo Levi, Elie Wiesel, Bruno Bettelheim, Victor Frankl, and many others—breaking the silence, bearing the shame that is the inevitable legacy of victimhood, giving voice where no voice had spoken before, often in a language that had to be invented for the purpose. Then came other voices—warriors and allies, resisters and subverters on all sides, even perpetrators themselves (the seductive memoirs of Albert Speer come to mind, with their Nietzschean undertone: "'I did this,' says memory; 'I cannot have done this,' says pride . . . Memory yields."); ultimately even the diaries of Hitler himself—which quickly turned out to be a hoax, but what accounted for the immense momentary furor and excitement, if not the obsessive fantasy that somewhere in the bizarre private musings and ultimately banal ravings of the madman we would find the key to how he managed to touch so many other hearts in some desperate and perverted place? As if Hitler himself knew! As if the dream knew itself, and could explain itself to the dreamer, after the terrors of that one particular night were over. Or as if we did not have Hitlers enough around us, among us, within us, and thus had to look backward in time, again (always!) at some great and reassuring distance from ourselves.

And now we have the children. There are the children of the victims, as in Helen Epstein's moving chronicle, *Children of the Holocaust,* with all their struggle to find a place for themselves in a world shadowed by the enormity of their parents' suffering and the incomprehensible accident of survival. And now, in *The Collective Silence,* there are the children of perpetrators—including "accomplices . . . onlookers, bystanders," in the words of Sammy Speier, in his essay in the pages that follow. What both sides tell us is what we already know but somehow keep needing to forget, ultimately I believe for all the reasons outlined above: namely and simply that no man, no woman is an island unto him or herself. A break in the story—our common story, who we are, where we came from, where we belong in some larger whole of meaning—remains as a rupture in each individual psyche and is handed down unhealed (which is to say, not made whole) until such time as the rupture itself is faced and felt, and the whole cost is counted, and recounted, and grieved. Real change, as always, has to be grounded in a deeper encounter with what *is,* before we can move on to what could be, or should be, or is wished for. And the beginning of that encounter, at least, is in the stories—which means a willing storyteller in the presence of a willing audience, and enough support for all sides to risk talking and listening with an open heart. (That there are risks, and that support is required, are themselves issues which are sensitively discussed in Barbara Heimannsberg and Christoph J. Schmidt's introduction to the chapters which follow.) All this is the passionate human desire to know, which is at the Greek root of the words *story* and *history* (from *histor,* learned or wise), and the Latin *narrative* and *ignore,* also ultimately from the Greek *gnosis,* knowledge. What happens happens to each of us alone, but we come to know it only in the telling, which is to say together.

Against this passion, this knowing, stands the silence. The word in English, meaning "absence of sound," does not carry the full active feel of the original Latin *silere,* to keep quiet—or of the noun *Schweigen,* which is the same as the verb in German (the command "Schweig!" is not far from the English "shut up!") This is the silence which actively prohibits speaking and telling—the speech which, if given voice, would no doubt bring statues to life and make the stones weep. A *collective* silence—making us see that silence itself is never a purely private act, any more than speech is, but always a kind of agreement between people, born perhaps of guilt or fear but then sealed with some mutual bond of shame (guilt wants eventually to cry out; shame looks for ever new ways to hide).

That silence is the subject of this book. Informing the silence, challenging it, ultimately melting it are the stories. Stories we have not heard before—perhaps in part because we were not willing to hear them. Stories of the children and grandchildren of the Holocaust—and of their parents and grandparents as well, perpetrators, fellow travelers, in some cases resisters and victims themselves. Stories of families, then and now, where the lives of the sons and daughters—again in Nietzsche's words—"are the fathers' [and mothers'] secret revealed." This again is the essence of psychotherapy, and indeed all the authors here (and the German editors and the American translators) are themselves psychotherapists. But the subject of the book is far broader than psychotherapy itself—just as the Holocaust is broader than German history alone, and abuse (and the silence that follows abuse) belongs, sadly, to families everywhere. Moreover, by definition, all the authors are children of the Holocaust themselves, in one way or another (from various "sides," as Irene Wielpütz says, herself a "returnee," which is to say a child of a Jewish family who escaped, then returned to Germany after the war)—and with the greatest imaginable diversity of heritage, from the daughter of a high Nazi official to the children of Jewish emigres, and including both those who were born during or after the war and those who were themselves raised in the Hitler Youth movement and can give us an unparalleled glimpse into that world, so strange in some ways, so unexpectedly familiar in others. It is this fact, this doubling of perspective on the stories of the patients through the lens of the authors' own experiences, which lends an additional dimension of astonishing and moving richness to these essays, growing out of the creative interplay between the two, as the therapist/authors themselves struggle to respond to the material offered by their own patients, to deal with everything that is stirred within themselves by the stories they hear, and ultimately to wrest some creative meaning from their common heritage.

This struggle is at the heart of this powerful and unique book. At times the struggle is palpable on the page, as language itself almost seems to resist the attempt to render into words thoughts and feelings which are reaching for expression for the first time, without the support of a preexistent vocabulary and syntax (and where this is the case in the original, we have tried to preserve this quality in the translation). At all times we are gripped by that struggle and that interplay—subtle, powerful, sometimes astonishing—of the patients' stories, recounted here in gripping detail, with the therapists' own memories and feelings (horror, empathy, even denial and defensiveness) as the authors reach out for a new vision, a new diction that will encompass without numbing, empathize without relativizing, and move beyond a customary language whose limits are set by silence and shame.

For this is also a book about shame. The shame of the perpetrators, the shame of the victims—and the shame of the children, whose shame is a part, in the pregnant term of the analyst Christopher Bollas, of the "unthought known," all that which is felt, and known, and which colors the world, but which cannot be spoken. And the shame of the authors, which belongs in the realm of what analysts like to call the "countertransference"—everything that is stirred by the patient in the therapist. That limiting Freudian term, however, cannot begin to do justice to the complex and fertile interweaving here of patients' and therapists' stories, often in open dialogue, each inspiring and allowing and informing the other, until something new emerges, which is the promise, at least, of a new story, a "greater and less cautious truth" as Sammy Speier says, quoting the eminent analyst Alexander Mitscherlich. A truth which patient and therapist alike can take and use and build on, to go on with their own stories and lives. This is the therapeutic dialogue indeed, and of a kind that destructures the theoretical framework itself in which terms like "transference" and "countertransference" once held sway and were considered to be the complete account of everything that can happen in the "space between" therapist and patient. On the contrary, the view that emerges so vividly from these pages is of a real encounter from which—if it is a real encounter— neither patient nor therapist can come out unchanged.

For those who are interested, then, this theme of an ongoing challenge to established psychoanalytic orthodoxy forms another powerful subtext which runs all through this book. This challenge moves beyond the issue of "countertransference" (central though that issue is to the Freudian model) to questions of the nature of psy-

chotherapy, of relationship, and of interpersonal contact themselves—and in the process brings us to another question, which is
why this book is being brought out in English under the auspices of
a Gestalt press. To be sure, many or most of the therapist/authors in
the chapters ahead have trained in Gestalt psychotherapy and make
use of it in their work, often as a principal theoretical orientation.
But the book is in no way specifically or directly about Gestalt
therapy per se. Rather, it belongs to that rich and influential stream
of work challenging and revising the theoretical and methodolog-
ical assumptions of the once-dominant Freudian model. Central to
those assumptions and that methodology is the question of the role
of the therapist, whose ideal stance of "abstinence" (from any direct,
personal responsiveness) is often referred to and called into question
in the chapters that follow. That is, in the course of the meetings and
conversations between therapist and patient, in which (because of
the payment of a fee) the patient's needs are the subject of focus, is
there a "real encounter" between two (or more) people taking
place—or is the encounter only imagined, in a sense, by the patient
(as transference theory would have it, properly understood and taken
to its logical conclusion)? To be sure, as in any encounter between
people, the felt realities of the past are entering into, and significantly coloring, the felt reality of the present, often in ways
unknown or only imperfectly known to one or both parties. And certainly in psychotherapy (unlike most encounters between people),
this fact itself, with all its unfolding implications, is explicitly taken
up for discussion, examination, even experimentation. Indeed, that
discussion and those experiments (whether or not they are formally
labeled in that way, as in Gestalt work) are the essence of any psychotherapy—beginning with the unlikely interpersonal experiment
of coming to therapy in the first place. But is this confusion, if you
will, of felt realities, this "transference" of the past onto the present
encounter, all that is taking place—or is there also a significant and
significantly felt *new* encounter between two sentient human beings
also going on in the room, within the structure and the subject
matter of the psychotherapeutic discourse? Is everything transference (and not just within the therapy hour)? Or is not every
encounter structured in some way by a *tension* between the felt and
perceived realities of the past—on both sides—and the perceived
and possible realities of the present moment?

This question is at the heart of the critique which has been aimed
at the classical Freudian model almost from its beginnings by a
whole series of more relational and "present-centered" perspectives

—including prominently, for the past four decades or so, the accumulating literature of the Gestalt model. Put in these terms, the question seems almost to answer itself; but note that the answer given, one way or another, will have enormous implications for the conduct of psychotherapy, the kinds of questions the patient can put to the therapist, the kinds of answers the therapist can and will give—and ultimately, then, the kinds of stories the patient can and will create and tell (since knowing your listener, as we have suggested above, is crucial to the kind of non-self-censorship and supportive conditions required for facing difficult and abusive [and thus shameful] material in a way that allows a new resolution, a new gestalt, to form).

To be concrete, as Sammy Speier is in his brilliant essay, "The Psychoanalyst Without a Face: Psychoanalysis Without a History" (in German, *gesichtslose,* faceless, and *geschichtslose,* historyless; a beautiful play on words which points up the essential unity between the identity of the individual and the contextuality of the group): suppose that you are a patient in therapy, or better yet, an analytic candidate in a training analysis in postwar Germany. And suppose you fall to wondering, what was your training analyst doing, do you suppose, back during the Nazi years? This person is a senior professional in the field, your mentor and your guide, and simultaneously your doctor, your healer as well. He (or she) must have been doing something! And suppose you screw up your courage and ask. What if the response is (and remember, you are being graded, in a sense, as well as presumably healed): "You aren't curious about me the analyst at all (since I am not really here, as myself, but only transferentially, as your father, mother, etc.)—but actually about your own parents. *And*—you are not actually curious about their politics either, but about their sex life! This encounter, after all, is not truly real, but only a screen for other encounters, other relationships, which were themselves only the elaborations of your drives, your 'instincts and their vicissitudes.'"

You accept this answer (what choice do you have—your future livelihood depends on it, as well as your continued acceptance in a relationship you have come to depend on). And thus you are doubly interpreted and doubly abused—and doubly removed from the immediacy of the present relationship in a way that curiously recapitulates the projective or distancing relationship to abuse which we encountered above, with reference to Nazism itself. Thus shame sets the seal (again) on the door of silence, and abuse within the walls of the therapy office goes unchallenged, since the doctor—by virtue of not really being there as a person at all, fallible and available for confrontation and dialogue—is always right. And note the implications here for the whole sordid spectacle of doctor-patient abuse, including the sexual, the revelation of which is one of the sorriest and at the same time one of the most salutary aspects of the current therapeutic scene. If people—patients—have a voice, then they are well placed to defend themselves against abuse. But without a "real" audience, no real voice, no real discourse can develop and be sustained. These are the dynamics of the silence-abuse-silence model, so eloquently articulated in the pages that follow, by which silence itself is understood in a new way as the precondition as well as the consequence of abuse. And these are the ways in which the classical therapeutic model lends itself, in tragic irony, to the perpetuation of that silence and that abuse.

Speier's is perhaps the most theoretical of the chapters that follow—though not by that token impersonal or merely abstract. At the other extreme is Irene Anhalt's courageous and wrenching memoir, "Farewell to My Father," which deals only with her personal memories and her personal struggle as a human being to bridge the unbridgeable and forge a whole self out of a heritage made up of irreconcilable pieces. To read this chapter is to be gripped with a sorrow beyond words and then to marvel in gratitude to the author for the gift of those words, simple and elegiac, which give you that shared experience. It is humbling to translate such a piece; if, as Frost observed, poetry is what is lost in translation, then you can only imagine the full beauty of the original.

Lying between these two treatments of all these themes are eleven other chapters, most of them weaving back and forth between past and present, personal material and that of the authors' patients, students, trainees, family members, colleagues, adversaries, and friends. The range is vast, the material unfailingly gripping. Each reader will have her or his own favorites, particular authors he or she wants to know personally, so fully and unreservedly do they offer themselves and step off the page. One of mine is Richard Picker, a wise and somehow distinctively Viennese voice, who opens up for us—among many other riches—the story of his own youth in the elite training school for Nazi youth. Who will listen to this story, he wonders aloud; who can bear to hear it? The existence of this book is the answer.

To continue with the remaining chapters, more or less in their order, we have another story of childhood training as a Nazi youth leader—and another personal favorite of many early readers—Heidi

Salm's "I Too Took Part." In one of her stunning case histories, she works with three generations of women of one family, identifying and supporting each in turn: a grandmother of Salm's own age and background, a mother estranged from her own mother, and a young daughter who, without Salm's wise and personally courageous intervention, was well on her way to becoming yet another victim to the Nazi past—and to that silence which is so deep a part of its legacy. In confronting and supporting the grandmother, Salm must confront her own past in a new way, and the quiet heroism with which she faces the task is almost unnoticeable under the simplicity of her approach.

Margarete Hecker and Almuth Massing both take us deep into the *belief systems* of Nazi families—beliefs and assumptions which persist in families today, explicitly and implicitly, and thus continue to take a toll, sometimes a deadly one, on the lives of family members. Both emphasize the crucial importance of *finding out what actually happened,* through interviews, family records, public and private documents, as an essential part of undoing the silence and addressing the break. In this they parallel much new writing in this country on the subject of helping victims of sexual and other abuse (see for example the work of James Kepner [1992], which focuses on the need for support in *bearing the unbearable reality* as a crucial first task in moving through healing to growth).

Wolfgang Bornebusch takes us into a world of stories out of a different setting, an educational encounter group with the explicit intent of exploring and coming to terms with the shared German legacies of Judaism, Nazism, and the Holocaust. His provocative title, "How Can I Develop on a Mountain of Corpses?," illustrates the depth and moving frankness with which the group approached its task. Here as all through the book the pervasiveness and dynamics of the Nazi legacy (guilt, shame, phobias, and self-restrictions of every kind) are brought to living reality in the stories of the participants—in many parts of which we will recognize ourselves.

Waltraud Silke Behrendt takes up the question of the therapist's own personal blocks—in this case, her own—and their role in supporting or blocking the patient's emerging story. In the process she directly confronts the question which captures the first reaction of many people to the whole topic of this book: namely, why attempt to understand the mind and world of the perpetrator at all—especially if that understanding might seem to threaten our own clear faculties of judgment and condemnation? Her answers to these questions are both provocative in their personal exposure and persuasive in their urgency.

Helm Stierlin approaches the same issues from the perspective of family roles and intergenerational silence and dialogue—a dialogue which, as he shows, is as essential to the older generation as to the younger. Again we have the *stories*—and not merely the abstraction of theory—to show us in living terms how the break in history (which is to say, the collective story) is recapitulated and carried forward as a rupture in personal identity, and how the latter cannot be healed without addressing the former. And again we have before us the dynamics of a whole dimension of life—the interpenetration of the personal and the collective—which is not adequately addressed by the classical Freudian perspective and may even be perpetuated and frozen as a problem by therapeutic work under that model.

Barbara Heimannsberg, to whom we are indebted (along with Christoph J. Schmidt) for the original collecting and editing of this book, makes a further contribution here with her chapter on the "work of remembering," and the neglected question of the relationship of history to identity. Since the orthodox psychoanalytic approach has come in for such extensive and incisive criticism through many of these chapters (and in therapeutic discourse in general in recent years), it is well to be reminded by Heimannsberg's work that remembering itself is not just an act or an event, but a process of work in its own right—and that it is the psychodynamic perspective that first explained this fact to us and embedded it in a dynamic context.

With Irene Wielpütz, as noted above, we add the voice of a "returnee"—those few German Jews who emigrated, survived, and then returned to a land that was after all their heritage and their home for centuries past. In the course of "not writing" her assigned article, she sheds the most eloquent light on all these issues from a unique point of view. Again, her willingness to expose the struggle for articulation itself on the page, across a full year of deep personal anguish, is a pure gift of trust to the reader—and one that is in no way lessened by the grace and balance of the finished product.

In a postscript to her beautiful "work of remembering," added in 1992, Wielpütz takes us forward into a post-reunification world, the "new Germany," which has been so widely welcomed and so widely feared, and which now occupies such a dominant and problematic place in the order or disorder of today's world. More than anything else, it is the emergence of this powerful new state which lends such urgency to the issues and questions of this book, moving them from a discourse of moral and therapeutic concern to one of immediate practical and political necessity.

Next comes Dan Bar-On, like Wielpütz the child of Jewish refugees from Hitler, but unlike her a lifelong citizen of the state of Israel. With his courageous and provocative book *Legacy of Silence* (1989), Bar-On took his place as an eloquent new voice in the emerging field of second- and third-generation post-Holocaust studies—a field which is changing our understanding not just of the horrors of Nazism and their aftermath, but of trauma, recovery, human development, identity, and that most urgent question of all the pressing issues of the world today: namely, the overarching ecological question of the relation of the part to the whole, the individual to society, the self to history.

Finally, we have Gunnar von Schlippe, pastor, father, psychotherapist, and deeply thoughtful theologian, who emerged from Russian detention at the age of eighteen, already a veteran of war and Party, to encounter a nation, a way of life, and a personal identity in shambles. Psychotherapy has long taught us about relieving neurotic guilt, Schlippe writes; it has done nothing to help us deal with guilt that is real. In extended letters to his son, he makes us witness to a deeply erudite exercise in theological creativity, as well as to a deeply personal history of combat and resistance, courage and self-deception, humiliation, shame, and the dawning horror and disbelief of a sensitive young German adolescent struggling to maintain some sense of self in the face of the opening of the camps. Among the other riches of this piece, he gives me the first tangible, fully believable experience I have had of what it meant, as an ordinary young German of that era, *not to know,* and what attitudes and defenses permitted him to live under the Nazis, whom he abhorred without ever openly opposing.

And last of all the afterword, by my cotranslator, Cynthia Oudejans Harris, who combines, as I do, a deep sense of the urgency of our common need to *face* the Holocaust, with a lifelong appreciation of that great German humanist culture which Hitler took it as his mission to destroy. But where the animating passion of my work has always been the question of *relationship,* for Cynthia it has long been the question of *language.* These two passions—and this urgency and appreciation—are all expressed together in the stories in this book.

Today we have a new Germany, and possibly a new world. And

yet the injustice and suffering of the world have not changed, while the destructive powers of victim and perpetrator alike only increase from year to year. And everywhere we hear the siren song of the projective theory of evil, which is the very heart of Nazism, deluding and enticing us away from the real tasks, sacrifices, and hard choices to be made if the world is ever to be different from what it has been and survive. In the end, we have only our stories to guide us. If it is the curse of our human imagination to be moved by hatred and fear of each other, our redemption lies in the fact that we cannot *listen* to one another, really listen, without being softened, connected, and changed. Here are the stories, the voices. We have only to listen to find the way.

CAMBRIDGE, MASSACHUSETTS   *Gordon Wheeler*
JUNE 1993

THE EDITORS

Barbara Heimannsberg, born 1947 on the lower Rhine; studied sociology, psychology, and ethnology at the University of Heidelberg, receiving an M.A., 1975; worked for many years with substance abusers in therapeutic communities; received psychotherapeutic training at the Fritz Perls Institute, Düsseldorf; maintained private practice of psychotherapy in Frankfurt am Main since 1982.

Christoph J. Schmidt, born 1947, grew up in Bremen; studied Protestant theology, philosophy, and pedagogy in Münster, Munich, Heidelberg, and Frankfurt am Main; has worked as editor since 1978; received psychotherapeutic training at the Fritz Perls Institute, Düsseldorf; maintained private practice of psychotherapy in Frankfurt am Main since 1982.

THE TRANSLATORS

Cynthia Oudejans Harris, born 1923 in San Francisco; B.S. in modern European history, Radcliffe College, 1945; studied at University of Salzburg and University of Munich, 1949 to 1956; M.D. Case Western Reserve University, 1963; psychiatric training, 1963 to 1966; a founder of the Gestalt Institute of Cleveland; extensive clinical practice and teaching experience in psychiatry and psychotherapy in the United States and Central America; currently a translator and writer living in northeastern Connecticut with her husband, Leo.

Gordon Wheeler, born 1944 in Texas; A.B. in history and literature, Harvard University, 1967; studied at the University of Munich; MAT in early childhood studies, Harvard University, 1970; M.Ed. and Ph.D. in counseling and clinical psychology, Boston College, respectively 1974 and 1988, with additional training at the Gestalt Institute of Cleveland; currently in private practice of psychotherapy with children and adults; teaches the Gestalt model widely in both Europe and the United States; author of several works of fiction and of *Gestalt Reconsidered: A New Approach to Contact and Resistance* (1991); lives in Cambridge, Massachusetts, with his five children.

THE TRANSLATORS

THE CONTRIBUTORS

Irene Anhalt, born 1940 in Berlin; studied German and psychology; received her psychotherapeutic training at the Fritz Perls Institute, Düsseldorf; works in private practice in Berlin.

Dan (Bruno) Bar-On, born 1938 in Haifa, son of a family which had emigrated from Germany in 1933. After 25 years as a member of Kibbutz Revivim, where he worked as fruit plantation manager, organizational development consultant, and therapist, he began university studies in psychology in 1970; received Ph.D. at the Hebrew University in Jerusalem in 1981. Occupied since 1985 with research into the effects of National Socialism on subsequent generations. His book *Legacy of Silence* (1993), has appeared in translation in Germany.

Waltraud Silke Behrendt, born 1944 in a small city in western Germany; in addition to studies in theology and philosophy, concentrated in psychology (graduated 1968); training in behavioral and speech therapy as well as in Gestalt psychotherapy and integrative psychotherapy (Fritz Perls Institute, Düsseldorf); active in social psychiatry and for the past ten years in the Speech and Hearing Department of the Hamburg University Hospital.

Wolfgang Bornebusch, born 1945 in Dinslaken; studied Protestant theology in Bethel, Tübingen, Munich, and Bonn; since 1974 has been a minister in Schermbeck/Lower Rhine; received training in Theme-Centered Interaction (TCI) and in couples and family therapy; counsels in a Protestant welfare center for marital and other problems; deals with the history of the former Jewish community in his town, an important part of his parish work.

Margarete Hecker, born 1932 near Greifswald; studied social work in Munich as well as education, history, and sociology at the Berlin Free University; trained in family therapy in Munich and Philadelphia; for the past twenty years has been engaged in the undergraduate training as well as the advanced education of social workers at the Protestant Professional High School in Darmstadt.

Almuth Massing, born 1941; psychoanalyst and analytical family therapist, active as the Physician in Charge of the Division for Psychotherapy and Social Therapy at the Center for Psychological Medicine at the University of Göttingen; has research interests and publications dealing with sociohistorical change and its effects on individual and family life.

Richard Picker, born 1933 in Vienna; NAPOLA Traiskirchen, 1942 to 1945; educator; Roman Catholic pastor, 1961 to 1968. Professor of religious education; student pastor; trained in psychoanalysis, group dynamics, Gestalt therapy; worked in residential treatment; presently in private practice, Vienna.

Heidi Salm, born 1922 in Hamburg; graduated from high school in 1940; trained as gymnastics physiotherapist; active in drug counseling, 1969 to 1974; advanced training in TCI, psychodrama, Gestalt therapy, bioenergetics, and since 1975, in family therapy; training therapist at the Institute for Family Therapy, Weinheim; private practice in family therapy, Heidelberg.

Gunnar von Schlippe, born 1927 in Riga; 1943 to 1945 soldier and Russian prisoner; 1947 to 1952 studied Protestant theology in Bethel and Göttingen; since 1955 Protestant minister in Dortmund, Münster, and Hamburg; since 1966 psychotherapeutic training (in individual psychology), with advanced training in TCI, psychodrama, and bioenergetics; since 1970 director of a psychotherapeutic center in Hamburg; retired 1987.

Sammy Speier, born 1944 in Israel; psychoanalyst (German Psychiatric Society, International Psychiatric Association) in private practice in Frankfurt; publications deal with peace research, psychoanalytic training, and Jewish identity in the West German Federal Republic.

Helm Stierlin, born 1926 in Mannheim; studied medicine and philosophy in Heidelberg, Zürich, and Freiburg; received Ph.D., 1951, in Heidelberg and M.D., 1955, in Münich. Worked, 1955 to 1974, at various psychiatric clinics and research institutes, including in the United States; trained as psychoanalyst; since 1974 Medical Director of the Department for Basic Psychoanalytic Research and Family Therapy at the University of Heidelberg.

Irene Wielpütz, born 1947 in Bogota, Colombia, daughter of Jewish emigrants; living in Germany since 1957; has studied psychology in Cologne; began psychotherapeutic training in 1973; was a training therapist at the Institute for Family Therapy in Weinheim until 1987; is a psychotherapist in private practice in Cologne.

THE COLLECTIVE SILENCE

PSYCHOLOGICAL SYMPTOMS OF THE NAZI HERITAGE
Introduction to the German Edition

Barbara Heimannsberg
and
Christoph J. Schmidt

The father's silence becomes the son's
speech, and often I found the son to
be the father's secret revealed.
Friedrich Nietzsche, 1883

A central concern in psychotherapy is dealing with one's own history and with the individual and collective development which extends across generations: Who am I? Where do I come from? What influences have marked me? In this effort, psychotherapy today must deal with the rupture in civilization of our Nazi past. In confronting our own history and that of our parents and grandparents, we can feel the hole in our own identity even if we were born after the events. How can we regard a house as our own and settle down comfortably in it when we know there is a corpse in the cellar? What are our possibilities for personal integration or integrity if we do not split off much that is sinister and ominous and bracket it out of our consciousness?

A widespread symptomatic pattern today is the silence within families. There is no longer any innocent tradition of storytelling between the generations. The questions of the children to their parents—"What did you do back then?"—go unanswered, and the children have learned early on not to ask such touchy questions in the first place. Horror, guilt, and suffering are all hard to bear, scarcely to be named or spoken of. But silence is paralyzing, and things which have been kept secret and repressed return in other forms. Often in psychotherapy we encounter people with a peculiar emotional numbness and emptiness; they can tell us nothing about the causes and precipitants of their sudden anxiety attacks, and if asked about their parents, they reveal a broad field of ignorance. In the psyches of those born after 1945, diffuse anxiety and feelings of guilt can be the half-erased traces of the Nazi past.

Here we encounter the paradox that on the one hand, since concrete reminiscences are not permitted, the Third Reich seems infinitely far away; on the other hand, since the memories are repressed, they are very much present beneath the surface, showing themselves in fear of the sinister and in secret fascination. The passionate insistence with which the criminal Nazi ideology and the incomprehensible Nazi crimes are altogether separated from the everyday world and "normal" life histories in the Third Reich in no way contradicts this fascination, nor does it contradict the defiant idealizations which surface again and again. The threatening, the guilt inducing, the humiliating, and the monstrous all coexist and are entangled with an innocuous naiveté. It is hard to bear this coexistence and to bring this entanglement into awareness.

When specific personal entanglements are involved, there is often a collusion of silence, whether in family discussions, legal proceedings, historical studies—or in psychotherapy. In psychotherapy there is a tendency to blind oneself to ethical categories because of our understandable reluctance to indoctrinate or to moralize. Actual guilt receives little attention in therapy, compared to neurotic guilt feelings and blaming. But guilt is a fact in relationships between people and is not merely a psychic introject and the differentiation between normality and crime is an ethical matter, not an empirical one.

It is certainly true that the entanglements in guilt and the psychic consequences of the Third Reich (the conflicts, the traumas, the identity crises) should have been central themes in psychotherapy after 1945. The identity problems, which were to be expected, afflict particularly those who were not yet grown at the time: the girls who were in the BDM* (League of German Girls), the Hitler Youth, *pimpfe,** the NAPOLA* students. During the years when their own identities were being formed, those young people drank in the spirit of National Socialism and gave their youthful enthusiasm to the values of their own time. An entire generation seems stamped in essential ways by the Nazi period; many Nazi values were retained and unconsciously passed on to the next generation—as were the traumas.

---

* See Glossary, here and wherever an asterisk appears. —Trans.

The fiction of the "zero hour"*—May 1945 (the date of the Nazi surrender)—shrouds the events that preceded it and erases its social and psychic traces. In addition, this "zero hour" fiction levels out the unique, individual, and indeed quite varied experiences of that historical moment: for some it was the hour of "liberation," for others the hour of "collapse." Depth psychology seems to have clung to the "zero hour" fiction even though the social/analytic diagnosis of failure to grieve was made long ago, above all by Alexander and Margarete Mitscherlich (1967). This phenomenon is analogous to the minimal interest on the part of professional groups in investigating how the Nazi ideology has permeated daily life since 1945.

Assuredly, none of the various schools of psychotherapy consciously wants to neglect the historical context or to wipe out the Nazi past, but wherever possible, they overlook how profoundly the Nazi ideology and the Nazi feeling-world continue to permeate our daily reality. National Socialism is not only context and background; it is itself psychic reality and part of interpersonal relations. The experiential world of the Third Reich, with all the things that seemed self-evident at the time, leaves behind effects which can easily cause development in a direction quite opposite to conscious ideological positions, just as in those days the enthusiasm of the masses grew in part out of an underlying receptivity for certain rituals and images and was by no means only the expression of rationally conceived political decisions. There is no reason to think that this receptivity has ceased to exist. Indeed, it continues to lead its own peculiar life, quite apart from the official standards of political education.

Alongside the enlightened critical rhetoric about National Socialism, there exists a world of Nazi feeling, whose naive, enthusiastic expression is rightfully taboo, in light of the mass murders and death camps. But what happens to these subliminal traces when they are not raised to the level of speech and consciousness? We sense them occasionally behind a relative impoverishment of feeling and in the rigid, lifeless language in which the Third Reich is spoken of. It is important not only to analyze spontaneous words and expressions but also to examine in-depth the common usages in our language and the unconscious thoughts and meanings which they reflect. It is productive to explore ideas from the Nazi era, and it is therapeutically necessary to bring to consciousness the meaning of these ideas and the feelings they evoke. It is also necessary to encourage the authentic expression of the client's own ideas about these matters in the present.

Imaginative therapeutic interventions, reconstructions of past scenes in the present, and guided focusing on affect are all helpful in making unconscious struggles available to consciousness, thereby opening up the possibility of reexperiencing the great enthusiasm for the Nazis and their obsessions. But without an ethical grounding of our own—a background against which the acceptable can be integrated and the unacceptable can be rejected—how can we work through all that the client has experienced? To do that, we require a differentiated language which allows us to move beyond demonizing cliches and also beyond the terms in which National Socialism saw itself. We who were born after the war know the tenor of war stories: the language is technical and uninvolved as long as the talk is of shootings, and then it turns nostalgic and sentimental in the gushing about comradeship. Between these two extremes lie worlds of confusion, mystification, and attempts to ease the burden.

Uncertainty and irritability frequently characterize the atmosphere when people talk in public about the Nazi past. For this reason, a groping approach is far better suited to this subject matter than a facile formulation based on cliches. Talking, as such, is not healing; language can make us forget, repress, hide, wound. But if we recognize that the house of our consciousness and identity is built on the foundation of language, then therapy can become a creative dialogical process, embracing metalinguistic communication as well as nonlinguistic expression, and may unfold in its healing power.

In this context, where do we stand as psychotherapists with our work? What language is available to us in the face of this widespread silence? Perhaps in the diagnostic process we should include and emphasize questions about the effects of the Nazi period. To what degree can psychic engrams out of the Nazi time be recognized and known—even by those born after the war—for what they are? And if the engrams are not recognizable, what is it that disguises them or makes it so hard for us and our patients to see them?

In this volume, materials from practicing psychotherapists are brought together which illuminate this complex from very varied perspectives. There are practical contributions from the realm of psychotherapy as well as several autobiographical essays about the vestiges of the Nazi time and the psychic injuries which followed it, and about successful or unsuccessful attempts at coming to terms with them. As editors we have had our eyes primarily on the children and grandchildren of active participants in the Third Reich and of convinced Nazis, since this is where the taboos are particularly virulent and the working through especially difficult. This became very evident to us in the difficulty we had finding collaborators for this volume: we wrote or spoke to about sixty people. Many of the therapists we approached—and we usually knew ahead of time that they had something to offer on this theme—were unwilling or unable to speak out and make a contribution. Others didn't receive their patients' permission to write about their stories. (It goes without saying that, in the cases presented here, patients' names and personal data have been made unrecognizable.) And several of the texts printed here are the result of unexpectedly laborious struggle, since the authors were confronted with some of their own wounds and taboos while writing.

Our interest as editors of this book lies in the exploration of each individual's own contribution to the creation of taboos and the corresponding speechlessness, as well as a possibly undetected secret fascination. In the course of dealing with the texts which were sent in, and in our editorial work, we sometimes had problems with particular terms and formulations (especially in the case of authentic descriptions of experiences), which sometimes seemed to us a return to Nazi ideology. This is the expression of our own bias and leads to a further paradox: on the one hand, the requirement of authenticity, and on the other, that of renouncing Nazi language. To overcome the ongoing unconscious heritage of guilt or injury, we seek to help our patients achieve consciousness through language—which is to say, through a language of their own—even if there are no simple answers. As for ourselves, we seek neither to blame nor to assign guilt, nor do we wish real guilt to be made to seem innocuous. In psychotherapy we must shed light on this guilt in a dialogical process so that, even if we ourselves were not among the guilty, we may assume the responsibility for our own history.

Editors' Additional Remarks on the Publication of the Second German Edition

Some four years have passed since the first edition of this book appeared in the fall of 1988. This relatively short span was a time of dynamic and rapid-fire change. Familiar political constellations, enmities, and ideological labels have been shifted or dissolved. The East-West conflict was so all-determining in the post-war period, politically, socially, and economically, that with the dissolution of the old power relationships, some (in transatlantic perspective) were declaring the "end of history." Europe was restructured, and at the same time we were seeing a resurgence of regionalism and nationalism.

But the disappearance of the wall which divided Germany does not erase the boundary in the mind. The internal image, the inner topography, is still bipolar, just as the past is bipolar: the Nazi past, in the eastern view and mentality, remains the past of the "other" side; reunification has not changed that. Meanwhile in the West, the challenge of the opening of the files of the East German secret police, or "Stasi," has come into the foreground as the past of the "other" side.

From a West German perspective, it is not that two "Germanys" have been reunited, but rather that new provinces have been added to the old. The fall of the wall was first greeted with euphoria, as the reunification enlarged one's "own country" toward the East, leading to new territorial claims and an expanded field of economic activity. And yet the sense of responsibility for the new territory has not kept pace with this expansionist drive.

Geographical names which had formerly been included in a wholesale "over there" now became more common. And it is true that there was a rapprochement of lifestyle and habits. But in many respects the people of the other side were not taken in as part of "us," but rather remained "the others." And the national "we" was then asserted all the more aggressively against asylum seekers and foreign workers.

Of additional concern is the phenomenon and paradox that on the one hand, the shared past of National Socialism is not remembered and reflected on as a heritage to be worked through together, but rather is lost in the mist of a seemingly distant time—while on the other hand the ideological content and symbols of "back then" are taken up ever more vigorously. To be sure, the increase in racist expression and violence is experienced as distressing to the majority of the German people, but on the whole the tendency toward aggressive self-assertion and chauvinism is underestimated, not overestimated, in its significance as a symptom of underlying developments.

If there is indeed such a thing as a collective German identity, then historical consciousness has to mean seeking out the traces of the Nazi experience in this identity, reflecting critically on them, and keeping the memory of these things alive.

Reactions to the first edition of this book were varied. As a result, additional material was taken into the second, expanded edition, which was undertaken by Edition Humanistische Psychologie (EHP), with our grateful appreciation.

Not the least of the reactions and responses were those of the editors and authors themselves; examples include the additional material from Irene Wielpütz and new contributions to the second edition. We experienced on the one hand a deepened sensitivity to our own constraints, blind spots, or prejudices in the face of this material, and on the other hand a growing attentiveness to these particular problematic constellations in therapy. The following additions to this expanded edition also bear witness to this growing sensitivity.

Dan Bar-On has been conducting research in Germany these past years through interviews with the children of Holocaust perpetrators. He presents here one aspect of his findings; namely, the question of the nature of the morality of the perpetrators themselves and of their children—a morality which he terms "paradoxical." Barbara Heimannsberg is concerned with the problems of identity, of memory work, and of collective consciousness in Germany.

The subject of National Socialism is not closed and cannot be closed. Indeed, with the new turn of historical events, it is again current, in a new way.

1

PSYCHOTHERAPY AND THE NAZI PAST
A Search for Concrete Forms

Richard Picker

I would like to offer some preliminary remarks having to do with the terms in which the themes are cast: "psychotherapy" seems clear enough to be useful, but what about "Nazi past"? This term refers to people still living, particularly in the German-speaking states of Central Europe, who were the witnesses of the times (among them former Nazis, their victims, and others who were involved), as well as their children and grandchildren. In these families there is a palpable relationship between the present and the Nazi past. The Nazi time belongs to the recent past; there is no feeling of distance here, as there is with other historical pasts. If any sense of distance is felt, then it must be from some other cause. Very often, however, all subjective distance melts away.

How past *is* the Nazi past? This is a question which concerns many people in these times, myself included. For my contribution here, this means that I do not know how to come at my topic in such a way that it is not influenced, or even engulfed altogether, by the Nazi past itself. From what standpoint can I survey the phenomenon of Nazi past without being forced to discover that my standpoint itself is a part of that same phenomenon? Thus I am left with the possibility of a concretely subjective approach and a concrete report about how the Nazi past emerges into present experience, and how the process of that emergence and that encounter takes shape.

My approach begins with my awareness that I live in one of the cradles of Nazism, in Vienna, here in the city where Hitler indulged his youthful fantasies, where the cobblestones of the Linzerstrasse still exist, along which he passed in his Mercedes at the time of his triumphal entry into the city in 1938. Back then, after the hours-long entry march of German troops was over, there stood the "Bavarian Relief Train," not far from my home. There, hungry Viennese received a free bowl of German army rations. Although my parents were not poor, we went along with many others to the field kitchen of this special train to take a "German meal," the "brotherly offering from the Reich," a sort of holy communion with "Greater Germany."* We passed over this exact same cobblestone pavement, which was to outlast the war years ahead, the occupation after the war, the reconstruction period, the economic flowering of Vienna, the tourist invasion. . . .

And perhaps these stones were here long before that, as was the famous view of St. Stephen's Cathedral from the Graben, which Hitler sketched a dozen times, or the Heldenplatz, where he delivered his "Justification at the Bar of History" (Hitler's speech defending the annexation of Austria, March 14, 1938). There are so many scenes and settings which are the scenes and settings of the Nazi past. To me they are the scenes of a Nazi present as well—the tourist buses and parking lots, the rush of visitors, all those things seem to me like a thin veneer over "German soil," "eternal German earth," which is to be defended "to the last drop of German blood." And if I travel just a few streetcar stops into Vienna's 21st District, I will come to the spot where a certain Major Biedermann was hanged. He did not want to see Vienna defended "to the last drop of blood." In place of the lamppost of 1945 there now stands the tall, unwieldy column of a streetlight, but other than that everything is the same.

Everywhere the Nazi time arises before me. In the lovely southerly Vienna Woods stands the centuries-old Cistercian Monastery of the Holy Cross. The choral chant of the monks is a commentary, in its fashion, on the fact that one of their number, Lanz von Liebenfels,* left the monastery some hundred years ago and became "the man who gave Hitler his ideas." Traveling on up the Danube, I follow the "Nibelungen Trail" and reach Linz, site of the former Hermann Goering Works (today the United Austrian Steelworks), and on into Germany (still following the Nibelungen), Land of Dreams, over the Valhalla* (by Regensburg) to Nuremberg, city of the Nazi Party Congresses. Everything I experience today is automatically infused with connotations from the Nazi period, and this occurs through the propagandistic misuse of words.

What are my own words? What language could be my mother tongue, when my own mother sought so ardently to speak the language of the Nazis—the so-called "German word"? The dubious

---

* See Glossary, here and wherever an asterisk appears. —Trans.

Viennese dialect was hardly the "proper medium" for the expression of hopes for a "glorious future"—a "world dominion of the good, the pure, the noble, of Nordic devotion to duty, peopled with heroic mothers and fathers who give their lives in the front lines of battle for *Führer, Volk, und Vaterland.*"

"Short and sweet" was the German word, "crisp and clear" as well; Schiller and Goethe wrote it, Bach and Beethoven set it to music, and the Führer spoke this German word. And when it was transmitted on the radio, then I for my part was to sit there, attentive and still, and to rise for the closing German anthem.

In what language, what German language, can I capture the Nazi past in words without repeating the old words of domination, which for the most part were stolen from our tradition? For me, the Nazi past is a phenomenon of usurpation. Its very essence is infectious; every attempt at a concrete approach is threatened by a complete loss of distance. Perhaps it is for that reason that in the realm of psychotherapy, the Nazi past comes up only as a private issue.

Between 1967 and 1975 I was undergoing my psychotherapeutic training, in the course of which I studied three different schools of therapy: group dynamics, psychoanalysis, and finally Gestalt therapy (which was to become "my" method). In all alike, the place of the Nazi past remained "private." In the beginning I did not appreciate this fact. It seemed to me that psychotherapy was a domain that offered security against the threat of an encounter with the Nazi time. The vocabulary of psychoanalysis was not "pure German," and its psychic dimensions were not those of the "German soul." Sigmund Freud, Kurt Lewin, Wilhelm Reich, Jakob Levy Moreno, and Fritz Salomon Perls had all fled to England, America, or Africa after the occupation of Central Europe by the Nazis. In no way did they transmit a Nazi ideology, a Nazi language, or a Nazi point of view when their scientific work was passed on to us. The world of psychotherapy was a different world from that of the Nazis. And that felt good. It gave me and my colleagues a certain security—even in the face of the Nazi past itself.

Could we not capture many threatening pasts in words? Had we not learned to deal with psychic dynamics, to grasp and even influence their processes? As therapists just setting out, were we not grounded in social criticism and relativism to a degree that placed us out of reach of the Nazi world? Thus the Nazi past was transformed into just one problem among many to be approached technically and classified diagnostically. And so it happened that whenever the Nazi past threatened to show up in therapy, we met it

as therapists, under the cover of a correct methodology, determined
to hold to therapeutic boundaries. The clients behaved accordingly.
There arose a sort of collusion: we were all of us more interested in
"positive" things—the human potential for future development,
the resolution of neurosis, emergency intervention in cases of psychosis, further development of therapeutic methodology, and many
other such matters.

The Nazi past, by contrast, came up quite differently. It had
always seemed to me to be unfathomable, and thus it was probably
just as well that it should remain private, buried, even though eminently present.

Typical of this state of affairs, it seemed to me, was a training
seminar that took place in 1973 in a nature preserve in the middle
of the alpine foothills of southern Germany. Some twenty candidates
of a psychoanalytic society who wanted to learn group therapy
plunged for some days into the experience of inner realms. The
world of dreams, the relational configurations that were manifest in
the group itself, the discovery of our own potential—all this had
touched us, changed us, brought us into a shared process. One
evening a second group arrived at the conference center and sat
down in the main hall, right in the middle of our accustomed places.
I was surveying the new faces curiously, when suddenly I was
addressed by the somewhat older woman who was the group leader:
"I hear you are from Vienna. We will be sharing space here for a few
days. I must tell you something: In 1938 I had to flee the city. I am
a Jew. This is the closest I have come to returning to Vienna since
that time; I have never made it any closer. Can you somehow understand that? It would mean something to me, to feel that you do."

I was thunderstruck. Everything that had transpired in our group
was suddenly inconsequential—all the dreams, the relational issues,
the agonizing and marvelous common processes of our group's
development. The shrill, sharp-edged words "Nazi past" hung in the
midst of the room, among us and between us. All at once there was
no detached point of view, no place of "suspended awareness" to be
found, from which some explanation could be offered. Here no
interpretation, no intervention was possible. I came from the same
city from which my colleague had had to flee because she was Jewish.
And while I could drive around through southern Germany without
thinking about it, the same terrain was a land of painful return for
her. My colleague left me alone while she plunged into the dancing
that was starting up, into movement, contact, wine, and fruit. I
remained for some time sitting at the edge of the commotion, stirred

up and distressed. The real world, the political, historical world had broken into the world of psychotherapy with a vengeance.

A second training experience belongs to this same period. This time the Nazi past erupted in the middle of a Gestalt training group. Here the process was confrontive, direct, more personal from the start—at least the therapist was more available. There was an elderly Jewish woman in the group who beseeched us for help. We didn't know how to help her. For three hours we listened to her depiction of horrendous concentration camp experiences. It was three hours too many, and at the same time far too few to work through all that we heard. At last we could not bear any more. Nor did we want to. But no one had the courage to admit this openly. And the "safe framework" of therapeutic encounter? What form could that have taken here? We had no idea. Was it that we were too young, in years and perhaps in training? What was to be done? An abyss yawned between the habitual approach of group therapy and the Nazi past.

Finally, the woman left the group room, leaving us with her image: a face shadowed with clouds of horror. With this face, the Nazi past stepped into our present. We had come up against the limits of psychotherapy as a craft which can be taught. The Nazi past forced us to encounter this boundary. I have often reflected uneasily on the feeling of being at a loss in this situation. My thoughts turn to my teachers. I ask myself, what about *their* Nazi past? But I can give only a very fragmentary answer to this question. This is because they themselves presented only a bare minimum of personal material—despite a great deal of supportive patience on those occasions when we did stumble onto the Nazi past in the course of working through our own biographical material. This material seemed to me always to be individualized, in myself and in others, as a purely "private" problem. Never was it—I think I can say this—a *shared* encounter with our shared Nazi past—unavoidable, affecting everyone, filling us with shock and horror, and leaving us all at a loss together. It was always "I have something to work on," but apparently never something that would challenge us all to a common therapeutic task (or any other task), to a shared questioning, to discoveries in common. And there might have been much to discover there, though at the price of being confronted with our own shared, immediate, historical roots.

This is how I see the constricting effect of our contact with the Nazi past. In order not to have to face it, we have developed into clever methodologists, avoiding it together. When I think of the loneliness that is tied up with this constriction, many scenes come to mind in which I, with my Nazi childhood, met with no interest, no resonance when I began to speak, for example, of my own school days. Certainly I am not alone in this. Over and over clients report that their fathers and mothers speak only reluctantly of the war years; to the question of whether they themselves wanted to listen to their fathers and mothers on the subject, the answer is in the negative. "The world has changed. Nobody would understand, after all," to which is added, "Let's talk about the present!" But in my opinion the Nazi past is not really past. There are the sites, there the perpetrators, there the victims, there the accomplices and witnesses, there their children and their children's children. Where, then, are all these horrors supposed to have gone? Who has exposed all this immeasurable weight to an open accounting?

And so by its *lack of closure,* the Nazi past occupies the present. In this way, it is still with us and poisons the present like a living corpse. I am thinking of an old man who had served as a police functionary after his army service and who came to the clinic because of "bad dreams, anxiety, and sleep disturbance." He needed help, but he also presented his helpers with the question of the Nazi past. His own Nazi past was coming back to him in the night—that much was clear to anyone who was willing to listen to him. And what became of this Nazi past, which was then awakened in his helpers? Everyone joined together in a soothing diagnosis: WHO-ICD #298.0: "reactive depressive psychosis." Separated from his wife and the families of his children, he was enclosed in the isolation of clinic life. This example illustrates for me the poisoning of the present by the living corpse of the Nazi past.

And so I turn again to all of you, my teachers, and pose the question that we, your students in psychoanalysis, should have asked you long ago: I beg you to join us in confronting the Nazi past. What was it like for the one among you who survived as the child of a Jew in Prague, only to come then to Vienna and encounter someone who had been in a prominent position under the Nazis—this time not employed as a chief physician but rather as a court consultant? We students heard somewhere that he had unburdened his soul with an (unpublished) novel. Was that enough?

And I think of the one among you who served as engineer on a submarine, completely integrated into the Nazi war machine, now above water, now below, hunted and hunter of others. After the war he sat for decades as an analyst behind a couch, ever more rigidly, until finally he fell ill and died, much too young for us all. Was there some connection in all this to the Nazi past? Can it possibly be that there was *no* significant connection?

And the one of your number who, as a Jewish youth, likewise had to live under the Nazi terror. He was tortured and survived it. Human kindness was united in him with an acute concern for fitting in with established authority. Psychoanalysis in its driest and most orthodox form became his backbone. This was inviolable. Why could he not, why *would* he not share his memories of the Nazi time with us? I cannot believe that such openness would not have been healing.

I think of the one from your circle who outlasted the war as a psychologist in a small Viennese psychiatric hospital. Deeply cultured and politically engaged—how did he pull it off? Psychoanalysis itself has its own Nazi past. How was that trick accomplished? This studied world-weariness, this bemused resignation to the inevitable futility of things human ("Now see here, gentlemen, this touches on your own fascism! And analysis cannot cure that, I'm very much afraid. . .")—can all that really be? All that, in answer to the question of how the Nazi past can even be possible?

I have an entirely different memory of my teachers in group dynamics. You called yourselves "trainers" and made up a "staff." That communicated a vigorous, pragmatic atmosphere and a kind of hope: organizations can be humanized; power can be controlled; the group has more capacity for solutions than the individual. Your ideology was in one respect the exact opposite of the Nazis': you had no use for führers. But what about the Nazi past? Two of you had visible wounds as a result of the war. Both of you could talk about that; but the Nazi past, which each of us carried within us, was not mentioned. The "here and now" of social psychology yielded a different emphasis. I remember in the last phase of our training, how the phrase "In cases of doubt, the group is always right," seemed unacceptable to me. After all, I had often heard that in my own school days: "The Führer is always right," or "The Party is always right." How can anyone be always right? The Nazi past plainly lurked under the surface of the discussion, but it remained frozen at that level. More and more, hope was invested in the group, in the "whole." But if at first these were small groups on which our hopes were pinned, they were large groups in the end. And I had the feeling of being in a world where the countless prisoners, the helpers, and the "quiet" resistance fighters of the Nazi time had been lost from view.

It seems to me all too cynical and unbearable to go along with pronouncements of that kind when I think of those who lived out the war and the Nazi years completely isolated and removed from the public consensus of the times. For example, a colleague who as a ten-year-old schoolboy at the beginning of the war was told privately by his mother how she saw Hitler and the war: "All Nazis are criminals! You'll see, the war will be lost! Don't believe a word of what your teachers say about all this. And don't tell anyone what I'm telling you now. This is for you alone—because it's the truth!"

How shall this colleague, lost and alone in the group consensus of a Nazi schoolroom (and yet supported by the contradictory reality of history)—how can this colleague ever put his faith in group consensus as a guide to discovering reality? Obviously this working hypothesis breaks down in the face of the Nazi past and its educational methods.

And how is such a consensus to be arrived at? Was the *dynamic* of the moment of the group process, which was the object of your research, so fascinating for you? Was the *harmony* of the emotional climate of the group so much more important than the discovery and articulation of the immediate past, in the conceptual landscape you presented to us in our training?

Of course, you knew all this well enough intellectually; you will refer me right away to some publication you can cite (and which I quite possibly am unaware of). But none of that helped us to come into contact with the Nazi past. That past remains exactly where it was: right under the surface of consciousness—close enough to be intellectually available, but emotionally out of touch.

I believe that this is an important aspect of the Nazi past and of how it actually comes up: *namely, that one cannot merely study it without being seized with the horror of it.* The "unthinkable" ("Now just a minute," as people said back then, "after all, Hitler is not a barbarian. . .") nevertheless became reality. It was possible, and it really did happen. When can we, when may we go on, after the encounter with the Nazi past, to the next order of business of the day, the next chapter in the curriculum? When will this horror be laid to rest?

With Gestalt therapy I found a working method that was immediately accessible to me. I was given a new foundation for my therapeutic training, in a sense learning anew everything that I had learned thus far—more clearly, more concretely, more penetratingly. Here, it seemed to me, I was learning to live, to apprehend life as a phenomenon, to have a sense of awe in the face of what "is." From you, my Gestalt therapists, I learned openness, contact, and a faith in new growth; here, it seemed to me, everything was possible, everything could come into therapy, as material and as experiment, because the encounter with reality was seen in a phenomenological way.

Thus it pains me all the more to see clearly now that even you, or we together, were unable to encounter the Nazi past in other than a "professional" way. We knew much more about each other than was the case in my previous training experiences. Gestalt therapy with its principle of "selective disclosure" made this possible, but still we could not come to any decision to face this past together. Instead, we transformed the Nazi past into concrete instances: Ingrid's father, the SS officer; Irene's industrialist parents, who fortunately escaped to South Africa in time; Roland's father, a solid Bavarian, who was away in the war for years (and. . . ?); Ulrike's current home, which resulted from her flight from Banat north of Belgrade. . . . Thus we confronted the moving episodes of individual development, but what had become of the Nazi past? Where was the memory of the Hitler songs, which our ears had certainly heard? Where were the shoulders rubbed raw from carrying the knapsacks of the Hitler Youth? What had become of the terrifying sound of air raid sirens, warning us of Allied bomb attacks? Where had our bodies gone, crumpled with fear while the bombs fell—where had they gone, in Gestalt therapy? Did we not *all* sit in the cellars crumpled with fear? Did not most of us—practically all of us—hear the sirens? Whose shoulders, whose feet were not rubbed raw with marching and singing and fleeing to bomb shelters? This I ask you, my trainers in Gestalt therapy—and you, my colleagues, who as adults must have had a Nazi childhood, or as young adults, parents who were involved in a Nazi past.

With all our expertise in the dynamics of human problems, with all our insight into personal development, how have we managed it so that it is precisely the Nazi past, of all things, that we avoid confronting together? Had we become mere Gestalt technicians? Did we suddenly belong to those who always knew all the answers in advance? Had we in the end studied and therapized the thing to death? Have we arrived at a point, after countless interventions, discussions, and "mini-lectures," where we can no longer encounter the actual thing itself, namely the Nazi past, as such, without any therapeutic labeling and categorization?

This therapeutic professionalism, I suspect, has made it easier for us to avoid the issue! This professionalism—which we have taken such pains to cultivate, because we have been so focused on public

recognition for Gestalt therapy—has made us forget that an uncon-
ventional therapeutic stance is exactly what is needed in dealing
with the the Nazi past: to taste its taste, see its colors, take in its
stench, its fascination, its horrible noise, and its crippling silence.

And one more suspicion: could it be that we were so captivated
by the pleasure and the positive things in life that in our exhaustion
with shouldering responsibility for our own neurotic suffering, we
were less willing to see life's negative sides?

However that may be, at any rate we became more and more the
conventional psychotherapists, conforming to the conventions of
psychotherapy, of clinical psychology, of psychiatry, and so on. The
Nazi past simply *didn't fit* in this conventional picture. It was a disturbing element, even if it actually had its conventional side. It
actually did happen, and one of the most depressing implications lies
in seeing how much the orderly machinery of the German and Austrian states served as a vehicle for the spread of Nazism. Many of its
horrors, such as the persecution and extermination of the Jews and
other "subhumans," were carried out through normal institutional
processes, centrally directed from Berlin. It did happen; the danger
of institutionalization and the power of unchallenged convention
are all too clear.

We were determined—as if nothing had happened—to famil-
iarize our training candidates with the usual therapeutic require-
ments: "Pay attention to the problem of the mother, don't forget
sibling rivalry, be sure to deal with sex and aggression, watch out for
signs of decompensation, don't forget to make a well-founded dif-
ferential diagnosis. . . ." We taught our candidates everything. We
wrote it into our curriculum, and certainly we were accomplishing
something objectively necessary when we did. But only the most
immediate thing—our common Nazi past, that of the therapists
and that of the clients—escaped our close attention. How could we
be so sure that this too was not a training requirement? This most
concrete of historical antecedents, of all things!

We know from our therapeutic work with ourselves and with
others, that one can fall ill from one's own history, but that one can
also be healed by that same history. To wipe out the Nazi past, in this
view, is a serious omission. A colleague who was an officer in the war
once wrote to me, "We have had altogether too much experience
with Hoefer [in Germany] and Waldheim [in Austria]. Have we ever
once taken up the theme, 'Our parents in the Third Reich!' How
would we then conceptualize working it through? I believe it could
not be done without recourse to normative-ethical standards; for

example, the distinction between *guilt* and *guilt feelings*. And not without honesty and an element of plainly old-fashioned *active repentance*, either!"

The confrontation with our Nazi past forces us to face the following contradiction: Accustomed as we are to regarding our own and our clients' guilt feelings (and the more diffuse "bad conscience") as neurotic symptoms that can be unmasked and worked through therapeutically with liberating effect, we often found this viewpoint confirmed in our experiences in family therapy. The question would not be to find out who was guilty of what, but rather to understand the individual disturbance that led to that person's guilt feelings. But when confronted with the Nazi past, this whole approach loses its validity. It strikes me as a mockery to regard the Nazi past as a systemic environmental disturbance or the neurotic personalization of a problem external to the self "which we, in our human limitation, can do nothing about."

Fritz Perls understood responsibility as "response-ability," the capacity to respond or, still better, the capacity to allow an inner resonance to a given event. This makes me think of a woman in Vienna during the Nazi period who was suddenly torn from her daily routine by the doorbell. When she opened the door, there stood a Jewish woman, begging to be taken in. She was a woman who lived in the same little street and was thus a nodding acquaintance. Nothing more. "I couldn't help myself. When I saw this woman at the door, I simply felt such pain that I took her in. Naturally I knew that the Gestapo would be looking for her." That was an act of "responsibility"—out of the capacity to answer to a situation. And for psychotherapeutic understanding, it raises a question of *values*.

I believe that we all felt reluctance, even anxiety, in the face of questions of this kind. Perhaps it was the fear of coming up against religious or philosophical categories. It seems to me that we did not want to deal with things at this level. But if we do not, it also seems to me that I can never confront the Nazi past. Moreover, while various concepts from humanism are accepted on the psychotherapeutic scene, anything that smacks explicitly of the Christian tradition or the church encounters problems. This amounts almost to a taboo, which is all the more contradictory when one compares the newer worldviews with the Christian one. Of all the spiritual worldviews, it is the Judeo-Christian which is the closest to the therapeutic.

Just as all of us, by necessity, have a Nazi past, so do many of us have some kind of Christian or specifically churchly past as well.

These two pasts have a great deal to do with each other, as Friedrich Heer (1968) has shown in his book *Hitler's Religious Beliefs (Der Glaube des Adolf Hitler)*.

I look at the Nazi past in relation to psychotherapeutic training— to my own various psychotherapeutic trainings. These three training paths which I have followed fell into three different groupings, with different methods and teachers as well as different colleagues. This is how the Nazi past has entered into psychotherapy, in my experience, *and insofar as it has affected training, to that extent it also affects the work of the trainees.* That is my thesis. And it is this thesis that I find disheartening.

I believe I have something else to add, before the Nazi past is prematurely relegated to the list of "curriculum topics" and filed away in its self-contained scientific category. As I confront the Nazi past, it is clear to me that I too belong among the witnesses, even though I was a child at the time; I am not dependent only on the testimony of others.

At the time the war ended, I was just twelve years old. I had watched and listened when Hitler paraded into Vienna, past our apartment house in the Linzerstrasse; I had sat on my father's shoulders in the Heldenplatz, the entire area black with people. I saw Jews on the main street of Eisenstadt with yellow Stars of David on their chests. I used to bring our shoes to a shoemaker in the ghetto. I was "informed" that there were no concentration camps. I had a school friend whose father bellowed fearfully at his family every night (he was quite audible through the wall separating our apartments). My father was embarrassed about the situation, inasmuch as the man was a prominent member of the SA* and our Party Block Warden, which is to say one of the "New Germans" the Nazis promised to produce. (I met him again later on; in the meantime he had become a leading member of the CSU* in Augsburg: "One cannot just stand by, when the community is in need"—this was 1951!) And more images upon images, to the point where they threaten to overwhelm this essay: the gleaming shovels of the National Work Corps*, the smell of leather, the fabric of the flags, the ring of the fanfares, the brown-red-gold firelight in the provincial courthouse in Eisenstadt on the occasion of a christening ("Deutschland, o holy name, in all eternity!" sang the men's voices of the SA choir); the German newsreels at the NAPOLA* where my parents sent me (800 cadets presented themselves for the daily rollcall, among them not only me, but figures who are prominent today: a National Council president, a cabinet minister, a mayor, a diplomat).

The National Political Education Institute—NAPOLA! I notice how I am beginning to rush ahead—it's as if I want to begin at the end. But it is the beginning that showed the true monstrousness of Nazi pedagogy. For a whole week we had to take entrance exams. I was only nine years old, one year younger than the requirement, but I had the "honor" of being allowed to take part. I was the only one from my school district to be admitted. The hopes of all Eisenstadt (today a seat of provincial government), and also those of my father, my mother, my relatives rested on me. With courage born of desperation I clambered ten times up the climbing pole in the gymnasium, dove from the five-meter board even though I couldn't swim ("if you don't dive, you don't stand a chance"), survived a boxing match, ran the five-kilometer endurance race, and— although I had never seen the broad jump pit—managed to clear 3.1 meters! The courage born of desperation, the honor of becoming a "cadet" (this is what is written on my certificate: "Service rank in the Hitler Youth: troop leader. Service rank in the National Political Education Institute: cadet")—such were the mainsprings of psychic survival in my absurd two and a half years of NAPOLA existence. At our morning exercises we had to run barefoot around the great parade grounds—on hard gravel! From 1943 on we also had to go barefoot all day long, from April to October: "Cadets, our soldiers need leather for their boots. Your feet will heal by themselves—so shut up about it! Right face! All together, march! A song . . . !" These were the words of our center leader, with the commonplace name. But there was nothing commonplace about him. Enveloped in a cloud of heroism and mythic sacrifice, he stood before us 800 cadets at reveille. Rumor spoke of a severe stomach ailment, of sleepless nights and desperate races over the obstacle course, over walls and across the pits and hills, to master the pain. He was the pinnacle of the hierarchy, Hitler's representative among us—the Führer directly under the Führer*!

All this world of party members and SS pedagogues! Everything was masculine, everything was uniformed, every shirt, every pair of underpants had a number and its obligatory place in the locker (which was simply a clothes closet to me, before NAPOLA), and all for the sake of *control*. When the troop leader came on inspection— or even the cadet squad leader, or just the platoon leader (platoon = class!)—then approval or disapproval was registered with a single glance out of the corner of his eyes. In the latter case the locker was flipped over and some five minutes given till the next inspection. However, if the least error (literally, "reportable offense") was still to be found at that point, then the most gruesome game was set in motion in the group: "All your comrades will just have to wait till your locker is in order!" Naturally this was a task almost impossible to accomplish, which then led to *taking it out on the group*—supposedly an old Germanic custom of the noble northern master race. Everybody would now receive a punishment—for example, clearing out weeds with a tablespoon—"because you still don't have your locker in order. It's a pile of shit, that's what it is." This "everybody" now vacillated between sympathy and resentment; this could happen to anyone, had already happened to everyone. What happened to me in particular was more a matter of the *pecking order* of the squad. At the top was the strongest, at the bottom the weakest. Those who were in a position to be suspected of physical weakness were careful to avoid an open showdown in the boxing ring. But then even in the NAPOLA there was such a thing as personal friends; would they perhaps be able to help? Not allowed! If the platoon leader or the cadet squad leader or the regimental leader noticed anything of the sort, then an *ear-boxing* match had to be held. The two friends had to take their places in front of the assembled platoon and box each other's ears, until one of them began to cry. Bravery was useless, crying was much better—only it had to look believable. That at least ended it, and often ended the friendship—and likely any remaining pride as well. Yes, I am often asked, but didn't you also get something out of all this hardness? Certainly we did, we got hardness out of it! Just the kind of hardness we had suffered ourselves.

And were there then no women, no girls in this world of men? A lone woman was housemother. She had an illegitimate son to care for. As housemother she was in charge of the "cleaning and mending hour." Each week we patched and sewed on our uniforms, so that the various leaders would find all our buttons and all our buttonholes and all our shoulder straps and all our German eagle insignia in perfect order for the morning and evening inspections. Beyond that, every morning she inspected the bedsheets of the younger classes. Seventy percent of the cadets in the lowest class were bed wetters! They received a dose of ground raw eggshell (one teaspoonful daily) in the infirmary. Anyone who had no yellow urine spots on his sheets got a piece of candy. Unimaginable luxury! Anyone who kept on wetting the bed sank lower and lower in the pecking order.

One of my platoon mates (today he is manager of a clothing chain), for want of any lower position to put him in, was summarily locked up in an empty goose coop. For an entire day he remained there, to be stared at . . . so much for the housemother. Other than her, the only females to appear at our institute were the choral troop from District 511 (Baden-by-Vienna). That was an experience beyond comprehension: crowds of pretty fifteen- to seventeen-year-old girls from the League of German Girls!* We stared at them, amazed. They sang Mozart in the musical competition: "Quick shine forth, to announce the dawn . . ." from *The Magic Flute* (a wholly foreign world). The seventh and eighth classes (already in the uniform of political leaders) were permitted to attend a gala evening dance with them. We were not allowed to go. We marched instead for the hundredth time through the village of Traiskirchen with fanfare and drums . . . and so on and so on.

There would be so much to tell, there would be—always in the conditional tense! In reality I did try to bring up the subject once, in a circle of my colleagues. Right away some thirty people expressed an interest, but after one evening of exchange, in which I discussed (somewhat more extensively) the pedagogy of NAPOLA from my own experience, some of the participants reported feeling ill—from the atmosphere of the Nazi past, which came across so strongly: This atmosphere of order, blood, fascination, and destruction in all its forms.

How did it happen that I was not able to communicate better with these colleagues? Why did they pose such insensitive questions, like "Yes, but then didn't you ever stop and think about these things?" or "Can a myth really have such power?" At last the Nazi era did come to an end. Even in the NAPOLA we could not fail to see its approach. We were bombarded. After the bomb attacks we climbed to the roof terrace and looked for the hardest-hit sections of Vienna by the size of the flames. "Where does my mother live? I hope she sends me a survival notice!" (preferred mail—no postage required).

The bombs, the wounded, the combat decorations in the seventh and eighth classes—Vienna burning, the silent disappearance of my father (he was "missing" . . . just "missing." The German army was missing someone, who happened to be my father) . . . Stop! Stop! Stop! before the Nazi past in all its multiple forms inundates everything. And I haven't even mentioned the sight of the liberated concentration camps at Mauthausen and Gusen. And then the images of the burning train car in which we were escaping, and the low-flying planes that buzzed me as I crouched in a field seeking shelter, not far from the lovely monastery at Goettweig. Such are the images from the end of the third class at the NAPOLA.

Thus my attempt to bear witness: only a detail, but gravid with meaning. Perhaps it will help in the introduction of a kind of healing and liberating process, which starts with the sharing of personal experience and can lead to a more general exchange. "What comes to light becomes lighter"; what has come to light can no longer haunt the darkness. (Freud: "Where id was, shall ego be!") But it is late in coming! How is it things have come to this point at last?

Here I want to consider the conflict about the candidacy and election of Kurt Waldheim as president of Austria. Suddenly the Nazi past —his and that of us all—stepped into the spotlight. This was first and foremost a matter of publicity in the form of media attention, interest, political action, reflection, discussion, documentation; a sort of "Waldheim industry" sprung up, perhaps best understood as a unique kind of *large group process*. And thus in the process the *Nazi past came out into the open*. It was not to be held back any longer, no matter where one might stand with regard to the actors and actions of this process. Suddenly there were the protagonists out of the Nazi past; suddenly it became clear that a figure was needed through whom the large group ("society") could define, view, and deal with its problem. And suddenly a vague current, which had flowed underground till now, swelled and slowly emerged as a broad river.

I will never forget one session of a training group, which had already spent a great deal of time in sermonizing against the generation of the perpetrators. All of them were well informed, all were intelligent, all were wearing white hats, so to speak, all were united among themselves. But the Nazi past was more immediately present than they imagined. A young woman began to speak of her mother. She held back: "What more did you want to tell us?" A silence ensued. And then it came out: "Mother lived in a large German city, and next door lived a Jewish family with an eight-year-old daughter. One evening the mother of this family came over and said, 'We have definite information: tomorrow morning at dawn we are to be transported to a camp by the SS. Could you take my little daughter and hide her?' My mother told me this many times. And in fact the SS did come with a van the next morning and hauled the Jewish family away. Including the little eight-year-old girl. My mother watched the proceedings from behind the curtain at the window of our room. And thus it was that my mother didn't incur any difficulties. And thus it was that I too didn't incur any difficulties and had a normal childhood." Silence, embarrassment, then horror spread through the group.

And so I encountered the Nazi past in this training group. And then later in an individual therapy session as well. When I read the book *Born Guilty*, by Peter Sichrovsky (1987), I did not notice something which a client at the time told me later, that one of the stories in it was his own. Thus the Nazi past entered into my subjective world of therapy. This acted as a brake on therapeutic zeal. A sort of stillness set in. I paused, and began to reflect.

This then is the place to think of those clients who were particularly affected by the Nazi past. They were my co-conspirators in silence; I had made them into that. Now I can see them, in all their woundedness from those times, not just as individual cases, but rather as human beings, through whom in the realm of psychotherapy our Nazi past can become more clear as something we share.

There is a certain old woman to consider, who came only once for a consultation. She had been involved in the concentration camps, and after this first groping conversation, she made no further contact.

There is Herbert, with his twin brother, Otto. The parents were officials and Nazis. When the father came back from the war, he naturally had to straighten out the twin brothers, who after all were his own children. Every night in the bathroom he gave them a thorough beating, ritually, all according to regulations, for their miserable behavior (they didn't sleep quietly enough in their little bed!). The mother said nothing. This silence of the women in Nazi families! This silence which always made excuses for the husband, always sought understanding for him. This silence, which always had the odor of a loyal follower and so seldom that of despair, weakness, fear.

There is Helga, whose father was a prominent Nazi physician. The family lost everything, including its integrity, and never found any of it again, not even through the kind of forgiveness which might have been possible.

There is Maria, whose grandparents were murdered in a concentration camp. Maria brandished her grandparents' fate before her like a banner, wherever she was politically active—no matter in what context—and held it up like a shield to hide behind. The grandparents had been murdered. And Maria kept their memory alive and hid herself behind it. But where was Maria?

There is Erika, whose father was married to a half-Jewish woman in the midst of Vienna in the midst of the war. Not only did he not abandon her to protect himself, but he even managed through bribery to keep her out of the camps and to bring her through the Nazi time alive, and then lived on as a small businessman, without recognition for this achievement and without thanks. Once he was able to explain all this to his daughter, he promptly died, as if he had only wanted to live until the time when the Nazi past—his own particular kind of Nazi past—had been witnessed, noted, and preserved in memory.

There is Helmut, whose father was a monarchist, Catholic, conservative, utterly incapable of surviving military service in the Second World War without being broken by it. His share in the Nazi past crippled him. He returned home a broken man and proceeded to break everybody else who was not strong enough and clever enough to keep away from him. These crippled family members are the direct progeny of his Nazi past—no resistance, no flight, only crippling, an infectious crippling.

There is Helene, whose father, for want of any other professional qualification, went straight from the German officers' corps to the rank of general in the Austrian army (with a brief intermission in between). He lived on, but in reality he was dead, incapable of any feeling, any thought other than the structure of his principles. A man held up by his uniform and by uniformity in general. His wife and his children—did he ever really see them? Helene, was your father ever aware of your existence at all, other than to correct you and give you orders? Is this how you were touched so young by the death of someone still physically alive? Helene, is this how you encountered his Nazi past—and as a consequence, your own?

There are Franz and Albert, whose parents had to separate in order to survive. After the war their father could not establish any viable relationship to "civilian life." He continued to hold a job, but stagnated in his own development, until he finally became a piece of rotten, poisoned flesh, from which others had to be protected. This his wife did, drifting in the process into crazy fantasies, which were actually not so crazy at all when one considered what she was up against in her marriage. But then who had time for all that? She was kept out of the hospital with medication. Both sons saw their own marriages fail. They had no models and had not been able to draw a glimmer of hope from their parents. Where had hope gone? For them it was fixated in the war, which had been lost—for the second time now—because of an "international conspiracy."* As a pensioner, the father waits in isolation—but for what? Can one round out one's life still brooding on one's Nazi past, still waiting bitterly for final victory? Will the Nazi past then triumph over death? (The end of the first verse of the song "Our Flag Unfurls Before Us": "Yes, the flag triumphs over death!") And who can help the "eternal victor" to achieve closure in his life?

I have come to the end of my attempt to confront the historical gestalt of the Nazi past. Of necessity, mine has been a highly subjective contribution.

At this point I feel the temptation to write a comprehensive, reconciliatory, or categorizing conclusion. I will not now do that. Kurt Waldheim—intentionally or otherwise, which is beside the point here—has given us the possibility, through his tenacity, of not coming to premature closure in the incipient process of a public confrontation with the Nazi past. (The subjects of Erich Hoefer and the 1938 Anschluss* disappeared from public view in Germany much more quickly.) From this I draw encouragement that we will keep the question of the Nazi past and the question of psychotherapy open, for now and until such time as they reach a natural and public closure in their own right. For this reason I would argue for more "Nazi past" and less "psychotherapy."

Perhaps under these circumstances we will be able (at last) to bear the trauma of facing the Nazi past—something which we have learned not to do, but which, I believe, may now be accessible to us once again.

2

FAREWELL TO MY FATHER

Irene Anhalt

Discourse and dialogue, you always told us, were the most important forms of encounter between human beings; as your children we learned from you to take pleasure in the use of words. You encouraged us to enter into discussions with you, even to contradict you. No subject was out of bounds; every topic we brought in served for a lively exchange. Most of all you loved discussions of German history; philosophical issues were welcome as well. And yet, as we gradually grew older, and our worldviews grew ever more distant from yours, you began to cut off our questions with historical illustrations, and the lively dialogue of earlier times now ended more and more often in your wide-ranging and abstract reflections.

What was it that imprisoned us in these ritual conversations, in spite of their growing emptiness and our mutual avoidance? Why could we not break through this frozen quality between us? You entered as willingly as ever into all my questions about you and your political past; you responded to my attacks and reproaches. And yet you said nothing, gave me nothing that I can take today, months after your death, as a satisfying answer.

Did you flood us with words, that we might not hear your inner silence? And was it not true that our well-measured questioning helped you maintain a semblance of order over the abyss of your own memories? And now that you have taken everything with you that could furnish me with an honest answer, I know that I never asked you the real question.

I know the stations of your life. I have an overview of your career. I know all the details; what is it, then, that I would still want to hear, if you were still able to answer?

It is true that you never made any secret of your support for Hitler. You were not among the ignorant and the misled; you were no fellow traveler. When you joined the SS* in 1929, you did it freely and with a conscious sense of the importance of the moment.

---

* See Glossary, here and wherever an asterisk appears. —Trans.

Some years ago on one of our strolls through Berlin, you showed me the spot where you first heard a speech by Goebbels. We stood together on the street and watched the door of a bar, from which a group of merry young people emerged and marched right up to us, demanding laughingly if we wanted to hear some "hot music." We joined for a moment in their laughter.

I wanted to hear from you what it was that was so important, half a century ago, as to make you abandon your earlier career plans so willingly. No longer was science to be your goal, but rather collaboration in the construction of a National Socialist state.

You reached that goal. Just four years later, when the Nazis seized power, you too were among the victors, those whose personal success was only made possible through their domination. Your rise was rapid; I am dizzied by the tempo. In the papers you left behind I found documents of your promotion from SS stormtrooper to first lieutenant of the SD,* the security service of the SS. I still falter when I pronounce the word that more accurately identifies you and your office: Gestapo.

Holding the papers in my hand, I felt as though I had never before taken in the power of this word, in all its horrible significance. The explanations from your own mouth, years before, as we cross-examined you ever more searchingly about your past, did not carry the weight for me of these yellowed sheets. Not even my own intensive study of fascism, or Eugen Kogon's book *The SS State,* had shaken me so deeply as this document, which connected your name so closely with murder and terror.

What might I have done if I had seen these papers while you still lived? Would that have made the struggle for understanding between us impossible on both sides? And would I then have condemned you once and for all, and turned away? I do not know. And would I have taken the occasion to judge you even more decisively than I had already done, years before? Meaningless questions which have no answers, inasmuch as we met as daughter and father, not as prosecutor and SS official.

In one of our most heated disputes in the early 1970s, I called you a murderer and hurled at you, "I wish you were dead!" I was horrified at my own words. Would we ever speak to one another again, now that we both had heard something so monstrous? Despairing and spent, I began to cry. There was a long silence between us, before you answered very softly: "My death would solve nothing, neither for you nor for me." You were right, your death would not have helped me find answers to the ever-recurring questions: how could you have mired yourself so deeply in guilt?

And yet I remained alone and impotent in my rage after this battle, which you had ended with a gesture of reconciliation. You, the most powerful figure of my childhood and youth, had been prepared to give your life, if it were demanded of you—just as you declared the lives of others to be insignificant—for the sake of an insane idea, a racist ideology, a political concept. For you for many years, death was an everyday matter; to me it remains to this day something senseless and inconceivable, if it strikes violently, and not at the close of a life infused with meaning. My despairing wish for your death was nothing other than my longing for a life with you— free of guilt!

Today it seems to me as though in all our discussions, whether in anger or in mutual searching, we were trying to ignore the unbridgeable gulf between us: our fundamentally different outlook on existence and living. Life for you, going back to the Kaiser's time, was first and foremost a challenge which one must rise to, without failing the demands of duty, dignity, composure. By these principles you lived; the stakes were high, bringing both success and defeat. Yet nothing, not even the complete collapse of your fascist world, could shake you in your basic beliefs.

By contrast, how different my life: when I was born, Germany had been at war for a year. In those days you were celebrating your victories and conquests, and nothing of the violence and destruction that surrounded you every day penetrated into my protected child's world.

You became City Director of Berlin; wealth and power converged around you. Pictures from this period show you as a man accustomed to success, in the circle of his happy family. I still carry with me today the security of those early untroubled years without the dark secret that hovered around you and without the awful certainty that came later. Daddy—that was a word to conjure with, and the magic spell came true every evening with your return home. We were happy; your presence meant storytelling and wonderful gifts at a time when food was already being rationed and the rising production of weapons made toys a luxury.

And yet the longer the war went on, the more frequently did shadows fall over my world: the news of the death of your cousin; Mama's brother reported missing; your brother, an officer in the

General Staff, gravely wounded; the maiming of a favorite uncle—the two of you could not always hide your sorrow from us. Horror and death had taken up a place in my life, and I began to realize that beyond the love and security that surrounded me lay something violent, something against which you could not shield me, because you yourselves were afraid.

As the city began to be heavily bombed almost every night, you transferred us to an estate some two hours by car from Berlin. There we were to live until the end of the war, undisturbed by bomb alerts and increasing shortages. To you, the end could only have meant victory, even in the spring of 1944; otherwise you would never have chosen a refuge for us that lay so far to the east, in what is Poland today, not far at all from your enemies. Did you not take seriously the steady encroachment of the Red Army, or were you still blinded by the idea of your superior military abilities, to the point that you could not see the actual progress of the war in Europe?

For us children, the departure from Berlin brought the first extended separation from you. With every sound of an oncoming automobile we broke off our game in the stables, ever ready to run to meet you. You did come on several occasions, sometimes alone, sometimes accompanied by men in uniform, but never without marvelous presents—sometime in winter you came for the last time, bringing with you a doll with long pigtails. I cried as you drove off again. Mama tried to console me, but I was not to be reached by her tender words and remained alone with my own pain. For eleven years I waited for you, always with the memory of our painful farewell, and always in the passionate hope of your return.

You did return, at the end of 1955; yet in the eleven years of our separation lay the time of my childhood, my growing into young maidenhood, and my gradual realization that there lay about you some terrible secret, which had kept you so long from us.

My fantasies about you, the ever-adored father, came to resemble some forbidden game, to which only I knew the rules. If I were to let anyone else in on it, you would never return. What did I know of you in these years? Mama told us you had probably been killed, like so many other fathers; and then in 1948, when we first heard news of you, you became for us a prisoner of war who would someday come home. "Returnees" was the name for those emaciated men with the grave, gray faces; I had often seen them. I waited for you and prayed every night for your return.

And yet slowly my longing for you detached itself from any real desire that you would actually be with us. I learned to live without you; my memories of you belonged to early childhood days, which were long gone. Yet I never stopped waiting for you; I was obsessed with the thought that only your return could lay to rest something dark and threatening within me. Your arrival would put an end to the war that raged inside me; no one but you would have the power to make me at peace.

In my dreams I relived over and over the end of the war and the first months that followed; I awoke crying out, ran to Mama, to lose my fear in her arms. The flight before the Soviets in 1945, long-range bombers overhead, bombs exploding around us, shrapnel, Mama's back gashed open, my foot shot through, the long weeks alone in the clinic with all the wounded soldiers, separated from Mama and my brothers. The time in the Polish orphanage, until finally my faltering hope was rewarded: Mama found me, after months of searching.

Although Mama never abandoned me in my nightly despair, I soon began to feel guilty for my inability to overcome the past. To me it was as though only I still suffered from the horrors of the war. The brothers played contentedly again on the street; around me life seemed to have taken on its old order anew. Why could I not forget?

Meanwhile we lived in a small Hessian city, which the war seemed to have passed by without leaving visible traces. Only the refugees, packed together in barracks on the outskirts of the city, never to be seen without their bag or backpack, served as a reminder that things must have been worse in other places.

I began to have the suspicion that something else must have taken place, and that it was something much more unspeakable than the war itself. It was as though beyond the war something else had happened, something evil, which must not be touched on lest it bring on disaster—a curse, like those in the fairy tales Mama read to me at night. The brothers made me swear an oath never to pronounce the name Hitler again; it was this name that seemed to me to be the key to the secret, which the grownups kept to themselves.

Sometimes we were visited by men who came from afar, bringing news to Mama. I was not allowed to hear their conversations, but I sensed they had to do with you. One time Mama called us to her, laughing and crying at the same time, and told us, "Daddy is alive!" The man was crying too; then he told us how he had met you in a Moscow prison in 1946, how you had been condemned to death, and then how, in a later trial, your sentence was reduced to twenty-five years' forced labor in Siberia.

I could not comprehend what the man was telling us. Why

should you not have been allowed to live?—only soldiers who had fallen in the war were dead. But you were still alive, and the war was over! What had you done, that you had to go to Siberia, and this man did not? And always I saw soldiers arriving—the father of my friend Renate was home now, and you were not. What did that mean—"reduced to twenty-five years' forced labor"? My hope that you would be with us for my next birthday—my eighth—was shattered.

Gradually I began to grasp that you were not one of those men for whose return we prayed on Saturday evening in school. You belonged to those of whom the grownups spoke only in a whisper. But why such a malicious grin on their faces, and why always that word "Nazi" again? Something shadowy, something unknown till now, entered into my longing for you, and I felt guilty about it, and ashamed.

More and more often now I sat down on the damp stones that led from the courtyard to the cellar, and scratched swastikas into the dry skin of my shins. The left leg, the one that had been shot, which still dragged a little when I walked, I scratched especially deeply. I placed the crosses so close together it seemed as though they were taking each other by the hand, and all the while I whispered the forbidden names, Hitler, Stalin, Goebbels, Goering. I did not stop until both legs were smeared with blood.

The brothers had heard of Stalin's mock trials and persuaded me that men who were in particular disgrace were made to kneel for years on stones strewn with dried peas. I waited till I was alone at last, to share the punishment with you. But after only a few minutes I gave up, exhausted; the peas had pressed painfully into my knees. I clung to the idea that you would outwit your guard and secretly push the peas aside. I wanted to write a letter to Stalin and beg him for mercy for you. Mama took me in her arms, as she always did when she saw how tormented I was for you.

It happened too in this period that the brothers took my doll, the last memory of you, stripped it naked, cut off its head, and jammed the head under its arm. I was paralyzed with horror and could not take my eyes off Jutta, as I had named her. Not until evening could Mama tear me from the awful sight. What was it that drove the brothers to destroy so violently the only thing I had saved from untroubled childhood days? Was there no other way for us as children to come to terms with the destruction within us than to act it out on each other? I was already on the road to self-destruction, and the brothers banded together and drew strength from my humiliation.

As I watched one time while D. stoned a harmless grubworm to death, accompanying the gruesome game with loud laughter, I sensed that the war could not yet really be over. Outwardly, we had escaped it by our flight; within ourselves, it was still going on.

My growing fear of the brothers became a new and serious menace for me. I doted on them tenderly, and yet I had to recognize that there was danger for me in them as well, which I could not avoid. Their favorite game was "war"; they played it across the millennia, as Romans who enslaved other peoples, as marauding knights, or as the conquerors of America slaughtering the Indians. They played scenes from the Second World War and killed the Russians. And in every war they required a victim, a guilty party who could be condemned to death; this role they forced onto me. At the end of every game they pardoned me, but the ever-renewed threat of my sacrificial death had the effect of ratifying my deepest conviction of my own guilt. I, the youngest, the girl, powerless in the face of their fourfold male superiority, lived only through their grace.

I clung all the more closely to Mama and longed for her return every evening with the same passion with which I had once waited for you. Without her I felt defenseless against my own frightening fantasies, helpless in the face of a world in which I could no longer find my way. Yet her tender care could only scatter my fears for a moment; her love did not reach my inner torment. I sensed too well that she also carried something within, from which she was fleeing; behind her sad smile there was something hidden which paralyzed me. In order not to touch her pain, I withdrew deeper into my own loneliness.

And how could she have helped me? She was Mama, a woman; I sensed that the menace—and yet also the salvation from this menace—came from men, from fathers such as you. Soldiers, warriors, heroes, liberators, even the dead were all men. Mama and I could only love each other; we could not put an end to what was seething within us.

Over and over I sought your presence, imagined myself in prison, in a Siberian work camp. In our town there was a house with bars on the windows, where criminals were held till they could be transported to the nearest city. Often I stood below these windows; once a man pressed his face against the bars. I returned with an apple and threw it up to the window with a shout. It bounced off the bars and smashed on the street.

I began to tell the neighbors that you were a criminal, now serving out your sentence. The brothers heard of it, and I was forbidden to speak of you. I had turned into a traitor who could no longer be trusted—even Mama was disappointed with me. Now a deep shame was added to my feelings of guilt; my schoolwork suffered, and I was sick more and more often.

Gradually I lost the hope that something would happen that would bring you back soon; it had been used up by the passage of time. I adjusted to the idea that I would never see you again, until the eternity of twenty-five years had gone by.

And yet the bond which held us together was not broken. We had news of you. Three or four times a year you were allowed to write a card; twenty-five words were permitted. We sent you photos and packages regularly; many went astray on the long way; some arrived. On my eleventh birthday I received one of these precious cards, addressed only to me. In twenty-five words you told me of your love for me, your pride in me, and named books for me to read. With only three lines you leapt over more than ten thousand kilometers, introduced me to the world of books, and once more gave me courage, just as in the days of my childhood. Courage to last almost another four years, until you actually did return.

In school I had learned the adage from Heraclitus, that war is the father of all things. War and father, those belonged inseparably together. Now I saw the fatefulness of this phrase for my own life as well—why had I tried for years to deny it? If war was "the father of all things," then there could be no life without war—why had I refused to understand this? Wasn't war even right, after all? My teachers never spoke of the wrongness of wars, only of their existence. I began to resign myself to the eternal recurrence of war.

The war had been over for more than a decade; the guilty from those times had been punished, the bombed-out cities were all rebuilt; the refugees no longer lived in barracks, but in new housing developments. Even the war cripples, whom I had looked on so fearfully as a little girl, were gone. It was as if their missing arms and legs had grown back. The time of my daily nightmares had passed too; nothing more tied me to those horrors. Hitler was agreed to be a madman, Stalin was long dead; the other names had apparently disappeared from memory. As for the hints and suspicions about terms like *Nazi, Gestapo,* and *SS,* which had tortured me for years, these seemed to be covered by a veil that screened and obscured whatever lay beneath it.

When Adenauer signed the agreement with Khrushchev in 1955 releasing the last prisoners of war, the news of your imminent return struck me quite differently from the way I had pictured it all those years. Anxiety, nervousness, the fearful question of how you might be—all this I experienced more clearly than my joy.

I had finally found peace in the last few years. Two of the brothers had left home; soon D. followed. Only G. and I were still there. At last there was space for me in the two-and-a-half-room apartment; at last Mama found time for me. G. and I had forgotten the malicious games of our childhood; we laughed together. School, girlfriends, evening strolls with Mama, the first furtive encounters with boys— would I have to give all that up for you? I was uncertain—did I really still want you? Did I actually still need you?

My relationship to you consisted of waiting for you. If you came back now, I would have to give up my longing and give you a place in my life, not just in my imagination. The memory of the gray, careworn men, the returnees of the first postwar years, came back to me: would you too look like that—perhaps even worse? I made an effort to suppress my doubts; I wanted to be happy about your return.

In the movie newsreels I found my worst fears confirmed: endless freight train cars rolled into Friedland, the first transit station. Iron doors were shoved back, revealing men trying to laugh, but the stress of the seven days' journey twisted their smiles to grimaces. They climbed out of the trains: felt boots, gray padded jackets, Russian caps with ear flaps, backpacks still trailing the straw the men had lain on for days—everything was different from the picture of you my longing had given me.

Week after week the transports rolled in, filled with onetime soldiers returning home. Then all was still again in Friedland. Then came several more trains, but you were never on them. Gradually I tired of hearing the long lists of names that were read out daily on the radio. Your name was never among them. Not until the very end did you come, at the end of the year, along with the former generals who had led the German troops in the attack on the Soviet Union, fourteen years before.

"Don't cry, I'm here now!" With these words you took me in your arms and tried to bridge eleven years of separation, as though you had just come home from a business trip. At first I was enchanted by your efforts to take a tuck in the fabric of time, as you tried to overcome everything separate and strange between us in the space of a few weeks.

The day after your arrival we bought you a suit, shoes, and shirts; you went to the barber, made an appointment at the dentist, threw away your felt boots, and were ready to begin a new life—with Mama, who meanwhile had become an independent woman who had fed and raised us alone, and with us, your almost-grown children.

Your return was celebrated like a holiday in our little city; everyone wanted to see you, to wave to you. In a newspaper article our family history was compared to the *Odyssey*. I was embarrassed; Mama had raised us with simplicity and modesty. Yet in one respect the reporter's simile rang true: no one asked Odysseus on his return why he had gone off to war against Troy twenty years before, just as here no connection was made between your return now and the war you had taken part in. You were received like a hero. Even my own faith was like that of Telemachus: Homer doesn't write that the son was filled with anger at the father. Uncomplainingly he had accepted growing up without a father, just as I first realized as a grown woman that my longing for you had covered my rage.

The state council honored you with a reception, speeches were given, an orchestra played. I was proud of you. Men in town to whom I had curtsied as a little girl now addressed me formally, at barely fifteen years old, as *"gnädiges Fräulein"*—mademoiselle. With Mama, they kissed her hand; you they gazed at respectfully. Waiting for you had been worth it! The mayor said he would do everything possible to help you find a position suitable to your capacities; hopefully you would place your abilities at the service of the city. I had no idea what he meant.

But then that was unimportant; what was important was something quite different. My dark inkling, the awful secret that had surrounded you, was gone. You had never been guilty; it was only the frightful war that had thrown its shadow over you as well. You yourself were good. Otherwise why would they grant you so much respect? I was ashamed of myself; how could I have doubted you? The weeks went by in mutual storytelling, as we tried to fill the gaps of the past eleven years with reports; enthralled, we listened to each other. In the retelling I once again lived through our flight in the midst of the bomber attacks, the time Mama and I were wounded, my stay in the military hospital, the months in the orphanage. I quickly suppressed the old fear that arose; I wanted to speak of the past just as you did of your time in the Russian prison and the years in Siberia. No mention of hopelessness and despair, but rather something like a fearsomely beautiful, dangerous adventure, a challenge which one had to meet, so your stories ran. While I listened to you, pictures from ancient tragedies arose in my mind, laced with scenes from the novels of Alexander Dumas, recast in the gloomy world of Dostoyevski.

You spoke of the months in a windowless cell, where you kept up your spirits by arguing questions of military strategy with the other prisoner, a famous general. How you had recited poetry to each other so as not to hear the monotonous sound of water dripping from the ceiling onto the stone floor. You told how you were taken out one morning to be executed, only to be brought back to another cell after two hours of anxious waiting.

You spoke too of the many dead of those first years, whose names you wanted to make note of in order to seek out their relatives later on. Your voice was serious; it had nothing of the self-pity of tipsy men exchanging war stories at the annual hunters' fair. Yet your seriousness seemed strangely detached from what you were talking about. In your voice was an echo of something that rang of fate, tragedy, inevitability. Without your using the words *duty, bravery, honor,* still I sensed that every sentence you spoke carried with it an unshaken framework of values according to which one was to act.

For several years I was your eager pupil; I wanted to be like you, strong and dutiful. And once again I despised myself for my secret tears, my weakness; I wanted to abandon self-pity and face life the way you did.

Only once did your face soften, your voice grow uncertain. You wanted to see where my foot had been shot. Trembling, I removed my shoe and stocking, as if I were exposing something that should be kept hidden. The scars had grown smaller with the years; they looked like stars on the right and left sides of my ankle. I had nearly forgotten them; only on lengthy walks did I get a reminder. You looked at the scars, carefully drew your finger over them, and said something I did not understand. I sensed how shaken you were. As though in these tiny scars you were seeing for the first time the full measure of mindless suffering brought on by the war. You had lived through the bombing of Berlin, had seen our home and the home of your parents in flames; you had seen wounded and maimed soldiers—you knew how many millions of people were killed by the war. You had defended yourself against all that. But the idea that your own family could be injured, that a four-year-old girl had been shot, filled you with helplessness.

I was moved and embarrassed by your pain and quickly drew on my stocking. I wanted nothing to do with your emotion. I knew it would undermine my resolution to be brave. Your sympathy for my wound came years too late; I no longer wanted it.

This experience of direct contact with everything we wanted to forget determined our future relations, without our being conscious of it. I believe it was then that we stopped speaking of ourselves directly. We made use of some third object; we took examples from literature and history, and gave these figures our thoughts. The moral dilemma of Kleist's Prince of Homburg, the loneliness of Schiller's Don Carlos, or the question of right and wrong in the Thirty Years War—these we took as metaphors to cover our own vulnerability. For hours on end we could talk, argue, grow excited, learning better and better how to keep ourselves hidden, both from each other and from ourselves.

Gradually I grew curious about your life before 1945. Now I could approach this dark time, now that I was certain that there could not have been more than a coincidental connection between Nazism and you. You told of your time as City Director, of state dinners, of important economic decisions, of your pleasure when you were conducted through the Prussian museums to select paintings for your offices in City Hall. A marvelous world of power and glitter arose before my eyes. Berlin, my home, a city of four million—and you had ruled it. I do not know which impressed me more—your glittering past or the naturalness with which you accepted our modest life in the little postwar tract apartment.

Only once did I see how these two worlds were still at war within you. We sat at the table in the living room, which became your bedroom by night, and suddenly you asked in astonishment why we did not use knife-rests at the table. I had to laugh. I hardly knew what a knife-rest was, but I knew at once it was something absurd. Mama became angry, tried to answer you, broke off, and left the room. I heard her crying softly in the kitchen. I have often thought back on these knife-rests. For you it seemed that they were the frame and the support you needed more desperately than any other. Not your long years in Siberia in unimaginable misery, not even the loss of your high position or our current poverty seemed to shake you. All that you could face with composure, but the small disorder at the table that resulted from the absence of knife-rests threatened your most basic convictions.

From your amazement at how Mama had managed all these years without knife-rests, I sensed that you had remained in the Old World, the time before 1945. A world in which the question of meaning was answered with outer forms. Today it seems to me as though it was this rigid clinging to forms that made it possible for you to become so deeply mired in guilt.

Soon we moved to Hamburg. You had found work in a government office there. My interest in you and your life slackened; I turned to my own affairs. I was a young girl, confident and curious about everything that lay before me.

One day at the house of some friends a book with pictures of Auschwitz fell into my hands. Even before I could grasp what I was seeing, I was overcome with a single thought: Daddy. I laid my hands over the open book, as if to hide the pictures from myself, to make them not true. I was bewildered; this was what I had suspected all those years, the dark secret, an unimaginable crime.

What was the relationship between you and this horror? There must be one; otherwise why the insinuations about your past? Now all the small pieces fit together that had been scattered across many separate moments in childhood, sometimes only in gestures, like Mama's painful smile. Now I remembered the ruined Jewish cemetery, overgrown with weeds, where I once was taken by children whom I admired but also feared for their coarse games. When one of the boys ordered us to pee on the upturned gravestones, I ran away; I swore to myself never to speak of this experience.

Now I remembered terms like *denazification** and *paragraph 131**: both had to do with you; they were the reason why Mama never received a pension or stipend in all those years, like other wives of prisoners of war. Now I recalled the letters from Berlin which she had to sign a receipt for, and which she hid from me. All that belonged to you.

After days of inner torment I asked you about Auschwitz. You reacted gruffly and evasively; I had never seen you like that. You had had nothing to do with that, was your answer. As I tried to show you and Mama the pictures, you pushed them aside angrily; you wanted to forbid my pursuing this. Mama was pale; she said nothing. In other words, you knew the pictures, you knew what had happened in the concentration camps; only you had hidden your knowledge from me. Why? For the first time I felt let down by both of you, betrayed. I wanted to get away from you.

Was it you who tried to win me back? Or was I still too young then to bear the internal distance from you both any longer? I no longer know, but soon we were speaking again. I began to question you: what were you, before you became City Director? I hoped you could take away my fear. And as before, you captured me with your tales, and I made your view of National Socialism my own. I saw your party membership and your entrance into the SS as unavoidable necessities, without which you could never have entered government service.

Gladly I put my faith in your assurance that you had had nothing to do with the murder of the Jews. The other question, whether you had known about it at the time, I answered for you myself: never, impossible! You would have intervened, you could not have lived if you had known.

And I—how was it I had made myself so deaf and blind as not to hear of this crime for so long, not until 1958? How had I not taken in the many hints that could have enlightened me? I was filled with the old feeling of guilt that had run through my childhood. Now I had proof of my guilt at last: I had been indifferent to the suffering of the Jews.

I was not aware at the time of how my readiness to take guilt onto myself protected me from seeing the guilt in you. I divided my conscience between sympathy for the Jews as victims of fascism and loyalty to you—you, the champion of law for the good of the majority.

I forgot my penetrating questions about wrongs and crimes and let myself be seduced by your memories. As before, when you told of your time in prison in Moscow, I followed you now through the years 1933 to 1942. I joined you on your path through the Berlin Ministry of Police, followed you into the Prince Albert Palace— Gestapo headquarters. Could I have gone on listening to you if I had known that thousands of people were interrogated, tortured, condemned, and murdered there? Inconceivable.

Dark, mysterious, and exciting—so I imagined your life in these years. "Security Service": did I let myself be blinded by the word *security,* or was I really so naive as not to know the truth about the SD? The same SD which together with the Gestapo wielded unlimited power, which controlled the concentration camps, which penetrated the entire state with its surveillance system, from which there was hardly any escape.

Your reports of the SD and the Gestapo sounded more like a dangerous detective game, more like an espionage movie than the criminal organizations they actually were. With a shiver I listened to your description of how you kept a secret watch on Goebbels, because Hitler doubted his unconditional devotion to the Party, or how Goering surrounded himself with his own security service, for fear of yours.

I was enthralled by your stories: the names which in my childhood had been the symbol for everything evil, you reduced to timid little figures. As though I could take a belated revenge on them by listening to you now. You initiated me into the secrets of the apparatus of political power; you made me your confidante. It was as if I held your hand and stepped behind the curtains of a theater, only to discover there that the fearsome scenery looked quite harmless, almost laughable when seen up close.

Why did you do that? Why did you feed me on exciting anecdotes about men who were responsible for the death of millions? Did you need me, the devoted daughter, faithfully by your side so that I would stop asking you about your own guilt? Did you need these stories to defend yourself against the question of the responsibility you shared? Did the memory of the everyday, eccentric aspects of these men help you to comprehend at whose service you had placed yourself so unconditionally? I do not know. At the time I was proud to be your audience and your confidante, and I gladly let myself be burdened with what you did not want to bear alone.

I owe it to a coincidence, an accidentally overheard telephone conversation, that I was able to break free from the inner warfare I felt at the time between my loyalty to you and my knowledge of the crimes. Once again there was a secret, only this time it was not in relation to the past; it was quite current. I learned that you had been working for years for the government intelligence service, the secret service of the West German republic.

I was stunned. While I was still coming to terms with your old guilt, you were already building up a new secret system, similar to the old one, which spied on people, pursued them, and punished them, even if today the victims were no longer tortured and murdered. You tried to counter my reproaches by saying that your work was necessary as a defense against Soviet espionage. But this time you could not draw me to your side. Even as you tried to explain, I realized that all these years you had been using your secret agent strategies on me as well, to inspire trust and at the same time obscure my view of the wider implications. In the process of your drawing me so close to you and sharing secret details with me, I had lost my objectivity. You took the twelve years of Nazi dominion and dissolved them before me into separate incidents; then once you had simply removed the murder of the Jews from the whole picture, it all seemed to me more like an adventure than a systematically constructed crime. In your stories the suffering was taken out; the victims were missing, and along with them the perpetrators.

Just as you never mentioned your own suffering in prison in

Moscow, in the same way your stories about your work with the Gestapo and the SD made no mention of the suffering of the Communists and Socialists and all the others that you had hounded so pitilessly. You never defended Nazism to us, but you never distanced yourself from it either. You never spoke openly of your political connections, although you must have used those connections immediately following your release in 1955. How else could you have gone to work for the West German intelligence service? One could never tell by looking at you what you did or who you were. You bore no resemblance to the jackbooted, whip-cracking SS types of American films; you were charming, cultured, sympathetic. Yet suddenly I realized what danger lay in you. Just as you had long abused my childish trust, so that I was prepared to take on your political views, now you were again trafficking in abuse of political power—since working for the secret service could mean nothing else but that.

All at once I remembered how I had knelt on dried peas as a little girl, so as to share your punishment with you, and for the first time I felt impotent rage toward you. Yet at the same time I was enraged with myself, for having loved you unconditionally for so long. I hoped I would never see you again.

We owe it to Andrea that things never came to the point of a final break between us. Her love for you, her grandfather, reminded me of those first happy years with you; through her I could experience your many-sidedness again, to which I had blinded myself in my anger and my disappointment. Sometimes I watched you as you showed her the lands and oceans on the globe, told her little amusing stories, and I saw her child's face radiating happiness, and yours, grown old now, softened by love for your grandchild.

Still I remained guarded with you; we resumed our old habit of speaking of books, sometimes breaking off in mid-thought as we sensed the estrangement between us. I needed the distance: I still feared that too much closeness with you would mean entrapment once more in those powerful secrets of yours.

The shared sorrow over Mama's sudden death brought us closer again. A tumor had formed around a piece of shrapnel, lodged deep in her spine for twenty-five years since our flight, and it had destroyed her spinal cord. We were bewildered; we missed her so. With her tenderness, her sad smile, and her silence, she had given us the secure ground on which we could meet for all these years.

You seemed infinitely lost; your helplessness moved me. We siblings had each other; G. and I lived near each other in Berlin, and I had Andrea. You were alone. You came to us frequently, and your visits to Berlin, your own city, forced me into a fundamental and unsparing confrontation with fascism, and with you.

I found everything confirmed that I had long suspected and never quite believed. As I finally admitted to myself what your position in the SD had been, my illusion that you could have been ignorant of the death camps collapsed utterly. And with it went my last hope that as City Director you had been involved only with the administration and official functions of the city. You had taken on that position not as a civil servant, but as an SS official of high rank.

As gruesome as the certain knowledge was that you knew of the crimes of the Gestapo, were even personally involved in some of them, still I suffered less than I had as a child, when I was torn between hope, suspicion, and terror. The most awful truth was lighter for me to bear than that despairing search for your innocence or later for your guilt. I was a grown woman now and could make an independent decision whether despite everything I still chose to have contact with you. Still there came moments of deep despair, sometimes triggered by an anniversary date, such as July 20, 1944* (the attempt on Hitler's life) which you and the other authorities had taken as the occasion to order the murder of five thousand people. But even at my most unhappy I no longer felt guilty, the way I had when my identification with you had kept me from taking up an independent perspective. My self-respect grew in proportion to the clarity with which I saw you—with features which remained irreconcilably contradictory for me. I had to give up closing my eyes out of fear of discovering some new horror; but I also had to give up wallowing in your guilt, which I had made my own. I could turn away from you and gradually release myself from that which had oppressed me. Not until I was free could I discover my responsibility for myself, even if I could not yet translate this into political action.

The more I left you in peace and kept my sadness to my self, the more eagerly you initiated conversations about your own past. You took our walks through the city as occasions for these reminiscences; you stopped in front of buildings that awakened memories for you; you went all the way back to the beginnings. Once I saw you angry: we were on our way to visit Andrea in her first student apartment and passed by the guard barracks where Hitler had the leaders of the SA murdered following the "Röhm Putsch."* You were involved in making the arrests.

For the first time you seemed to grasp how as a young man you had subscribed to a system to which millions of human beings were to fall victim. What you had seen as duty and obedience, strengthened by an oath of loyalty, was the beginning of a process by which you would gradually sign away more and more of your own responsibility. Then as more and more responsibility was entrusted to you, you were no longer in a position to pose questions to yourself.

I was unpleasantly moved by the fact that it was precisely this event that shocked you and not something that in my value system counted as more than the murder of SA leaders. I still could not give up my hope that you would feel remorse. But I no longer dared to ask you; I was too afraid.

When you knew that a fatal illness no longer left you much time, once again you drew me into the abyss of your memories and confided one more secret that you had carried for over forty years. At the same time you extracted a promise from me never to speak of it again. As of this moment I still feel bound by that promise.

We saw each other again a few days before your death. I sat by your bed; you seemed to be sleeping. I was shocked by your appearance. G. had prepared me, but not for this! Memories rose up of horrible pictures of human beings reduced to skeletons.

At some point you opened your eyes and tried to smile, as you recognized me. After a time you spoke, quite softly, about Gottfried Keller's novel *Green Henry,* and how he waited with joyful anticipation to quit the old world and discover the new. The effort was too much for you; I went on speaking for you, till you fell asleep. For once I was thankful for our symbolic code, which enabled us to express our feelings while masking them at the same time.

Later I sat with you again. You became restless. With infinite effort, as if you already had to call up the words from another world, you spoke: "It was wrong of the Spaniards to murder the Incas and steal their land." My throat tightened with tears as I answered you: "Yes, Daddy—thank you."

The next day you lapsed into a coma from which you never awakened. You remained for eleven days in this deathlike sleep, till finally peace was granted to you, and you yielded to death. In these eleven days I relived the eleven years of waiting for you, and all my longing, and then the joy and soon the despair, which now, like my love for you, will be with me always.

3

I TOO TOOK PART
Confrontations with One's Own History in Family Therapy

Heidi Salm

In May of 1987 I was asked if I would write a chapter for this collection on the subject of my experiences with children and grandchildren of the perpetrators of the Third Reich—which is to say, of convinced Nazis. I agreed quite spontaneously, since an abundance of images out of my therapeutic work came immediately to mind. I began to leaf through the records of my twelve years of practice as a family therapist, in search of specifics. In the process it struck me how much importance I have attached, in my work with individuals, couples, and families, to handwritten life histories of the parents of my clients, and how the time between the two world wars and the Nazi years in particular had come up again and again as themes in the sessions. But the tapes have all been erased or else taken by the patients. Thus I am thrown back on myself alone, on my memories, my handwritten notes, and my images. But then after all, isn't the issue really one of my own experience and self?

I was born in 1922, and thus was eleven years old when Hitler came to power. I participated in these times; they marked me as a child and a young woman, and I too was involved. In this chapter the subject is supposed to be perpetrators and convinced Nazis. But who actually considers himself a perpetrator or is defined as one? Does that really mean only those who killed other people, either by denouncing them or by taking a direct part in their murder? Are people not labeled with the smear word "Nazi" today whose behavior was quite the opposite? In my first case report, in 1984, a daughter called her mother a perpetrator—an accusation which made me realize that I too must consider myself to be one.

When I asked not long ago, in my own family, about the political activity of my late father, I was told plainly and clearly that while my father did admire Hitler, only I had been a "real Nazi"; the others had tended more to hold back. It is true: as a young girl, prone to enthusiasms, I was for some years a leader of ten- to twelve-year-old *Jungmädels* (the youngest members of the *Bund deutscher Mädel*—the BDM, or League of German Girls*) and was promoted in the course of time to council leader, before I was drafted into the Workers' Corps in 1939 after I had finished high school. In the years of this leadership role, to the extent that I had been influenced by Nazi ideas, I passed this worldview on to the ten- to twelve-year-olds. Therein I see my participation, my co-responsibility, and my guilt.

A few weeks ago I was speaking with a twenty-one-year-old student of education about this question of responsibility, which was on my mind, and about my own history. This student asked me how I could possibly see myself as a perpetrator, since after all I was obliged to do what I did, just as today people are required to do all kinds of things; the real perpetrators were different people entirely. This question made it clear to me once again how many of the younger generation, because of our silence, have a vastly over-simplified image of "the Nazi," seeing him either as a threatening monster or else as a hero to be admired. It is likely that they really know very little—precisely because of our silence—about the majority of Nazis, who were neither the one extreme nor the other, but rather just tended to conform, without thinking much about it, and just did what the authorities demanded of them. Given these images of extreme villains, it was relatively easy for many of us of the older generation to say that we never belonged to "those Nazis."

I have long searched my memory again and again trying to answer the question of whether I did not actually know something of the atrocities in the concentration camps—did not indeed have to have known something! This question which I posed to myself, about what all I might have forgotten and repressed from that time, left me uncertain and hesitant in speaking of the Nazi period. For a long time I was in the grip of self-doubt as to how much I might be minimizing the actual mass murders through my memories of many positive experiences in those times, and how valid my own testimony could actually be, for this same reason.

In the framework of psychotherapeutic work, I stimulate others to review their past and their history, and to place them in relationship to the present. In the process I am constantly confronted with my own history—and differently from the way it happened in my own therapy. It has long been clear to me that my choice of profession was closely related to my own family history. What is only

---

* See Glossary, here and wherever an asterisk appears. —Trans.

becoming clear to me now is that my therapeutic activity is obviously an unconsciously chosen way for me to try to deal with my political past as well.

These thoughts were the final stimulus for my participation in this book. In what follows I would like to portray my own memories from the Nazi era in relation to the experiences of my patients. Out of the multiplicity of possible examples, I have selected three case presentations through which I was confronted anew with my own Nazi past.

First Case

Frau Ursel N., born in 1944, came to my office in 1984 with her daughter, Anna, who had just turned nine years old. She depicted the situation as follows: "I am helplessly locked in conflict with my own mother, whom I depend on to run the household and look after my daughter, since I am divorced and working. With all this conflict, I am worried about my daughter, Anna, who cries a great deal and is obviously suffering from the constant arguments." As she told me her own life story, I was struck by the similarities between Ursel and her mother. Both the mother, Frau Leder, and Ursel were only children. Both had married at the age of twenty-four and each had married a teacher. Frau Leder's husband was declared missing in action in Russia shortly after their daughter's birth. Ursel's husband obtained a divorce soon after the birth of their daughter. Frau Leder, born in 1920, was a nurse, while Ursel was an elementary school teacher. Ursel explained her mother's career choice to me in the following terms: "My mother more or less grew up in her profession because of the war, and many of her ideas and much of her thinking were shaped by this period as well—ideas which we argue a great deal about and have very different views on." On account of this, it seemed necessary to me to invite Frau Leder to my office for the following sessions.

In the subsequent meetings, at which three women from three different generations sat opposite me (with Anna constantly swinging back and forth between mother and grandmother), we quickly got down to the similarities and differences between mother and daughter. For Ursel, not only was a nursing career completely incomprehensible, but above all she felt a deep shame that her mother had practiced this profession in the Nazi period and still found much to admire, as she put it, in those times. This led to a heated discussion between mother and daughter, while Anna hid behind a chair in the farthest corner of the office. I offered my services as mediator. Frau Leder reported that at the age of fourteen she joined the BDM, the League of German Girls, and that "like many other girls in my class," she was very proud of receiving her black neckerchief with the brown slide and of wearing a uniform. I told her that I too, two years younger than she, had admired myself in the mirror in the uniform of the BDM. Only then did Frau Leder have the courage to go on with her story, despite the physical agitation and the caustic side remarks of her daughter.

She told of excursions with girls her age outside the city, which she, as an only child accustomed to playing only on city streets, had especially enjoyed. She told us too of accordion concerts and singing, and repeated once more, with a nod in her daughter's direction, "And it was wonderful, even if you refuse to understand that." At this point I asked her daughter, Ursel, whether she couldn't understand what her mother had been saying, and what she imagined it would be like, to be out in the countryside, having fun along with the group. Ursel answered that that had nothing to do with what her mother was telling; she too enjoyed things like that and was in a women's group that still made weekend excursions to the country. But then they would talk about quite different things; there was no political component—they weren't even interested in politics. In that regard the two things were not even comparable. The daughter seemed then to have great difficulty in even listening, as Frau Leder tried to convince her that those weekends were not political either, that the political education in the BDM had taken place once a week on the so-called home nights, which for Frau Leder had been in part as boring as a school lesson, but which she was required to attend.

I too remember well the day when the bestowal of the black neckerchief and brown slide in the course of a formal ceremony marked my entrance into the ranks of the *Jungmädel,* after some three months' probationary status. Just like Frau Leder, I too was swept up in a flood of lovely, positive memories of the fellowship of these ten- to twelve-year-olds. I too enjoyed singing, making music, hiking, and putting on plays together. And in my memory too, the home nights, in which I took part for two years as a *Jungmädel,* were much like school: there was a lot of mischief making, and we paid only intermittent attention, all according to the authority or inspiration of the leaders at the moment. But in my case it went further than this: at thirteen I took over a beginning class of ten-year-olds, and what is more, I was quite proud to be entrusted with this responsibility. But as a so-called *Führerin,** I now had the job of presenting political topics at the home nights once a week. I still remember vividly the lesson I was to give on the life histories of the "great leaders of the Third Reich." (It strikes me as an irony of my own history that at the age of thirteen in the Nazi period, I had already begun to concern myself with the life histories of others.) Other themes of these home nights were special moments in history in which the Germans were depicted as the chosen people. In school I learned history from a very one-sided point of view, and I passed it on in this form to the members of my group. All the themes stated generally that it was "granted to us to live at the dawn of a new era, and we must prepare ourselves and be ready for whatever might be demanded of us."

When I write that here and let these thoughts and images pass before my eyes, and feel what it all meant to me then, I am shocked at how blindly and uncritically I passed on to the younger girls this Hitlerian worldview, which held up the Germans as the "chosen people" and race, and took every sign of difference as grounds for expulsion, and which ultimately led to the mass murder of the Jews.

At the same time, my memories of these times, whether as an eleven- or twelve-year-old or later as a youth leader, are always bound up with feelings of fear. Thus, for example, I could ask Frau Leder whether she too had experienced this fear, as I had. At this, Frau Leder told how in her class there were groups of Nazis and non-Nazis. Of course, all of them were supposed to wear uniforms. Nonetheless, she admired—without at all understanding them—the two students who refused to wear the uniforms, who were always very much on the outside and were treated unfairly by the teachers. She told too of how the political pressure grew ever more intense. "But that was more a problem for the ones who didn't go along; we didn't think much about it." Such remarks by her mother enraged Ursel, who was also unwilling at first to compare any memories on her side of the time when she was fifteen or sixteen years old. "We didn't have any concentration camps or mass exterminations," she cried out. "And that's the whole point. That's what can't be glossed over."

In spite of the strong recurrent objections of the daughter, we were able to contract for further sessions, where we would go on talking about similarities and differences in past and present. I asked Frau Leder to bring in photographs of the old days, and Ursel was to prepare all the critical questions she liked. While mother and grandmother were quite uncertain whether Anna should attend the sessions, Anna herself declared her firm intention to be there.

The stormiest debates had to do with the daughter's questions about what her mother had known of the concentration camps and the persecution of the Jews. Frau Leder insisted over and over that she had known nothing about it and could not say anything more. Ursel refused to believe this and continued to accuse her mother vehemently. In this session I reacted, probably quite defensively, and reported that I too, so far as I could remember, had known nothing of the concentration camps.

I still experience helplessness in the face of this theme of not being told and abandonment by those who failed to tell me. I knew, for example, that the Jews were in danger, because my father was helping Jews to emigrate. But apparently at that young age I did not inquire any further, and so far as I can remember, nothing more was told me about the exact nature of the danger. Thus I must have learned to close my eyes and ears to certain dangers, but the fear associated with those dangers stayed with me.

But then as far as I can tell I was surrounded by people who kept out of it, did not want to know, people who held their tongues and did everything they could to avoid conflict. Just as the young now accuse us of silence, so do I now question and accuse my elders in retrospect: my own parents, my teachers, pastors, and other caretakers, who were likewise silent. Did not their decision to stay out of it enable others to go to such extremes of involvement? But those "silent ones" I knew by name are no longer living, and others are only nameless faces in my memory. Thus I have never had any opportunity, since these questions first began to occur to me, to discuss or argue these issues with people whom I knew personally from the older generation. I feel a deep grief that my parents and I never discussed the Nazi time, that neither I nor they could touch on the subject during their lifetimes.

In the framework of the therapy session, through comparing photographs and exchanging life experiences, the two women gradually were able to hear each other better and allow each other more space. In the process a further secret came to light: according to his wife's report, Ursel's father was apparently a convinced Nazi, who also taught his beliefs in school. This had been kept from daughter and granddaughter until now. At first Ursel seemed close to a complete breakdown in this session: long sobbing and weeping now took the place of accusations; Anna too wept and pressed close to her mother, while the grandmother seemed to me to be paralyzed. An image of her father which had been built up for decades was now destroyed for Ursel. Only with time could she begin to understand that the part of her father which taught school as a convinced Nazi— who felt, as her mother put it, "understood and accepted in the Party"—did not completely eradicate the other part, which her mother described as a sensitive, warmhearted family man. A conversation with a living father had never been possible for Ursel, and on this account her anger at her mother, for showing her only one half and holding back the "real Papa," was quite understandable. Frau Leder was shocked to see that her silence had not served to protect the image of her fallen husband or to help her daughter, as she had believed it would.

In the following therapy sessions with the Leder family, Anna could begin to form an image of her grandfather for the first time, and by her continual confusion of father and grandfather, she elicited ever more information and explanation about the men of the family, now present only as empty chairs. Frau Leder could now speak more openly about her fears and feelings in the time of growing oppression during the Nazi regime, and her relief at being able to translate this fear into active physical caretaking for others in her work as a nurse. At the same time, the daughter's attacks on her mother's past began to lose some of their sting. But despite this greater openness between them, a certain alienation came up again and again, as for example when Frau Leder would say to her daughter, "Why don't you try to do something, instead of just complaining!" or when her voice would suddenly change, and she would talk about how easy the current generation had it, how you couldn't make comparisons anyway under such different circumstances, and how on that account nothing like that could ever happen again.

Remarks like that were and are like a cold shower to me. All I can do then is to ask the younger generation whether they themselves really feel that they have it so easy, and whether similar things might not be repeated at any moment. To this, I would cite the answer of a twenty-five-year-old, in 1987, which left me totally speechless: he told me in all seriousness that as far as any lack of information was concerned, nowadays the computer could easily fill this gap. How could I have so little faith in computers? Nor could the economic situation be in any way compared with 1933. Thus for his generation there could be no possibility of any recurrence of Nazism. All this was just the fantasy of the older generation!

Second Case

The setting was a nine-day therapy seminar (family reconstruction[1]), within the framework of a family therapy training course, with twelve participants, which I led with a colleague in 1985. One of the group members, Friedrich K., born in 1942, married and the father of a two-year-old son, had already learned a great many new things about his family of origin in the preparatory work required before the seminar. In the process much had been stirred up, in him and in his family as well. In the construction of a life history of his father, who fell in the war in Russia, Friedrich had come up against many gaps and contradictions, so that along with his mother's reports, he had interviewed two surviving sisters and an old school friend of his father's. Through his father's friend, Friedrich learned, to his complete surprise, that his father did not die as a combat officer in Russia, but rather had been an active member of the SS from 1937. This information hit Friedrich like a body blow. He himself had been politically active for many years and counted himself among those who react with great sensitivity and aggression to any gestures or remarks in his presence that seem to him to smack of Nazism. Friedrich had devoured, as he put it, all the reading material he could get his hands on having to do with the Third Reich. He described his own feelings of helplessness in encounters with older politicians, none of whom ever seemed to have been involved, when he asked them about the Nazi period, so that no direct confrontation was ever possible. Now it seemed that his own father had been one of those directly involved, and even in the "black SS"—which is to say, actually one of the perpetrators! Once again, no direct confrontation was possible.

Friedrich was also filled with anger at his mother, who had knowingly allowed her son to take up a false position: that of pursuing former Nazis as enemies from the standpoint of one who was supposedly not involved. For him, his equilibrium was shattered by this new information. His conceptions of his family, of his own political activism, and of his identity were thrown into question. His sixty-six-year-old mother too seemed to have lost her customary composure through the accusations of her son; she cried continually and spoke for the first time of her fears, then and now. His two older

---

1. The techniques of "family reconstruction," based in part on the work of Virginia Satir, are explained in the case description that follows.

siblings reproached him for stirring up the distant past and for having no consideration for their mother.

It was in this frame of mind that Friedrich came to the seminar with the question, "Who was my father?" In the course of the seminar, with the use of the material he had brought in (life history, photographs, reports), and above all through family sculptures, we attempted to capture an image of the personality of his father, Ulrich, and the imprint on him of his own family of origin. At the same time, we posed hypotheses about the possible rules of that family. From all of this, as well as from the feedback of the group member chosen to play the role of Ulrich, came the following picture: Ulrich K. was born in 1913, the only son and youngest child, following four daughters. His father was a civil servant, his mother a housewife. The father was drafted into the army shortly after Ulrich's birth and fell in France in 1917. The remainder of the family seemed to have the following survival rules: "We all stick together," "We are very special people," "Open conflict is not allowed." It was confirmed by Ulrich's two surviving sisters that they all made strenuous efforts to live up to this last rule and that no conflict of any kind was ever allowed to come out into the open. For the most part Father Ulrich seems to have conformed to all this as a boy; at the same time, however, as the youngest child he did try to draw special attention to himself through school pranks and naughtiness. In order not to be forever the "little one" (which his mother still called him when he was six-feet two), he did all he could to prove his manhood and his strength (height, a steel physique, evidence of physical and intellectual achievement, among other things, were all criteria for admission to the SS). There is much evidence that Ulrich needed groups with whom he could fit in, as well as ones of whom he could make high demands, as he did of himself.

In the course of family reconstruction, role plays, and sculpturing, we arrived at the following scene: three group members were asked to feel their way into the role of SS members, who would wear the black uniform with the death head, and to give expression to this role in their physical carriage. They formed a group marching in lockstep in front of the then twenty-one-year-old Ulrich—as best as could be reconstructed through our work so far. The more regimented this group became in its movements, the more confident the ring of the marching boots, the more uncertain Ulrich looked, until he began to fall in line and march with them, "following the undertow, wherever it might lead," as the member playing this role expressed it afterwards. I can still see and hear the agitation of the man who played Ulrich in the feedback after this scene, as he reflected on the sensation of a physical pull toward the group. Friedrich too was very moved as he watched.

In the course of the therapeutic work we reached a confrontation between father and son, which of course in reality could never have taken place. But even in this form the encounter showed how difficult it was for Friedrich to sustain his rage and his accusation— "How could you, Father, be so blind and remain so blind to the role that the SS, and you with them, played in the mass extermination?"—in the face of his father's reply: "At first I was fascinated by fine-sounding ideals, by the elite nature of the group; later on we SS members were especially sworn to an oath of silence, and we learned to live with this silence under the threat of death."

I feel now in writing about this just as I did when I experienced it in the seminar: when the son's accusation was countered on the father's side by expressions of fascination, of silence, and of fear, the effect on me was one of discomfiture and incomprehension, and I was left with a feeling of helplessness. For me, the son's accusation only takes on its full validity when I hear the other side. For is it not this very silence between the generations that leads to the ever-increasing uncertainty between us? To what extent do many older people assume that the young share the uncertainties and fears that they themselves experienced? And to what degree do they con- sciously make themselves available for an encounter with the young and their differentness?

This group portrait from family reconstruction also stirred many memories in me. Images arise, for example, of the May Day festivals, where every year I spent hours on some square or other. Endless standing goes along with these images, as well as heat and bad air, singing, and listening to speeches, but also the feeling of belong- ingness and identity through the uniform and the great mass of people. It was a "we" feeling, and when I think back on it, there is sadness as well, because it was also my birthday, which after all should have belonged to me alone, especially in those years from eleven to fifteen. And I remember too how at times I had to use all my strength to stay on my feet, because I felt fatigued to the point of dizziness. But the group pressure I felt as youth leader carried me through, as well as the code of conduct I learned at home: "Pull your- self together." I stuck it out, just as I have so often done in later life.

But other memories as well came into this picture of the group to which Friedrich's father was drawn—memories having to do with fear. I see myself standing on a street corner, and the SA marching by with ringing steps. I knew that they were carrying out some mission; more than that I did not know, but it was enough to inspire every kind of fear in me, which I still can feel today whenever I think of the sound of boots on pavement. But what fears must have been felt at the time by those youths who grew up not as I did, in sub-urban villas, but in cramped apartments and streets, experiencing directly, perhaps, the persecution of the Jews!

Another image from those times surfaced in my memory for the first time not long ago, when I heard from a close friend about a house search. In those days, around 1937 (it must have been at the beginning of my role as girls' youth leader), one of the girls from my group came to the weekend training with the news that there had been an uproar at their home one evening. When she opened the front door, she was simply shoved aside by eight SA members who proceeded to search all the drawers and cabinets. Her father was not home, and she, her older brother, and her mother had been ordered not to move and not to say anything. Her mother had sat stiff and straight in a chair, and put her hand over the brother's mouth when-ever he tried to protest. Then with a "Heil Hitler" the SA men had left, taking with them books and papers from her father's desk. When she asked her father about it the next day, he merely answered that there was nothing to be said.

For forty years I simply forgot this incident. Now I see it again in all its details, including my own reaction as a fourteen-year-old youth leader: at the time, I took ten-year-old Annette in my arms, let her tell her story, but said little. I myself felt deeply afraid as I lis-tened, and through the weekend I made sure there were plenty of activities, sports, and games—which was one of my well-learned ways of avoiding anxiety.

Third Case

In what follows I would like to add a brief report of a conversa-tion in my office between a seventy-year-old father and his forty-year-old daughter, in which the subject was the father's involvement as a district leader in the Nazi period. Question from the daughter to the father: "What was so important to you back then about your position?" Father: "I no longer know; I only know that it was important to me, and that I was even proud, for you as well, that I could be district leader." Daughter: "Then what did Hitler and the other leaders mean to you?" Father: "I admired Hitler. When he gave a speech, I always tried to pick out a few sentences that particularly impressed me, and memorize them. At the time I admired him deeply." Daughter: "What was there to admire about him? This is what I can't understand." Father: "His voice, for example. His upright bearing; he knew what was right and gave me security. But you would have had to experience it yourself. You can't possibly understand." Daughter: "I don't want to understand." Father: "But then none of this has any point."

Yes, I too was fascinated by Adolf Hitler. When I was fifteen years old, on one occasion I stood almost a whole day in the rain, just to see the Führer drive by in his car. For many people Adolf Hitler had a kind of radiance, which reminds me in retrospect of the tale of the Pied Piper. In the story it was the rat catcher's flute music that drew out all the rats of the town, but also all the children, who followed him into a dark mountain, which closed again behind them.

The seventy-year-old father in my office ended the conversation with the resigned remark that "none of this has any point." For me every conversation contains the possibility of a new encounter. Not until I began to think back on these experiences in preparation for this essay did I fully appreciate how thoroughly we had learned, in the time under Hitler, to live with the silence of our parents, our teachers, and our superiors. "The enemy is listening" was the watchword not only for the news reports of the war years later on, but also for our everyday life as early as 1933.

To my own daughter's questions, of how I dealt with the collapse of Nazi ideals during and after the war, and whether I did not already feel guilty at the time, so far I can only give the following answer: My memories of the war, during which time I took no more part in Party activities and did not enroll as a Party member, are marked by the mortal fear I felt in the air raid shelters and by the events of war, and have hardly any connection to Hitler and his ideas. In the reconstruction period, I see myself caught up in every aspect of life by the search for personal and professional identity and the establishment of my own family. Certainly I will never be able to explain to anyone who did not live through the Nazi period what happened to me and within me in those times, any more than I can explain what an expanse of time, what external and internal events, were necessary for me to make all these forgotten things accessible once again. It only became clear to me how much I required an external push to overcome the silence and the forgetting of the Nazi period when the demand of the publishers of this book moved me to go beyond the sheltered preserves of family life, friends, and the therapy hour, and to declare myself openly as a one-time active follower of the Nazis.

4

THE PSYCHOANALYST WITHOUT A FACE: Psychoanalysis Without a History

Sammy Speier

What will finally determine whether our freedom is and will remain a worthwhile goal of our efforts may lie in whether we learn better to endure the truth about ourselves: a greater and less cautious truth than before. . . .
—*Alexander Mitscherlich, Address at the opening of the Sigmund Freud Institute*

For some years, German psychoanalysts have intensively debated the possibility and necessity of political commitment and the issue of reality in psychoanalysis. In what follows, I wish to bring this discussion to bear on the suppressed history of the National Socialist dictatorship and draw implications for the therapeutic work of psychoanalysts today.

Whoever works as a psychoanalyst in Germany today stands in the shadow of the reality of the Third Reich. The generation which carried out the systematic extermination of millions of Jews, Gypsies, and other groups who were excluded from the "racial community" is the generation of the parents and grandparents of today's patients. Even when they were not accomplices, they were onlookers, bystanders, and thus participants in this era. Our patients were thus brought up by these people, or perhaps not brought up enough. The early childhood, the formative years of our patients' lives can be correctly understood psychoanalytically only when this connection is borne in mind, and not, as often happens, when the attempt is made to ignore it.

For the microsociety of psychoanalysts, which mirrors the macrosociety, the same is true: the teachers who trained today's psychoanalysts belong to that generation whose life history bears the stamp of the Nazi dictatorship and the mass extermination it brought about. The psychoanalysts in postwar Germany were not, as one would like to imagine, men of the "founding hour" only, but rather men of the final hour as well, and that has important implications for the new generation of psychoanalysts. The fact that we have an unadmitted and unresolved history of genocide behind us is a state of affairs which we would prefer to suppress and deny.

Since Auschwitz, an important traditional precept of classical psychoanalysis, namely the idea that fantasy surpasses reality, no longer holds true. From that time on, we have known that reality is often far worse than our most depraved unconscious fantasies. Anyone who denies this is working in the service of the repetition compulsion; absence of discussion conjures up the return of the same material. On this issue, E. Simenauer (1982) wrote:

> The recurrence of war and persecution in psychoanalyses is only one aspect of the repetition of the preoccupation with war and persecution on the political and societal levels. . . . Both possess the characteristics of the return of the repressed. . . ; the underlying repetition compulsion reveals itself in the polarity of memory and repetition in life, and in the psychoanalytic process. . . . The present social reality with its ubiquitous latent violence means that the conflict of the generations cannot be understood and dealt with exclusively from the perspective of the theory of the Oedipus complex. The particular nature of aggression demands an interpretation of present reality as well. [p. 9]

The program of classical psychoanalysis was to confront the patient lying on the couch with his unconscious, which is to say, to make him aware of fantasies outlawed by the ego and superego. The confrontation with frightening, sometimes monstrous impulses was supposed to allow the patient to work them through and to integrate them, so as not to have to act them out. In the course of this therapy he would discover sexual curiosity, sexual fantasies, ambivalence toward his parents, and murderous impulses. Neurotic behavioral traits would be reduced by increased consciousness of repressed experience.

Keilson (1983) has described how, in the analysis of a child who had to "live" in a concentration camp, language was not adequate to represent the events and experiences there: "I have tried to throw

---

* See Glossary, here and wherever an asterisk appears. —Trans.

light on how difficult it is to translate into psychological, psychoanalytic terminology, events which occur in a world where language
fails to penetrate" (p. 925).

Likewise, reports from witnesses, historians, and therapists show
that the reality of the concentration camp far outstripped the possibility of capturing it in words. On the one hand, it is impossible to
enter completely into the experience of the concentration camp
inmates; on the other hand, it was never possible for the victims
themselves to express their experience fully in words. Nonetheless,
if we are serious in our desire and our struggle for a future, we must
confront ourselves again and again with this reality—and find language to express it. For language is *the* medium of psychoanalytic
therapy. "When the analyst is confronted with undisguised fantasies
of violence and extreme degradation, his generally recognized and
familiar world of psychoanalysis may threaten to collapse" (Simenauer, 1982, p. 9).

The fear of such confusion and destabilization leads many psychoanalysts even today to deny that the possibilities of "classical"
psychoanalysis are limited in dealing with both the monstrous forces
of impulse which were lived out unrestrainedly in the Nazi period
and the severe traumatization which resulted. There is a tendency to
deny the existence of traumatic childhood experiences which cannot
be directly verbalized afterward, as well as experiences which were
mediated nonverbally. In both cases a reconstruction by means of
classical psychoanalysis alone is impossible (see Grubrich-Simitis,
1984). Among psychoanalysts, the implications of the experiences
of concentration camp survivors for the psychic illnesses of their
children are much debated; even the use of the term "psychic illnesses" shows that the traditional diagnostic vocabulary of
psychoanalysis is insufficient here. It is difficult, often impossible, to
find a "classical" diagnosis for patients who have grown up with fear
of extermination (see Wangh, 1985, p. 51). And I would like to stress
that here I also mean the fear of extermination experienced by the
children of the perpetrators, onlookers, and bystanders, when they
looked at their own parents, relatives, and others.

From colleagues in the Netherlands I have heard that in Holland
there exist special programs (under the name "Recognition") for the
treatment of patients who are children of Nazi collaborators
(National Socialist Movement members). Although these patients
were not themselves collaborators, they are not integrated into
Dutch society the way other people are, and this causes them to
suffer. They can attend these programs anonymously to try to deal

with their quasi-stigmatization. How many such programs would there have to be here in Germany!

Psychoanalytic practices in Germany are full of patients who are the children of the persecutors, accomplices, witnesses, and bystanders; this state of affairs is, however, collectively denied. Apart from a few attempts to describe this phenomenon (Mitscherlich-Nielsen, 1981; Rosenkötter, 1979; Simenauer, 1982), it would seem that this "second generation syndrome" of the perpetrators, accomplices, followers, and witnesses is nonexistent; it has disappeared in the fog of fantasies of normality and the "zero hour."* The attempt in Germany to perform "classical" psychoanalyses, without taking account of the historical space in which the patients and therapists move, is symptomatic of the "inability to grieve" (one ought rather to speak of a *refusal* to grieve). Among psychoanalysts in training, this leads to an identity diffusion and to the much-lamented empty, apolitical psychoanalysis. Unbearable reality produces an impulse to flee: one would like, in memory, to leap over the terrible years from 1933 to 1945 and return to the "healthy world" of the years before 1933. That which is immeasurable, inconceivable, unimaginable and in part unutterable, is surely that which troubles us most deeply as people and as analysts, and which impels us to try again and again to flee to a supposedly "healthy world." And yet the repression, here as elsewhere, is doomed to failure. Nonetheless, it contains enormous explosive power: the denial of Auschwitz (see Wangh, 1985) can pave the way for a new catastrophe for mankind.

In what follows I would like to describe some of the manifestations of this denial of the past and point out how badly "classical" psychoanalysis stands in need of revision and amplification, now that our fantasies have been outstripped by social reality.

In psychoanalytic training, people who wish to devote themselves to psychoanalysis seek and find models with whom they may identify. But do we really have models? Do we find opportunities for positive identification in our training, and if so, with which models? For years I have felt at a loss when judging analytical work with a view to determining whether people are ready to become analysts and thus to treat neurotic people. This helplessness and disorientation, in my opinion, are the expression of the fear of asking ourselves the difficult questions: what are we doing? which criteria, what standards do we have for our work? I have the impression that the hesitation comes also from a fear of admitting to oneself that a part of one's own disorientation is due to an emptiness, a feeling of pretence in the DPV (the German Psychoanalytic Society). "When I came to the DPV, what struck me most about the conferences was something atmospheric, something in the air. I sensed a constant breath of something dead and rigid which seemed to lie over every statement like a fine and impenetrable shroud" (Vogt, 1986, p. 435). There is also the fear of admitting that because of Auschwitz, a malaise, an uncertainty, and a powerful self-doubt have arisen in ourselves as well, and that perhaps in the Nazi era something was destroyed that has not yet proven possible to rebuild—namely, the future.

In Germany the oral tradition, the transmission of experience from one generation to another, has been effectively shattered. Nor does it help matters to construct facades that are meant to conceal this break in tradition. When the relationship of psychoanalysis and Nazism was first broached, at the Bamberg Conference of 1980, some of the training candidates asked their older colleagues, "Where were you between 1933 and 1945; what did you do then, what did you not do, what did you know, what did you not know?" I became very troubled. How can one pose such questions *in real life*? Analysis, after all, is transference, and clearly the underlying question is directed to one's own parents and their past; but then that belongs only on the couch and not in everyday life, not in a psychoanalytic work group. Only later did I understand to what extent I had learned, at my parents' knee, not to ask about reality, and how deeply I had held in my psychoanalytic childhood to a seemingly self-evident and familiar "rule of abstinence" which forbade me to ask about the reality of my analyst or of psychoanalysis itself. Gradually it became clear to me that reality is often far more unbearable than my fantasies and that I had learned to escape this unbearable reality—even, if necessary, by a flight to the couch, to transference, to free association. I understood then the meaning of the dogmatic rule of abstinence, which dictates that the analyst say, "Do not ask! My person, my life, and my past have nothing to do with your analysis." "Everything is transference here; that is your only concern, and with that you must be satisfied." The usual response to a patient's question about the life reality of his analyst is, "What is your association, what are you thinking of?" This answer actually means, "What on earth are you thinking of, to ask me a personal question?" Gradually I came to realize that behind my fear, and the fear of my colleagues and patients, to question analysts and psychoanalysis was not the fear of opening the door to the parents' bedroom and witnessing its "primal scene," but rather the fear of opening the door to the gas chamber.

When I was introduced to Paula Heimann, the unorthodox London psychoanalyst, I thought at first, this is not a real analyst; the walls of her consulting room are full of pictures, and through them she shares something of herself which disturbs the transference. Then I looked once again at the photographs of Freud's office. The peculiar lifelessness, the emphasis on facade in German psychoanalysis became clear to me; there were facades being erected, but behind them lay emptiness, disorientation, and confusion. All of this is very far from a mature psychoanalytic confidence and identity developed from within. Here, there is much surface and little core. The break with the past that the psychoanalysts have accomplished has led their patients to lose their way. Empty, without sensing an emotional echo on the part of the analyst, the patients are left to fall back on themselves alone and on their own neuroses. The analyst, for his part, is uncertain and lacks the awareness and common courage to admit this deficit, but rather does everything possible to prevent its coming into consciousness. "Observations abound that malign forms and contents of transference, the so-called negative therapeutic reaction, the intensified regression in analysis, are to be understood first and foremost as reactions to a faulty stance and an unjustifiable lack of human resonance on the part of the analyst" (Stone, 1981, p. 647).

Some time ago a patient met a close acquaintance of mine "on the outside," then came into the analytic hour and began to tell me about her encounter: she was "disoriented." I asked myself, Why is she disoriented by a real experience? After all, reality serves to orient one. I understood that up to that point, in the grip of the rule of abstinence, I had largely held back from the patient emotionally; she was supposed to know nothing of my reality, she was supposed to ask me no uncomfortable questions, and as a result she could not understand me. Nonverbally, as a therapist, I had established a climate of taboo, in which questions such as "Who are you, where do you come from, what do your past and your present look like?" could not be asked. In the following sessions, the patient continued to complain of the void and the lack of an echo to her feelings in her own family. She remembered that her father was wounded in the war and that her grandfather was what was called a "half Jew"; at home nothing more could be found out, nor had she asked more. I said, "Here, I am as elusive and incomprehensible to you as your parents were; here with me, you find just as great a void as you did at home, because I do not tell you anything about myself." Up until this point, I had rationalized my feelings of gaping emptiness and my weariness in the countertransference as a narcissistic regression on the part of the patient, and interpreted it accordingly, which benefitted neither myself nor the patient.

With this patient (as well as others) it occurred to me that she entered almost exclusively into relationships that were "unreal." I asked myself whether she could learn to empathize with others and become capable of relating to them, within the frame of a therapeutic relationship in which everything is "only" transference and which is thus itself "unreal." I began to understand why we analysts are so eager to label patients as "borderline" whose problems we don't fully understand, who "have a little of everything," and are overly interested in the life of the analyst. And I began further to understand why there is so much talk of the "don't-care generation" (no past, no future), and why it is that analysis lasts so very long these days. The denial of the Hitler era and its consequences leads analysts and patients to continually beat around the bush.

Since Auschwitz there is no longer any narrative tradition, and hardly any parents and grandparents are left who will take children on their lap and tell them about their lives in the old days. Children need fairy tales, but it is just as essential that they have parents who tell them about their own lives, so that they can establish a relationship to the past. Nowadays, however, the parents' and grandparents' repertoire of stories is no longer made up of "simple" war and adventure stories, but rather of questionable, shameful, even dangerous and horrible stories, which can drive you insane. Too many fathers and grandfathers, mothers and grandmothers would rather tell their children nothing of the experiences that were decisive for them. What is erased reappears in the children, who are our patients today, as emptiness, identity diffusion, bewilderment, and confusion. With this distress (an understandable distress, since all of this is reality), they enter our practices and encounter silent therapists who are determined to treat them "classically," so that they themselves will not be confronted by the ghosts of the Nazi era. "Here, the so-called withholding of empathy plays a fatal role. Behind this lurks the unremembered anxiety that the developing yet still fragile ego core will be overwhelmed by the archaic primary process, with risk of psychosis" (Simenauer, 1982, p. 910). It is easier to talk with patients in psychoanalysis about the bedroom than about the gas chamber. However, the formula, "that's oedipal," does not make the repressed reality of Auschwitz disappear.

Both training and therapeutic analyses stand in the shadow of denial. In 1985, in Hamburg, a training candidate said to his examiners, "What do all of you *want* from me about Auschwitz? That played absolutely no part in my analysis" (personal communication, B. Vogt-Heyder). If society has become "fatherless," as Mitscherlich (1963) points out, this is not due simply to an actual absence of fathers, but rather to the fact that these fathers do not project any vital image of themselves. They remain unreal and are not available for life experience. In the face of unbearable reality, one erects the wall of the "rule of abstinence" and believes oneself to be protected. Yet today psychoanalysts must issue the challenge: where were our psychoanalytical mothers and fathers, during the Nazi era—those who later handed psychoanalysis on to us? What did they know or not know? What did they do or not do? What did they see? If a member of the first or second generation after Auschwitz is in psychoanalysis, and if the patient is to regain his lost orientation, the analysis must take up the theme of what his parents actually did or did not do, as the case may be—things which most parents seldom or never discuss.

From my own experience as an analyst, I know that the stories told by patients whose parents were in the SS or the Gestapo have been a disorienting element to me in the countertransference. In the process I was confronted with my own deeply buried aggression and destructiveness. The fantasy that one could spare oneself and avoid all this supports the evasion and denial of the unbearable reality. The result is that the patient does not feel understood, while a certain inhumanity on the part of the analyst creeps in, which he acts out because this material was almost certainly not worked through in his own training analysis. And acting out is always easier than analyzing. Herbert Rosenfeld, in the discussion at the conclusion of his address to the German Psychoanalytic Society in 1984, said in this connection that in psychoanalysis in Germany, the working through of early material with patients may fail to take place, because the evocation of the chaos of the Nazi period would lead to a confrontation with the analyst's own schizoid and borderline self-components, which we understandably try to avoid at any cost. "When a dynamic of psychotic omnipotence overwhelms an entire nation, then the healing impulse to face this insanity squarely becomes very difficult" (Rosenfeld, 1984, p. 80).

A patient came to me for treatment because of a fear of disorganization. Above all he feared the unstructured life at the university and had already been treated psychopharmacologically for this problem. His parents, who lived in an artistic milieu, remained unfathomable for him. Gradually we came to understand that his mother, in particular, had only a false identity and thus could not serve him as a model (see Mitscherlich-Nielsen, 1978). I said to him, "Your mother simply doesn't exist, emotionally. I have the impression of something hidden from you here, something not talked about. Very likely something to do with the Nazi era." The patient now began to look into the life circumstances of his parents, and at the age of 23 stumbled for the first time onto the fact that his grandfather had been a member of the SS. At first he was furious that I had set him on this track, and yet astonishingly, he found his orientation again and gradually lost his fear of disorder. Nor did he need medication any longer. The mere fact of paying attention to concrete reality led to a partial recovery of this patient. For the fact is that material which is not spoken, which is only transmitted nonverbally, cannot be directly recalled, and yet definitely has an influence on the patient's psychic consciousness as well as his unconscious. Only this focusing on historical context made it possible for me and for the patient to become clear about the traditions in which we live, and to work on these issues in a truth-seeking psychoanalytic way.

I would like to take up the problem of denial on the physiological level: Isn't an allergic person, whose organism reacts to environmental pollution, healthier than the person whose organism desensitizes itself to the new stimulus? Anyone who focuses his attention on Auschwitz is putting himself at risk of decompensation. Anyone who wants to enjoy life must deny Auschwitz. Ever since Auschwitz and Hiroshima, denial, which is actually a primitive defense mechanism, has advanced to the status of a "normal" one. And yet whoever denies Auschwitz and Hiroshima entirely, shares in the guilt for the destruction of mankind.

Johannes Cremerius (1984) has asked the question, "What does an analyst do if a patient comes excitedly into the analytic hour and reports that minority workers, Turks for example, are being beaten up just outside the door?" A therapist fails if he does not take real action in such a case; he will surely lose the trust of his patient. If he attends only to Mama and Papa, who perhaps thrashed the patient at an earlier time, then he denies both the reality of the situation and himself as a socially responsible person. The acting out of grandiose fantasy lies not in basing political action on psychoanalytic insight, but rather in attempting to reform the world from the couch. In our times, he who insists on remaining always behind the couch joins the army of those who, through their inaction, have made the atrocities of this century possible.

The reaction of many DPV members to the attempt on the part of a few to clarify the question of how psychoanalysts had conducted themselves in the years 1933–45 was monstrous. In the ensuing tumult, all standards were thrown into confusion; the facade which the DPV had built up over decades crumbled. The attempt to pierce through the comfortable legends and establish what position psychoanalysts had taken vis-à-vis the Nazi state was taken as an attack on the identity of psychoanalysts today: the questioners were accused of fouling their own nest. Rage and hatred rose up to meet them. As the Yiddish expression goes, the con man doesn't notice when his own hat is on fire. Many psychoanalysts in the DPV live with the fantasy that they received the Jewish blessing of the International Psychoanalytic Association in 1950. That date was to have marked the painless birth of a German psychoanalytic society after Auschwitz. But so far as I know, painless births occur only under anaesthesia; and all too many DPV members today still give the impression of being anaesthetized.

I am convinced that we psychoanalysts today—in departure from the classical model—must concern ourselves in psychoanalyses with reality, with denied histories and unbearable truths. The relational difficulties from which almost all of our patients suffer, stemming from the psychic absence of parents and grandparents, cannot be healed by the psychic absence of the psychoanalyst.

> By contrast, the relational space between active analyst and his patient is quickly filled with information about the analyst. (Nor as a rule will his office be neutral and impersonal; rather it is arranged to express his taste, so that he feels comfortable there.) From these elements the patient forms an idea of the thinking and feeling world of his analyst, of his wishes and fears, his private philosophy of life, his weaknesses and his strengths, and so forth. Provided that the analyst establishes an atmosphere of trust, in which the patient dares to express himself, whatever is stirred up in this way in the patient leads necessarily to a lively engagement with the analyst as a real person. The fantasies, impulses, wishes, fears that he now experiences can no longer be interpreted only as projections and pushed aside by a posture of classical refusal onto a fictitious transference level—"what is your association?" . . . What is more, the patient would never understand such a refusal. He would experience it as avoidance, sham, deceit. Ferenczi saw in all this a repetition of the dishonesty of adults toward the child, and accused analysts of professional hypocrisy. [Cremerius, 1984, pp. 792–793)

The young analyst, in order to find his analytic identity, must concern himself with the reality of his forbears. Many of these are still living; it is not too late for a dialogue, a telling of the past, to take place. We could still learn from the "errors" of our predecessors. Concretely, that means the following: If patients have grown up without models, then in some circumstances the analyst must be able to slip into this modeling role himself, in order to close the gap. If he remains systematically "abstinent," he leaves his patient to wander in a void. Deficits cannot be filled by interpretations alone. Always to interpret only the transference, while never entering emotionally into relationship with the patient, means for the patient a repetition of his traumatic childhood experience.

In society at large, as in the microsociety of the DPV, there is still a conspiracy of silence. And psychoanalysis, if it is not to be reduced to a mere magical ritual, must make it possible to break this silence. Psychoanalysts who take part in this general denial attempt to disappear as human beings in relation to their patients. Whatever lies behind the facade—aggression, horror, cowardice, complicity, murder—should preferably not come to light. Erdheim (1983) speaks of the "unconscious lying" which gradually creeps into our work. As a countermeasure against archaic forces which ever threaten to break through, an extremely strict superego has been erected—doubtless a professional or DPV superego as well—which constantly plagues the analyst in training. For he notices that what he is experiencing and doing in his analyses often deviates sharply from classical analysis as it was handed down to him by his teachers. And thus he hobbles along in pursuit of an unattainable analytic ideal. Only seldom does he find true confidants, colleagues who can admit their own inadequacies and feelings of failure.

The perfectionism of the West German system of psychoanalytic training, the erection of an extremely severe professional superego—all of it is a facade thrown up against Auschwitz. And thence comes the "shroud" over the DPV. He who denies, must repeat. Whoever holds back from politics today, and thus becomes a "fellow traveler," need not challenge his own parents, who were also "fellow travelers," need not question his "love" for them, is on the contrary unconsciously identified with them and need not become conscious of the flaws within himself.

The wish, the fantasy, that we are dealing in the main with oedipally structured patients, by no means creates such patients. The many patients who are not capable of symbolizing their inner conflicts, who possess no basic trust, should move us as analysts to question whether a method which was valid before Auschwitz continues to be usable today, without being adapted to the new reality. We cannot ignore, for example, the fact that in the age of television, the realm of fantasy and abstraction grows ever narrower. Without a doubt, this has its effects on the relation of fantasy to reality and must be discussed.

In a land in which there is not—must not—be consciousness of the worst atrocities of human history (and consider here the "Historians' Debate"*), the relationship of the conscious and the unconscious must also be discussed anew, by us, the psychoanalysts. For without a past, there is no future.

5

FAMILY RECONSTRUCTION IN GERMANY
An Attempt to Confront the Past

Margarete Hecker

Prologue

After many years educating and training social workers, with an emphasis on family counseling, I would like to offer the following experiences for discussion. In the context of training seminars, participants worked on their own families of origin. In these seminars we sought—using "family reconstruction" as originally developed and led by Virginia Satir,[1]—to see and to experience in a new way hidden family structures, family patterns, and emotional blockages. In the course of this work we oftentimes got to know families in which participants had to deal with the active involvement of their parents and grandparents in the Nazi regime. Out of the multiplicity of family histories known to us in this way, I have chosen three family profiles in which it becomes clear, in my opinion, what the suspension of the dialogue between the generations has meant, in terms of family life and individual development, for the children and grandchildren of the perpetrators, and of the supposed perpetrators,

---

1. Virginia Satir was the first to develop family reconstructions as a therapeutic instrument for working on families of origin. She led such family reconstructions in many different cultures. To my knowledge she has published nothing herself on this topic up to now. William F. Nerin, a psychotherapist practicing in the United States, describes his own experiences in working with family reconstruction (Nerin, 1986).

of the Nazi regime. I have led seminars using family reconstruction with various foreign as well as German coleaders. The first experiences I had were with colleagues from the United States, the Netherlands, and Switzerland who had had experience working with the survivors of the Holocaust and who helped and encouraged us to deal with the problems of German families.

Wolfgang, Uta, and Gudrun have given me their family genograms[2] and their permission to publish them, although names and places have been changed. Recently Peter Sichrovsky (1987) and Dörte von Westernhagen (1987) have presented to the public, from different personal perspectives, sketches of the life stories of "children of the perpetrators." My object here is not to add three additional histories to this impressive group, but rather to show how the instrument of family reconstruction can help to accomplish a piece of the working through of one's family heritage, insofar as this can be done at all in the first or second generation.

It is the goal of family reconstruction, using the therapeutic methods of humanistic psychology based on its image of man (see Bühler and Allen, 1974; Lockowandt, 1984), to dissolve any exaggerated or negative bond to any single part of the family of origin and to recognize possible entanglements and thus to become freer for one's own tasks in life. Being freed from family entanglements often means learning to trust oneself, one's contemporaries, and one's elders as well, in a new way. It is not that we adhere to a particular ideology about families which says everyone must be at peace with his forbears and have resolved all conflicts relating to his heritage. This is assuredly a lifelong task for each of us. But, in order to become capable of intervening in systems as a consultant, it is essential, in my opinion, to know one's own place in the system of one's family of origin and to know where closeness, divisions, boundaries, and blockages lie in the contacts with one's parents, siblings, and grandparents.

Against the background of the documents which were brought in—family passports and pictures from photo albums—and through the use of family sculpture, psychodrama, and role play, moments and scenes out of the family's history emerge, and a family dialogue

---

2. A genogram is a graphic representation of a family constellation which reaches over several generations. It shows which sibling positions the parents had in their own families of origin as well as which position the index patient presently has in his own family. Deaths, illnesses, symptoms, and the like can be entered and easily seen in overview (see Simon and Stierlin, 1984, p. 125). As an illustration, we have given Uta's genogram in the section devoted to her.

develops. In this way the attempt is made to put ourselves back into the scenarios of the past and to experience at a feeling level what up to now has been incomprehensible as mere historical fact. Unresolved conflicts and contradictions which lie buried in the family's unconscious become visible and accessible; they can be grasped in words and thus become potentially available for therapeutic work.

Members of the generation which participated in Nazism and must share responsibility for it let their children know, usually nonverbally, that they can only live in the present if their memories are reduced to a bearable minimum. Unconsciously they place their only hope in their children. But that isn't talked about. For attentive, loyal children this means not burdening their parents with questions and living themselves with a veil of forgetting, even with the danger of not really knowing who they are, where they come from, and whom they can trust. For the postwar generation the unspoken question about one's own family and national identity exists in a void. For instance, there is profound uncertainty about any sort of political involvement: "I can't tell which trap or whose I might be falling into," or "I don't know if I can appear self-confident, convinced, and competent." And behind this there is often a secret fascination with the people who thought themselves capable of *anything*.

The participants prepared for constructing a genogram (a graphic representation of all family members) by thoroughly gathering all the data. Some of them were thereby enabled for the first time to talk with their parents out of real interest ("How was that really for you at the time?") rather than out of accusation and reproach regarding their parents' participation in the Nazi regime. For all of them it was the first time they had broken the solidarity of silence which lay over their families, as they told, in a small circle of 12 to 16 people, about their parents' or grandparents' guilt and shame, and were able to admit to themselves how hard it was to gain self-understanding as a member of their own particular family. Without really being able to name it, the participants came to this seminar hoping to be freed of a "curse" or from a "negative legacy."

In the three family histories presented here, the confrontation with fathers and grandfathers takes primary attention; much less is paid to mothers and grandmothers, although the latter—as we know from other sources—had a not inconsiderable role in building up and sustaining the "heroes" of the Nazi regime. Going beyond individual cases we need more work, I think, on an historical study of the Nazi family.

Three Family Profiles

WOLFGANG

The following family history provides us with, among other things, insight into the relationships between fathers and sons through four generations. Wolfgang is a psychologist, the eldest of three brothers. He presented the material about his family—which comes, both on his mother's side and on his father's, from peasant circumstances in the Vogelberg—very carefully and comprehensively, back to the generation of his great-grandparents. His father's side interested him primarily, a side with which he had had relatively little contact because of the subtle avoidance strategies of his mother, Gerda, even though his paternal grandparents, Friedrich and Erna, lived in a neighboring village only three kilometers away. His mother kept her husband and her sons away from her in-laws. Wolfgang and his brothers are pacifists and conscientious objectors, refusing military service. Ulrich, the youngest, went as soon as he could to Berlin to study. At the time of the family reconstruction, none of the brothers were married (they were in their early thirties or late twenties).

Grandfather Friedrich was a convinced Nazi, and although he was interned in civil detention for two years after the war and the Americans sought to make a "good democrat" out of him, he never permitted himself to be reeducated. He was formally denazified,* but up until his death at the age of 83, he remained a member of a German Unitarian sect; this group gave him, along with many of his old comrades, "a fitting burial" in the best Germanic tradition.

Through the work on Wolfgang's family reconstruction, the following view of grandfather Friedrich emerged, as he seems to his grandson today. As a small farmer Friedrich was hard hit as a young man by the economic crisis between the two world wars and, because of his nationalist, conservative convictions, he looked to the fascist movement as a solution to his misery. Out of love of "German soil" and "German honor," he looked forward to something for himself personally, as well as politically, from the announced movement for renewal. He wanted to be able to be proud of his work once again and to create a future for his sons. By 1932 he was already a member of the Party and was therefore referred to as an "Old Fighter."* He

---

* See Glossary, here and wherever an asterisk appears. —Trans.

built up the local Nazi group in his neighborhood. His brother Georg, 16 years younger, became a leader in the Third Reich's work service; when he was killed in a motorcycle accident in 1937, his coffin was draped with a swastika flag.

Early in his life Wolfgang rejected this grandfather; in contrast, his mother's relations offered him some support. They considered the paternal grandfather to be querulous, inflexible, and greedy. Nonetheless, this rejection was hard for Wolfgang because the grandfather secretly fascinated him. He had been a self-confident man who stood by his convictions even after 1945. He had spoken genuinely and convincingly about his experiences of comradeship and his loyalty to his old friends. Particularly disconcerting for grandson Wolfgang was the experience that when he, as a leftist liberal, condemned the United States for the Vietnam War, for example, or the Soviets for the Prague Spring, grandfather Friedrich shared his opinion, which, given the grandfather's past, wasn't supposed to happen.

Observing the person of Friedrich and his role in the family against the background of his time, questions came up in the seminar: "Could he have made up his mind in some other way? How much elbowroom, how much free space did he have at the beginning of the thirties? How did the fathers and grandfathers of the other participants arrive at their opinions? Which life experiences and convictions led them?"

Further details emerge out of Wolfgang's reconstruction: the grandparents Friedrich and Erna married in 1926. Erna, coming from a miner's family, knew nothing other than to subject herself, in hard work, to the patriarchal family system. But she also knew how to enjoy free time. Photographs exist in the family which capture "People at Work in the Fields" and "Life in the Country," in all its austerity and unpretentiousness. Wolfgang sees in this something of his grandparents' shared burdens and their mutual capacity to form relationships. Erna and Friedrich had four sons, of which the eldest died as a small child in the year 1929, the same year the second eldest, Wolfgang's father, Heinz, was born. Following in his father's footsteps, Heinz entered the *Hitlerjugend* (Hitler Youth*) when he was nine years old, and while still a schoolboy, he took over running the family farm while his father was away in the war. In this way he pursued the contemporary educational aims of "manliness" and "early responsibility," which had been raised to ideals. When he was 13 years old, in 1942, he became a troop leader in his Hitler Youth group. In the winter of 1944 he went to work on fortifications on the western front and in 1945 to training in the *Volkssturm*.* His high school education was interrupted by these activities. Only in 1950, as a 20-year-old, was he able to go back and complete middle school and then go on to business school. When he was 24 he married Gerda. He had to promise her, as part of the marriage contract, so to speak, not to take over his father's farm: she didn't want to take on the farm work, which would have been part of it.

Father Heinz became, on the basis of his business schooling, an employee of a savings bank and laboriously served and worked his way up. Later on he became a branch manager. Outwardly he seemed to have mastered without a hitch the shift from being an enthusiastic Hitler Youth and member of the Volkssturm to the civilian life of the postwar years. But his profile remained strangely ill-defined. He gave the impression that, as the son of Friedrich and knowing of his father's past, he held himself back as a person. His wife not only distanced herself from her in-laws, calling them inflexible and greedy, but also withdrew inwardly from her husband. Her loyalty lay strictly with her family of origin, and this strengthened Heinz's tendency to withdraw, as well as his peripheral position in the family and his tendency to drink. He ate and drank a great deal, so much so that he sometimes weighed 275 pounds, and Wolfgang frequently had to drag him home from the bar.

As branch manager of a savings and loan office, he encountered, in 1982, a serious professional crisis. He had been more trusting than he should have been and had made loans which resulted in the bankruptcy of the debtor. After a short period of unemployment he found another good position in a nearby city as an inspector, but the experience gnawed at his self-confidence. He compensated for this professional blow by getting elected on a nonpartisan ballot to the honorary position of mayor. The marriage with Gerda was indeed stable but for long stretches during these years of professional development it was unhappy.

As the eldest, Wolfgang became his mother's confidant. Very early on she shared with her son her disappointment in the marriage. Gerda characterized Heinz's efforts to further his education and achieve additional qualifications and upward mobility as "Heinz abandons his family." Added to this was the evening beer drinking, when the men could again experience the comradeship of their youth.

Financially, the family had hard years to get through. Wolfgang felt this at his confirmation: he had to hand over all the money given him by his relatives in order to pay for his confirmation suit and the family party, lest the family's financial distress become visible to others. Heinz felt torn between his wife and his father in a conflict of loyalties that was insoluble for him. From Gerda he got: "You cannot like your father! The stain hangs over the whole family!"

The three sons went to the gymnasium (the academic high school), not just the middle school like their father. On their father's advice, they chose Latin as their second foreign language. Education and status were a way he sought to escape the dilemma. The sons received the nonverbal message that through one's own achievements one could leave the family trauma behind. In the first years after the war, when father Heinz was young, this escape had been closed to him. He supported his sons at school and expected them to succeed without ever saying so directly. Their success indirectly implied his own social movement upward as well. All three sons ultimately took academic degrees.

Wolfgang, in his early youth, was a delicate, sickly child, closely attached to his mother. She fussed over him and stuffed him with food until he became very fat. When he was 15 years old he began to diet on his own and soon became slender. He learned, at his mother's behest, to bring his father home from the bar tactfully and smoothly when Heinz seemed on the verge of settling in there— something Gerda could never manage. The strong coalition with his mother made it difficult for Wolfgang to interest himself directly in his father's family. Nor was he permitted, really, to like either his father or his grandfather. The fact that Heinz had mastered very difficult professional situations in the postwar years despite a limited education, that he continually furthered his training, that he was a prominent citizen in his own town who founded clubs and engaged in public life—all this Wolfgang was neither permitted nor able to see for many years. He held his father in contempt.

Using all the available information, including written materials, Wolfgang made a great effort to understand the Nazi period. In this way he sought inwardly to distance himself from his family's Nazi past. In self-criticism he admitted that, while carrying mail as a work-student in his hometown, he had never quite been able secretly to let the Nazi papers, to which Old Fighters still subscribed, simply disappear. He might have gotten into trouble, and thus he found himself in a conflict similar to that of his father and grandfather.

The key scene in Wolfgang's work of reconstruction lay not in the family celebration on the occasion of his confirmation, but in an imaginary conversation between Wolfgang and his grandfather, who had been dead now for six years. In a cleansing, explosive dialogue with grandfather Friedrich, Wolfgang was able to hand back all the political offenses which had lain so heavily on him as the grandson up until that moment, and he was able to distance himself from them without having to devalue Friedrich completely. Afterward, he could acknowledge that Friedrich had been a good-looking man who, for his time, had been progressively minded about certain things. The grandson was impressed by the fact that when Friedrich was almost 78 years old, following the death of the grandmother, he had chosen a new wife. In this conversation Wolfgang was able for the first time to free himself from mother Gerda's negative judgment about his father's family. Father Heinz had not been able to achieve this in relationship to his own father. The male members of the family were painted in black and white; they were not permitted to appear in their full colors. Thus a piece of liveliness was also lacking in the relationships between the generations. Everything that happened was gathered up and evaluated in such a way that the negative image of the opposing side always won out and got reinforced.

After the reconstruction, Wolfgang seemed freed from a negative legacy: the spell lying over him was broken. The unspoken prohibition against being a man, which meant being like his father or grandfather, dissolved. The fear had been overcome that if he became a man he might turn into someone like his grandfather and so propagate Friedrich's dangerous seed. Thereupon—and this sounds like a fairy tale—indeed that very night, he fathered a son and not long after married the woman who had long been his partner. Soon thereafter his brother Peter also married.

We are not claiming naively that now all the problems of the family were solved. But an important step in the process of clarifying identity was taken. Something remains of his old inner distance from the family of his father. At the birth of his son, Wolfgang gave up his job in order to give his wife the opportunity to continue working, and their son Jan bears his mother's maiden name, not the family name carried by Friedrich and Heinz. Only after the reconstruction did Wolfgang decide to look up his only living great aunt, a sister of grandfather Friedrich's, in order to find out more about the family history. Before that the pain and fear had been too great that crimes out of the Nazi time might possibly come to light. Another thing that still remains is a clear ambivalence about joining a political movement or a political party. It remains very difficult for Wolfgang to get involved in things whose effects he cannot see ahead of time.

Since the birth of Jan, the relationship between Heinz, Wolfgang, and Jan has become very close. Heinz is a proud and happy grandfather who very much enjoys being together with the young family. It was crucial for Wolfgang, in order to take on his own identity as a grown man, that he once again confront his grandfather—a grandfather at once fascinating, in some distorted way, and scorned. Now he feels that he can deal with the criticism of his family; he no longer needs to take part in the repressive process of collective silence.

Wolfgang attended the family reconstruction seminar after he had already completed various therapy training programs (including his own therapy). To experience once again the life paths of grandfather Friedrich and father Heinz was a decisive capstone in the long progressive chain of working through his family heritage.

Wolfgang's family history was presented in some detail for illustrative purposes. The following family stories from two women are considerably shorter, and they stand at the beginning of professional therapeutic development.

UTA

At the end of the basic training for social work, in a seminar dealing with the topic "family work with foreigners," we were taken by surprise by the following theme: the participants, who were in their early to mid twenties, asked how we can meet foreigners freely and openly if we don't know what "German" is. I was not really prepared for this shift in the topic of the seminar, but I proposed that at the end we explore some family histories in greater detail in order to pursue the question of our own identity. It was clear that Uta, a delicate, rather slender student who was specializing in the field of social rehabilitation, felt challenged by this idea. This was the background for her presenting her family to us. In a soft voice, and as if she were telling about something alien to herself, she confronted us with an unsolved murder in her family.

She told about the peasant origin of her forbears from the Westerwald. Her paternal grandfather, Philipp, had established the local Nazi group, together with others of his generation, among them his brother-in-law Friedrich, Uta's great-uncle by marriage. One of their duties was to guard a group of foreign workers and prisoners of war in the village of Allmenfeld, which had been newly founded during the Nazi regime. In the course of this activity, the foreigners were abused. Toward the end of the war, great-grandfather Hermann intervened and suggested to his two sons-in-law, Philipp and Friedrich, that they treat the foreigners in a more humane way since the tide was now beginning to turn. During one such discussion about changing their behavior, a heated argument developed. The still-convinced adherents of the Nazi ideology turned against the warnings of the 81-year-old man. In the presence of his family, Friedrich shot and killed his father-in-law with his army pistol. The men helped to carry the body outside. Publicly they said that it had been newly freed prisoners of war who, in the course of their plundering, had shot great-grandfather Hermann.

Up until today strict silence had been preserved about this event. There was no one who would have charged those who committed the murder. Uta is the only one in the younger generation who now, at the moment of the planned family reconstruction, knows this part of the family history. In the course of preparing for this seminar, her father, in tears and with great difficulty, had admitted to her the true course of events. It was only under the stubborn questioning of his daughter that he became willing to talk. Uta had felt the need to find out more about the family history: first, because there always seemed to her to be an unexplained pall hanging over the regular family gatherings and, second, because grandmother Maria, the mother of her father, following the death of grandfather Philipp, called her granddaughter Uta a "murderess."

In 1972 the paternal grandparents, Maria and Philipp, took a vacation in the Black Forest. The evening before they were to return, grandfather Philipp called home from a phone booth to say that they would be coming home by train the next day and wanted to be picked up. Uta answered the phone and was to pass on the message. On the way back to the pension, Philipp was struck by a young motorcyclist and killed. It was then that Maria made the apparently irrational remark that Uta was the "murderess" of her grandfather. Nobody made any response to her remark. Grandma Maria named the family theme, but the assertion remained in a void without commentary. Uta went on to say that up until now she had never asked for an explanation or rectification of this strange attribution. Something in the atmosphere of the family told her she had best be silent about it. At that time the family myth remained untouched, and through her own silence Uta helped to strengthen the process of repression.

Uta is the one in the family who thinks a great deal about her parents and the larger family. Clearly she is the person in the family who, on the one hand, breaks the taboo of silence about the murder, and on the other hand, takes on the role of "savior." Still, it is very difficult for her to make the connections conscious for herself.

UTA'S GENOGRAM

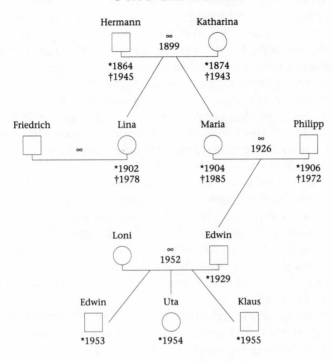

She told how, after the war, great-uncle Friedrich became a successful professional policeman. Several of his sons became prison wardens. At home as a girl, Uta had to fight hard for herself in order to get permission to leave the village to go to high school. She wanted to study social work in order to become a parole officer. She saw how her parents, Loni and Edwin, worked terribly hard after 1945, first in their own nursery and then in the garden-tool business, without ever really getting anywhere. They very much hoped to leave the house and the business to their children free of debt, yet their business decisions led them ever deeper into the red. In the beginning, they were able to keep their business going through the sale of cut roses; but when the competition from Israel and Holland got too stiff, father Edwin threw the valuable rose bushes from two large fields on a pile and set them on fire.

Uta related further that her parents were afraid of sickness and death but did nothing about their medical care. At home, Uta continues to hear very denigrating remarks about foreigners—despite the fact that father Edwin once, in his interim phase of working as a day laborer in a large factory, when he had had an argument with his boss, was greatly helped by a Moroccan co-worker. For instance, she hears things like: "All foreigners are stupid," "These people take away our work," "They want to live from our money but they don't want to do anything for it"—assertions which Uta has met with silence up until now, not wanting to burden her parents. She feels as if she doesn't quite belong in this family, saying, "We don't really have anything in common." But she is also the one who senses something of the burden her parents carry and feels herself in part responsible for it. Her brothers don't see how much the parents struggle for their living and yet never escape from the vicious circle of ever more effort and ever more debt.

Despite all her criticism of her parents, Uta takes note of the fact that they have provided her with the material necessities and a place to live. Of course it is true that she financed her social work studies herself by cleaning houses and tending bar, but she still feels gratitude for these basic things. At the same time, the parents have great difficulty understanding their daughter's choice of social work, a calling in which one has to devote so much of oneself to others and which pays so poorly.

At present Uta lives in a medium-sized city and works in a project dealing with unemployed youth. In her work she is particularly sensitive to the disparaging remarks the young people make about foreigners. She doesn't just let these remarks pass but instead involves the young people in discussions about them. At 33, she lives a very withdrawn life and doesn't really trust herself to enter into deeper relationships. She seeks out workshops dealing with self-awareness, where she can also meet with older people who experienced the Third Reich as victims. It is her desire to contribute to reconciliation. Yet in her own family she doesn't trust herself to open up any discussion of the taboo themes.

In Uta's case we did not succeed in working out a true family reconstruction. The seminar didn't provide the proper frame, and in that context I didn't feel it appropriate to elicit from Uta by therapeutic means a more profound examination of the family themes she had brought up. A first step toward an inner distancing was taken, nevertheless, since for the first time she became aware of why she was called "murderess." By her silence and her protection of her parents, she still continues to participate in the mutual process of repression in her family. In this case the speechlessness already extends over four generations. Her goal of working as a parole officer may perhaps be her way of living with the burden of the family past.

GUDRUN

Gudrun grew up in a village in Franconia. Her mother's family were peasants and also ran the village post office. Her father was a skilled laborer. His mother was a midwife. Among other duties, she was responsible for enforcing the Third Reich's Hereditary Health Code.* Nevertheless, she managed to protect her mentally retarded son from euthanasia. She gave her elder son, Hermann, Gudrun's father, prayers and pious sayings on loose sheets of paper to take with him into war. Her mother's parents were strict Protestants. They distinguished very clearly, almost rigidly, between good and evil, even though their daughter, Irene, Gudrun's mother, was born only a few months after her parents' marriage.

Father Hermann was a cabinetmaker. As a young man he was very convivial and enjoyed sitting around in the tavern together with his many friends. His bride, Irene, looked to him for release from the constraints of the bond to her strict parents. The pair had to marry because Gudrun's elder brother, Horst, was on the way. The night following their wedding, Hermann and Irene were in an air raid, which shocked and deeply terrified them. They looked to the future with dread. They were struck dumb by the sight of the red skies over the burning city. Irene feared being left alone in her pregnancy. The very next day, Hermann had to go off to his unit, and with only brief interruptions he was gone for many years in the war and then in captivity. During the retreat after the Russian campaign, he was wounded by a bullet through his lung and was given up for dead. A comrade nevertheless brought him to a field hospital and thereby saved his life. The end of the war found Hermann in a military hospital in Denmark, and he came home at the end of 1945. Only then did he learn of the birth of his son Horst.

After the war Gudrun was born. She is nine years younger than her brother. Hermann and Irene still cannot really talk with each other. During all the years of their marriage, they remained as mute as on the night when they parted. Their experiences during those hard years had been too different for them to believe they could share them with each other. Any points of connection were lacking. Nor did they have the strength to bear the feelings their memories provoked. They never took the time to develop a personal relationship with each other. Hermann continued to seek the fellowship of male friends in the tavern, friends who had been through similar things and among whom he felt understood and accepted. In the process, he drank a lot. Irene despised this behavior and so drove him even further away. Nor was she asked about her own fears and sacrifices; she remained alone with them, too. Work is the only thing that ties the two together: the building up of a mutual existence after the war and the two children.

The close relationship between mother Irene and son Horst, which developed during the years of separation and tormenting loneliness, keeps father Hermann from ever really growing back into the family. Horst feels himself a part of his mother's family, on whose farm he grew up. The strict religiousness of his grandparents was a model and a support for him. He studied theology and became a minister. He and his wife adopted two children who, according to information from the Youth Office, had had a very difficult family past.

Gudrun's life path hasn't followed a straight line at all. As an adolescent she rebelled with all her power against the life-style of her parents. She threw herself into everything they forbade her. She tried out many shifting relationships with men. She has a two-year-old daughter by a foreigner seven years her junior with whom nothing really connects her. From a south seas vacation she brought home a case of syphilis, which happily was diagnosed and could be cured. Gudrun became a social worker and works at present in a rural drug-abuse clinic.

During the family reconstruction, in the course of a confrontation with her father, Gudrun experienced how very much her rebellion had been a desperate attempt to reach him and to shatter the world of appearances into which her parents had fled. This attempt went to the very borders of her physical and psychic existence. Although the siblings have a good relationship with each other, the inner schism of the parents has carried over to them. Horst lives the life of a "saint," Gudrun that of a "whore." Gudrun, Horst, and their mother, Irene, know almost nothing about father Hermann's experiences during the war years. Only through photographs of young Ukrainian women in bikinis did they learn that the life there couldn't have consisted solely of privations. Gudrun surmises that possibly a child of her father's is living in Russia. She realizes that for the young men, the war had also meant adventure and getting to know foreign lands. She is disturbed by an unadmitted undercurrent of fear that her father might also have participated in war crimes. When the war comrade who had risked his own life to save Hermann came to visit, Irene threw him out of the house. Stories from the old days had no place anymore in the new postwar consciousness. And so the experiences of that time live on as ghosts between the marriage partners and between the generations.

Gudrun is one of the postwar children who has never felt really connected with the generation of her parents, even though at the beginning she felt very drawn to her father. Her feelings have remained in disarray, and she has fears about the future, which are incomprehensible to her. She rebelled vehemently against her parents' norms and sought to enjoy her youth—contrary to the prohibitions of her parents and grandparents. They had failed to communicate any joy in life to her and seemed rather to see life's meaning only in seriousness and work. She wanted to flee from this ever present burden but hasn't learned to pay attention to her own needs in the process.

A speechlessness, so far insoluble, permeates all areas of this family's life. They are unable to have any real exchange about such questions as work, personal relationships, sexuality, religion, politics, child rearing, or future plans. Gudrun summarizes it thus: "We have no connections with each other; my parents don't love me." The insubstantiality of the relationship to her parents makes it very hard for Gudrun to be trusting and to enter into any profound relationship. The only person she can trust is her brother. He always took her side, as if he felt she had lived out, in an opposite way to his, the other side of the cleft inheritance they both received as their family's legacy.

During the family reconstruction, Gudrun resolved to begin the conversation with her parents all over again, together with her brother, and to be more considerate than before. She has many concrete questions to ask her parents, and she can now see how, with her aggressiveness and defiant denigration, she has prevented her parents from answering honestly. She hopes that both of them, Horst and she, can thereby become more alive and more open, and that in the future they will no longer have to organize their lives in such extreme, almost schematic forms of good and evil.

Attempt at a Balance

Over and over again with members of the war generation, we find, beginning right at the start of the data collection, that those who actively participated in the Nazi era never really talked, following 1945, about those events and experiences, let alone worked them through. This is a very striking phenomenon. Even the date of May 1945 itself is referred to as "liberation" by some, "collapse" by others.

After the flood of propaganda speeches during the Third Reich, a speechlessness spread through the population. Any attempt to begin a clarifying conversation froze in the face of the incomprehensible dimensions of the crimes in which so many had been involved, knowingly or unknowingly. In this climate of emotional paralysis, questions could not be posed, nor answers sought. Each member of the family remained alone: the men with the experiences of being at the front and in captivity; the women with the experiences of the nights of air raids, flight, evacuation, and the worry about hungry children; and the children, prematurely grown up as helpful child-adults, with no childhood of their own but with all their strong emotions of rage, frustration, and sorrow. It seems as if, within the families and among friends and neighbors also, an unspoken agreement existed not to talk, not to open up, not to make any of the connections clear, and thus to protect each other. After all, an exacting inquiry and an honest search for answers could lead many to lose face.

And so in the children and grandchildren we encounter a new generation, whose fathers' faces in the photograph albums seem alien to them. Sometimes the stripes on the caps or on the sleeves of the uniforms have been carefully cut away; one doesn't know: was he an officer, was he in the SS, or something else? Children have crossed out the face of their father in the photo album and spoken to their mother about "that man," only later to discover with a shock that they look very much like him, that they can even feel his sudden rage in themselves and can't tell for sure whether this is a creative or a dangerous power. The mothers, too, preferred to stay silent and for their part were happy with the silence of their children.

In the face of a world laid in ruins, which had to be rebuilt and formed anew, the phenomenon of mutual protection mobilized immense energies around orienting oneself in a new way, learning a new language for the new everyday world, and creating a new public life. The process of denying and repressing the mental and emotional world of National Socialism was so complete and thorough that today, over 40 years later, it takes hard psychological work to admit to consciousness memories from that time, to reexperience the images of horror, and to tell others about them. When this happens, which is to say when fathers or mothers unpack their memories, it is astonishing how present and palpable the ideas become, together with the names, the places, the ranks, and the pressures that were experienced in all their inexorability. The listener senses that everything is still alive, but not at all sorted out or worked through. When the children are suddenly overwhelmed by the flood of such memories in their families—as for instance when the adults have had a little too much wine to drink or are standing around a sickbed—they find themselves helplessly exposed to the emotions that have been released. They take pains to protect their parents from such sudden explosions of old memories, and in so doing, they also protect them from the accompanying retrospection and the subsequent weighing and judging. By not posing any questions, they support the process of repression.

A high price is paid for this silent collusion and for the remarkable mutual loyalty of the family members: they don't really know each other, and in some inexplicable way they are cut off from their emotions and often have the feeling of not being able to rely on themselves and their own strengths. Many also have the sense that in spite of an enormous investment of energy, much of their life doesn't work out either professionally or personally; they feel as though they were carrying an invisible burden and must pay for something that they themselves didn't cause.

The children's silence, in my opinion, protects the parents in an additional way. To admit to consciousness the repressed memories stored in images, pictures, emotions, thoughts, and conceptualizations would also mean to experience them again with today's consciousness and to subject them to a new critical examination. For everyone concerned, it is an undertaking deeply fraught with anxiety to expose oneself directly and straightforwardly once again to the evil and to the brutal violence of that time. They really need an outsider to help them cope with their guilt, shame, and disgrace in such a way that they can manage to live with it. They cannot simply report the facts of the atrocities, reusing the same old language. A healing process would have to follow. It is as though an abscess were to burst without their knowing whether or how they can close the wound again. A dialogue would have to follow, offering a new humane orientation, which could make possible a transformation and a distancing so that the memories don't simply freeze into stereotypical images. This dialogue demands great understanding of the interrelationships and details of that time, because the memories come only hesitantly and falteringly to light. Often it is the language of the family which gives us the first access to the buried interconnections. In accidental, trivial formulations or in side remarks, the unconscious contents of what has been repressed surface, as we experienced in a drastic way when Uta was called "murderess." Such formulations can offer us the real key to understanding.

Usually it is the sensitive and loyal members of the family who have turned to a helping profession and who, in the framework of training in family counseling, for instance, begin to seek the complete picture of their family of origin. They want to bring out into the open the false reality and the half-truths which they keep hearing and from which they suffer. Then they find themselves in a dilemma. Words such as "family," "love," "care," "loyalty," and "comradeship" have always been filled with a double meaning. It is not easy to show the rage, frustration, and disappointment over these half-truths and false reality to parents who have gone through so much hardship themselves and who gave life to their children in an uncertain time and then went on to save them from bombs and war. In order to survive emotionally there exists, alongside all the opposition to these parents, a great need to love them.

Many parents whom we have encountered in the reconstructions, couples who married in the thirties or during the war, attempted, while the Nazi propaganda defined one reality on the outside, to live in a different reality on the inside, namely in a "healthy, innocent family world" with a strong longing for the time after the war. Over and over again we hear words such as "survive," "save," "worry over the children," "stick it out to the end."

The end of the war brought all Nazi dreams to an apoplectic end. Only a very few succeeded at the time in consciously and clearly comprehending this hiatus in their own understanding, and in recognizing and admitting their own share of guilt. Most people tried to forget and repress the past like a bad dream and to behave as if they could begin all over again as though nothing had happened. There was no place for such feelings as rage, anger, sadness, anxiety, or shame in the period right after the war. Only the level of present reality was tackled. They were astonishingly inventive in making survival possible under the most difficult of circumstances, and in building up new life structures. But during this process a new understanding of oneself could not yet be attained and reflected upon. For most people the spiritual strength for such a task was lacking. The children were the carriers of their hope, the guarantee that life indeed does go on. But these children don't know who they really are; their roots are missing. The facts about the Third Reich, which were transmitted in their school or in the media, could not provide them with the knowledge of their own roots since, as a closed topic in their own families, the subject found no personal echo.

We hear, for instance, statements such as "I have to prove to them that I exist, that I can do something, that I'm courageous"; "At night my father screams, he wails like a cat, but I don't know why. Maybe a tank is driving over him"; "I couldn't learn English because at that point we were about to invade England, so why bother?"; or "My father was a Nazi, but a good one!"

In the family reconstructions, we attempt to permit the memories of the unresolved attachments and conflicts to represent the conversations and confrontations which have never taken place in the families. We attempt to see both the historical facts and the concrete stages in the family's development at one and the same time. It takes a great deal of courage for the individual course participants to confront their parents' repressed emotions, to bring into consciousness their parents' failures, mistakes, and active participation in the Nazi regime, and at the same time to accept themselves as members of this particular family.

This intensive emotional work of sorting out and arranging is made possible because it is also being borne and shared by the other course members. The members of the group take over, in turn, the roles of authoritarian patriarchs; of enthusiastic young soldiers; of returning prisoners of war, physically and spiritually exhausted; of young widows who sacrificed to save their children and then become hard and bitter because life has passed them by; of nurses who save mentally retarded children from euthanasia or those who don't manage to do that; of mothers who haul their children at night into the air raid shelters while the foreign workers from the munitions factories remain outside, exposed to the bombs; of peasants who illegally slaughter their livestock so as to strengthen the soup of the war prisoners and the foreign workers, or those who brutally mistreat these people; of Polish volunteers who build streets and concentration camp barracks with the "Organisation Todt"* and then disappear as ordinary German subjects; of newlywed couples who are continually overshadowed by the "heroes" who fell; of opportunists who manage to land on their feet in every situation; of men and women who plunge themselves excessively into their work in order to forget; of German emigrants who want to escape everything and then come back because they can't make it; of ambitious young people who do well in exams, earn a lot of money, and nevertheless feel empty; of loving, sacrificing parents who spoil their children and give them every opportunity but never set any limits; of refugees from the east who hang onto their old pictures and are disappointed when their grandchildren don't want to listen to them anymore; of children who are secretly fascinated by their father's heroic bearing and appearance; of young women who become prostitutes or bring black grandchildren into the family in order to confront the old ideals of racial purity; of family members who vilify and reject foreigners in a grotesque way, and of others who glorify everything foreign in an exaggerated manner; of families who secretly hide and feed Jewish relatives or friends, or others who inform against them and then look on as they disappear.

It is often for the first time that through these scenes, the participants experience something of the subjective feelings of their parents and grandparents, something of their anxieties, the stresses they underwent, their mistakes and failures, all the way up to their crimes. Encountering the individual character types of the Nazi era with their own particular language, their ways of behaving, their ideologies, is shocking. In the group it is necessary to empathize, to share the burden, to give support. As this happens, understanding grows for the pressure to make decisions, for the fears, seductions, and human failures of this time. But it also becomes very clear that in every single situation the actors had the chance to decide for or against our common humanity. In the family histories of the Nazi time, it is very difficult to find any positive element in the things that happened. Crimes cannot be glossed over or excused, even if they happened long ago and have been deeply repressed.

It is immeasurably difficult to live with the knowledge that crimes have been committed in one's family or by close relatives, as for example in Uta's family. One cannot reconcile oneself to such events in one's parents' lives. We often find these children and grandchildren, as adults, among the members of the helping professions. They are extremely socially involved, often in seemingly hopeless situations. They adopt interracial children, concern themselves with the homeless, and fight the injustice that the Turkish workers suffer in our country. They often remain childless, as if it wouldn't be worthwhile to pass on their own family tradition, as if they had enough to do just gaining mastery of their own past. But there are also those, like Gudrun, who live out the "profane" part of the family, those who give the family a chance to scorn a scapegoat so they needn't seek in themselves the things they have so painfully repressed. These children live out the dark, negative side in order to take this burden from their parents. Thus they themselves remain entangled in the Nazi past.

After the shared process of clarification in the reconstruction seminars, it often becomes possible for the participants to enter into conversations in a new way, with more interest for details, and to approach others with fewer accusations and attributions of guilt and with more real understanding. There is a chance for clarifying, redemptive talks with those family members who are still alive. A "healing through encounter"[3] may come to pass. This is more difficult with the dead, but even that is possible, as Wolfgang showed us in his reconstruction.

It is not a question of finally ceasing to accept the old stories and of tearing the masks of honor and propriety from their fathers' and mothers' faces at the end of their lives. Far more, it is a question of giving such parents opportunity to take onto themselves their guilt for acts committed and to admit their guilt to themselves so that the next generation will not, by unconsciously carrying this guilt, have to become entangled in a new set of insoluble problems.

In many families there were also experiences of great sacrifice from the Nazi time, of comradeship and solidarity with others at the risk of one's own life. There was also much creativity in inventing survival strategies. These experiences also belong in the history of that time, and they contribute their existential share to many family histories. Countless people survived war and persecution only through such personal bravery. But even that can make it difficult to look openly and courageously for the areas in which one's own family collaborated with the Nazis.

After such seminars we all ask ourselves how we might have acted in our parents' difficult and conflicted situations. Would we have had the courage and the strength to say no, to see through the wrongdoing early enough—and at the cost of our own social recognition, of material and social advancement in our country, and perhaps of ourselves becoming objects of persecution? The answer to this question is hard to find; it can lie only in our own lives. Our families offer us innumerable positive as well as negative ideals and models: we can consciously decide for ourselves which ones to choose and which to reject.

---

3. Martin Buber writes in *Healing Through Encounter* that "the analyst must see the sickness of the patient as a sickness of his relationships to the world. True guilt doesn't exist within the human being but far more in his incapacity or refusal to react to legitimate demands and calls of the world. And the repression of guilt and the neurosis which arises from this repression are not simply psychological phenomena but far more events between persons" (Friedman, 1987, p. 232).

6

EFFECTS OF LINGERING NAZI WORLDVIEWS IN FAMILY LIFE

Almuth Massing

Göttingen today: a contemplative city with a 250-year-old university tradition, venerable churches, historic squares, which give no hint today, in their urban bustle, of what was played out here under National Socialism. Take for example the Albaniplatz, which surrounds the Romanesque church of the same name: it was to this square, called Adolf-Hitlerplatz at the time, that an enormous torchlight procession wound its way through the inner city on May 10, 1935, to stage a grandiose book burning, in an infernal act of mass enthusiasm: "A funeral pyre of filth and ordure was stacked up higher than a man's head, to be given over to the purifying flames" (Fussel, 1983, p. 98). Göttingen celebrated the victory of the national revolution and prided itself on having been one of the first islands of National Socialism.

Buildings, streets, and square show hardly a trace of all this since the war, nor do they evoke memories of the fascist scenes that were staged there. The Adolf-Hitlerplatz is called Albaniplatz once more. Its expanse of gray asphalt is given over to traffic. History has been smoothed over as well. And yet in the souls of men, it lives on. This violent relationship with the past has left its mark.

Let us raise this brief evocation of Göttingen's National Socialist history to a symbolic level. As therapists we are concerned with families whose inner lives still contain fragments of National Socialist identity which have not been smoothed over and thus still have power. This is why the rediscovery and exposure of these foundations are so eminently important for a broader understanding of pain and rigidity in the families affected. Only in this way can change become possible.

At the close of a family therapy session, I asked Herr K., now a chemist, formerly a student at a National Political Educational

Institute (NAPOLA*), whether he still knew the "Horst Wessel Lied"*
by heart, as I might want to use it in a talk. He spouted forth
spontaneously:

> Flag aloft, the ranks closed tight,
> The SA marches with confident treads.
> Marching in spirit by their sides,
> Comrades felled by Rightists and Reds . . .

Then, "Did you want the melody too?" Dumbfounded, I now listened as he sang the song—with his wife, five years divorced but
present today, trilling the tune along with him. At the end he added,
"Did you really need that for a talk, or were you just testing me, to
see if I could still do it?" Whereupon I repeated my intention. His
response was to assure me that the bad German in the song had
always bothered him.

Bemused and somewhat bewildered as I was at the time, it was not
until shortly afterwards that I was struck by the monstrousness of the
situation which had unfolded before my eyes—a monstrousness
that lay in the realm of the everyday: the fascist song par excellence
merely a question of style and grammar, of tests and memory? No
reflection on the *content* of the song, no curiosity to know the *content*
of my talk. The reenactment of Nazi normalcy on the one side,
confrontation and naiveté on mine. In retrospect I might have
wished for an embarrassed hesitation at least, hopefully even some
sign of struggling with the past. At the end I even received a little
lecture from Herr K. about the official character of this song as a
national anthem, along with the first verse of the song "Deutschland." "But then you know that one too: *'Deutschland, Deutschland
über alles. . . .'*"

Extraordinary, or Everyday?

In what follows, I would like to report on experiences from
everyday life encountered by the family therapist in which the
recognition of an ongoing National Socialist outlook turned out to
be of critical importance for a broader understanding and working
through of neurotic suffering. We (Massing and Beushausen, 1986)

---

* See Glossary, here and wherever an asterisk appears. —Trans.

have already offered a discussion of the importance of the historical context for family therapy. As recently as 15 years ago, the National Socialist past of family members was still surrounded by an atmosphere of silence in family therapy work. Before that, some remarkable cases came to the fore. I remember a highly placed pillar of the culture of those times who cited the Aryan heritage of his family and attributed the schizophrenia of his grandson to his daughter's marriage to a blood relative, which he regarded as "inbreeding."

I consider the focus on *everyday life* to be fruitful (as do Focke and Reimer, 1984; and Peukert and Reulecke, 1981), because under such a perspective the various aspects of life-style and social conditions can be examined from the point of view of people's own experience and the imprint on them of the history of the times. In the process of therapy we must then look for the interplay between intrafamilial and individual dynamics and the general effects of the social and political system. At the same time, as Peukert and Reulecke (1981) caution, this must not lead, in the name of "history of everyday life," to a complete scientific relativism, which exhausts itself in attempting to construct an abstract conceptual system, thereby avoiding a *clear, critical, moral position* in the face of Nazi atrocities— nor should it result in a cult of strictly passive observation and respectful speechlessness in the face of the experiences and memories of our grandparents' generation. Moreover, this retrospective view must not stop there, with the Nazi epoch, but rather it must serve to sharpen our critical awareness of "those constructive and self-destructive forces which are contained in modern industrial societies in general" (Peukert and Reulecke, 1981, p. 17).

I wish to draw attention to families who, in their capacities as representatives and participants, reacted and continue to react to the *worldview* of National Socialism. This worldview was laid down in the German legal code from 1933 on, with relentless consistency. In the process it drew upon certain ideologies of many years' standing, themselves built on particular concepts from the fields of biology, medicine, anthropology, and not least, psychotherapy—concepts which themselves had been subjects of debate over the past century all across Europe. These concepts include (1) social Darwinism, (2) racism, and (3) "racial hygiene."[*]

This worldview was deeply rooted in many families. As an illustration, take this marriage advertisement from those years: "52-year-old pure Aryan physician, veteran of the Battle of Tannenberg, plans to settle in country, desires male offspring through civil marriage with healthy Aryan virgin, young, modest, frugal, house-wife, accustomed to hard work, broad-hipped, no high-heels or earrings" (Focke and Reimer, 1984, p. 121). Nowadays, such an ad is greeted with a bitter laugh—but in those days it was the most normal thing imaginable, the vocabulary quite standard, and hardly occa-sioned either criticism or surprise!

On Therapeutic Practice

In what follows I would like to illustrate the intermingling of Nazi and familial determinants in a therapeutic context, making use of three exemplary cases[1] which cumulatively illustrate the compres-sion of these themes into neurotic symptoms on the part of family members. Briefly, let it be noted that an underlying concept of family therapy is that disturbances and conflicts always go back to more or less conscious conflicts between parents and grandparents—which is to say, between the marriage partners and their own parents—not in the sense of a linear chain of causality, but rather in the sense of a circular interdependence. In Göttingen, in accordance with our model of "multigenerational family therapy" (Sperling et al. 1982), we make a point of inviting the grandparents to the family sessions. Along with continuity within the family, this means the explicit introduction of an underlying historical dimension based in real experience. With an expanse of time of some 80 years before our eyes, we can shed light on the developmental patterns of individual family members in the course of their family history, while at the same time illuminating the inevitable connections with the history of the times through those persons who lived that history. The ther-apeutic process has to be a matter of remembering and working through, with all the difficult grief work that that entails; its goal is the creative reorganization of the present.

In a first example, we have the issue of the relation of present-day theories of heredity to the social Darwinist principles of the Third

---

1. These examples represent the combination and abbreviation of a number of cases, with a view to highlighting these particular themes.

Reich. A second example has to do with persistent racist ideology, which comes to light in a family's elitist mentality. By means of a third example, which has to do with "racial hygiene," and in particular the laws governing "racial purity," our role as therapists in these issues will be brought into focus.

WHAT IS THE SOURCE OF OUR THEORIES OF HEREDITY?

The identified patient was a 22-year-old son, Robert, a student with massive disturbances in the capacity to work, together with outbreaks of aggression. Robert was so preoccupied with feelings of hatred, disappointment, rage, and revenge toward his family that he had no space left for life plans of his own—nor could he give up his demand for compensation: "First my parents have to change. All my life I've been the bad one, no matter what I do. All right, but then this is what they get!" Indeed, as became clear in the family sessions, the parents were absolutely convinced that Robert had inherited a preponderance of "bad character traits." Both parents were distressed about the situation. The father made overdrawn and cynical allusions to "fate," while the mother reduced the son to furious despair when she maintained that with a great deal of love one could still try to ameliorate his evil nature. It was clear that themes of "heredity," "inheritance," and "hereditary traits" were particularly pronounced in this family. This had a direct parallel in the parents' occupation, which was forestry. Thus they were in command of a stock of observations and biological knowledge about the laws of heredity. This was the basis of their practical expertise, having to do with seed stock, or plant, tree, and animal cultivation and breeding. By a process of analogy, the parents were firmly convinced of the application of these hereditary laws to their family situation with their son. Thus from the father: "If you compare the genealogies of our dogs, you will also note that *there too* a bad-tempered dog always comes from a bad-tempered line, whereas one with a good disposition always comes from a tractable line. It is true that you can make a good dog bad with extreme mistreatment, but you will *never* train a bad-tempered dog to be a good one."

Although we therapists could feel our own revulsion—and could see Robert cowering more and more, in the truest sense of the word, "like a beaten dog"—we encouraged all the family members to say more about their own theories of inheritance. And in fact it was the case that the parents were convinced of an absolute correspondence between human beings and the observations they had made in forestry, "all according to Mendelian laws," as the father maintained. In Robert's case they had settled on the idea of a recessive trait in the paternal line.

We therapists insisted on the question, "What is the source of these various theories of heredity? Where and how were they taught and learned?" Old school and reference books in the family were now investigated, and at last the father brought in the proof of the correctness of his hereditary theories in the form of an encyclopedia which was *still in family use.* There it read, in *Meyers Encyclopedia* of 1939 (p. 1246): "The Mendelian laws are fundamentally and generally valid for humans as well, since all living things are governed by the same laws. The proposition that all human traits, healthy and pathological, physical as well as psychological, are passed on according to the exact same laws, has been proven in a great number of cases. Thus the previous assumption of equal genetic potential among humans, and the importance of environment in development, is proven false. This is the basis for the racial hygiene policy of the National Socialist state." (We call the reader's attention here to the fact that essentially the same theory can be found in the chapter "Man and Modern Genetics," by F. Vogel, in *Meyers Encyclopedia* of 1974!)

Not until we had emphasized and generally confirmed that this dogma reflected the normal teachings of the parents' and grandparents' school days, could a dialogue begin on the question, "Where does badness come from?" with regard to the biographical history of the family. The parents then became aware of a persistent archaic anxiety in the face of their own parents and their ironclad commandment: "Grown-ups are always right, even when they are wrong." Along with this was the underlying fear of punishment, which could be seen as a direct consequence of National Socialist influence. Thus the father, when he was still a Hitler Youth, had "trained" his own father to use the "Heil Hitler!" greeting, which became obligatory in 1934. The son overcame the father's resistance with the argument that he owed obedience now not to his father, but only to the Führer. Now, after the war, without the support of the power ideology, he rightly feared the resentment of his father, who had felt humiliated in his own parental authority. And indeed, the grandfather expressed this feeling quite clearly in the family therapy sessions.

In sum, it was clear that in this present-day family, alongside their own particular family dynamics, we were working above all with the aftereffects of National Socialist policies of "racial hygiene." For according to Lenz,* the foremost "racial hygienist" of the times, "The overriding goal of applied racial hygiene must be to insure that the talented and the sound reproduce in greater numbers than the incompetent and the inferior" (*Meyers Encyclopedia*, 1939, p. 1246).

In the next example I would like to take up the question of an ongoing National Socialist mentality of racism and elitism.

"DEUTSCHLAND, DEUTSCHLAND ÜBER ALLES," OR FAITH, DUTY, STRUGGLE

Here we return to the family mentioned in the introduction. The identified patient was the 19-year-old daughter, Brigitte, who came to us with her mother after repeated suicide attempts. The daughter's increasing decompensation had developed after the divorce of the parents, five years earlier. On the surface it seemed to be a typical "broken home" situation. The mother clung too closely to the daughter. For the daughter, because of her guilt feelings, the only escape lay in suicide: "Then, at last, the limits would be clear." And yet, after endless hours of discussion, "even with my suicide attempts I can't get through to them; they remain numb. What else can I do to make an impact on this fog?"

I felt this "fog" quite clearly. It rendered me impotent with this family and required the clarity of my colleagues in supervision. My countertransference feeling: "In this family you can't get any ground under your feet." This became a therapeutic key and clarified the subtly murderous strategy of the mother and the father, which came into play whenever the daughter made attempts to pin anything down exactly or came to any different conclusions from the model the parents offered out of their own lives. This model was untouchable in its depiction of the father as a brilliant scientist, and the mother's abilities were also outstanding. The superior intellectual capacities of the daughter were much emphasized, while her merely average high school marks were explained by her illness.

The picture that became more and more clear was of a family with an ongoing National Socialist elitist and racist mentality, expressive of the NAPOLA motto: "Physically tough, morally firm, and mentally supple," the motto of the elite schools, which were supposed to assure the Third Reich of a disciplined ruling caste. By the standards of those times, the father would not measure up to this elite ideal today, since he was only moderately successful in his career.

Shocking to me—gradually becoming clearer to the daughter—was the early socialization of the father. I emphasize "to me" here, since the father himself, who if anything was rather weak and ludicrous, was notable for the rigidity of his "character armor," based on a defense of contemptuous disparagement. He came from a middle-class merchant family. The grandfather's business had gone bankrupt after the First World War. The loss of independence, along with unemployment and a loss of class status, was one of the chief motives for the grandfather's entrance into the SA. This membership quickly paid off in the form of protection by his comrades in the building up of a new business. His marriage—"a catastrophe from the beginning," as he put it—had ended in divorce when our Herr K. was four years old. From this time on Herr K.'s mother called the shots: "We had to study for hours every day, or else we were locked in. That developed my concentration, and *that* never hurt anybody," explained Herr K.

When Herr K. was ten years old, the parents were remarried. Here too the chief motive, as I reconstructed it, was once again a National Socialist one. Under the divorce law reform of 1938, as the adulterous party in a past divorce, the grandfather would not be able to pursue a political career. Moreover, children from divorced families could not attend the elite Nazi schools. Those were the principal reasons for the remarriage: considerations of the grandfather's political career and considerations of the grandmother's elitist ambitions for her children. When I asked Herr K. for *his* feelings about this situation, which I found shocking, he had no response. He cited nevertheless the motto of his teacher from those days: "Better a hero's death than a coward's life." At this, the daughter began to scream, "But both of you are complete failures, don't you see that, with all your elitist drivel? And I'm supposed to be like that too, always at the top, always strong, always nice and tidy. And you want to be models for me! The truth is, you'd probably rather see me dead than have me see through your fraud. But what does your Hitler have to do with *me*?"

"Better dead than average," reduced relations with children to functionalism and drill, which led in turn to their internal destruction, to a "false self," which was basically modeled on the old Nazi pattern: with the father, through the idealization of his elite status; with the mother, through the mission of the "German mother." Her own mother had been "knighted," as she put it, with the silver "Mother's Cross."* She herself was still giddy to this day over the fact that as a child she had once personally handed flowers to the Führer.

With a voice near breaking, she repeated, "He looked me in the eye and said, 'You'll turn out well.'"

I want to emphasize that in these families, in contrast to those, for example, which show a neurotic-compulsive structure, I find not so much anger as incomprehension, despair, and horror at the ideologizing which led to the destruction of human beings. It also disconcerts me to think that people schooled in this way in the past, isolated from all present feeling and incapable of experiencing a connection between their own existence, their ethical categories, and political realities, ruled our world in both public and private realms, and still rule today.

These are the people already described so brilliantly by Heinrich Mann as early as 1914, with their hard-won mentality of submissiveness. So might his characterization of Diederich Hessling have been applied word for word to one of our fathers in therapy: "He was a soft child, much given to dreaming, who feared everything and suffered frequently from earaches. . . . More gruesome than gnome or toad from a fairy tale was the father, and what's more one was supposed to love him. Diederich did love him. If he happened to pass by the shop after being punished, sobbing and face stained with tears, then the workers would laugh at him. But Diederich would immediately stick out his tongue at them, and stamp his feet. He was sure of his ground: 'I got a beating, but it was from my Papa. You only wish you could get a beating from him too, but you're far too insignificant for that.'" [Mann, 1918, p. 5].

A CANCER PHOBIA, OR THE THERAPIST'S FEAR OF CONFRONTATION WITH HIS OWN PERSONAL AND PROFESSIONAL NAZI PAST

A family sought out our department because of the severe cancer phobia of the 18-year-old daughter. Elements of intrafamilial conflict became evident. The father talked freely about the Nazi background of his own family, and the continuing fascist views of his parents. The mother, by contrast, complained of the suicide of her father, now nearly 50 years in the past, which had brought great misfortune to her family. Because of the close bond to her mother which resulted from this event, she slipped into depression at the first sign of any wish on her own part to separate from her mother. On this account she first visited a psychiatrist in 1940, at the age of 20. In 1949 she began a regular psychoanalysis, "which did help—but still solved nothing at the core," as she put it. This "core" she described in terms similar to those the daughter used for her cancer phobia: "There is something bad in me, which is destroying me. The doctors always say it is nothing, just as they do to her . . . it's all imagination, they don't want to hear about it, they prove through laboratory tests that they are right . . . I've been hearing this since 1940. It's always my imagination, but all the same my siblings had to give up their studies, because nobody needed *that kind* of people, and my uncle was murdered, just because he supposedly worked in the resistance!"

We will not follow her history any further, but rather point out the tragedy of this woman, to have visited a psychotherapist in 1940 who interrupted her in the anamnesis to bid her *not* to discuss certain themes from her life history on account of the existing Hereditary Health Code,* which would apply to her family because of her father's suicide during his depressive illness.

We therapists felt clearly at this point that all the therapy that this woman had undergone had been fundamentally flawed. We had particular doubts arising out of her reports about her experience of analysis beginning in 1949. For according to everything the woman said, the therapist ascribed the neurotic fixations of the patient overwhelmingly to the suicide of the father and the mother-daughter symbiosis, thereby *neglecting* the existential psychic effects on the woman of being the child of a family that actually was assigned to the category of "unworthy life."

At the beginning of the eighties little had yet been published about psychotherapy and National Socialism. Nonetheless, many discussions with colleagues have confirmed my own direct experiences right down to the present day, even as additional literature on the subject has continued to appear (as for example Mitscherlich-Nielsen, 1981; Rosenkötter, 1981; Lockot, 1985; Bromberger, Mausbach, and Thannan, 1985, among others). It appears that a defense mechanism for our profession, when confronted with Nazism, consists in *not* believing the patient or rushing to "neuroticize" him.

We recall clearly how the woman in this particular family therapy not only struggled for the validation of her experiences, but battled as well for rehabilitation, for a kind of reparation. She was not to be satisfied with formulaic reassurances on our part, but rather was intent on undoing the ascriptions which caused her suffering—like the man in Borchert's "Outside the Door," who struggles desperately to give back responsibility. This woman too confronted us with the demand that we *seriously face* the reality of the Hereditary Disease Laws, the euthanasia program, and the sterilization proceedings by studying the legal texts of the time. On one occasion she brought in the text by A. E. Hoche and K. M. Bindung from 1920, "The Right to Eliminate Inferior Life." We never experienced this woman as moralistically or querulously accusatory; yet she forced us to shoulder a kind of guilt or shame for our profession, and thereby to experience a real therapeutic empathy for her suffering in the past, which had a *factual* basis—and to become aware of our own countertransference reactions. She had no doubt seen the familiar unbelieving look on our faces, since we ourselves, as mentioned above, had sensed it quite clearly and therefore certainly expressed it.

Conclusion

In the cases described here I have shown that severe symptom formation in the patients is to be understood as a melded interaction of family determinants and National Socialist concepts. Only through recognition and awareness of these facts does it become possible to work on these issues, thus permitting a restoration of *continuity* between the generations, with a living interaction out of their present personal reality as representatives and participants in the history of those times.

Therapies involving National Socialist issues and material are slow going, on the one hand because of defended feelings of shame and guilt, but also because of defenses against anxiety from the Nazi time, which remain unworked through and which feed on denunciations, mistrust, and repressions in the banality of everyday life. Thus for example a harmless joke could lead to the court conviction of a teacher under the Malicious Gossip Law of the time and to her dismissal from state service: "A farmer didn't know what National Socialism was. When he came to Berlin, he asked the taxi driver, who said: 'See the kids playing marbles in the park? If all the marbles belong to one kid, then that's capitalism. But if every kid has his own, then that's National Socialism.' So the farmer went home and told the other farmers, 'If all the marbles belong to one kid, that's capitalism. But if everybody has lost their marbles, that's National Socialism'" (from Peukert and Reulecke, 1981, p. 215).[2]

In our experience working with the "National Socialism

---

2. Originally, "'*Wenn die Vögel alle einem gehören, ist das Kapitalismus, hat aber jeder einen Vogel, dann ist das Nationalsozialismus.*'" "*Einen Vogel haben,*" in German, is roughly equivalent to being "soft in the head." —Trans.

complex," we have found that the *person of the physician or therapist* is drawn more than usual into the foreground—specifically, on the one hand, with regard to how the National Socialist past is reflected in his own family of origin, and on the other, with regard to the Nazi past of the psychotherapeutic profession itself, which has not been worked through. In the therapies we have carried out, we were forced to realize that before we can get to questions of refinement of technique, it is essential first to master social history, historical data—and above all the actual texts of laws—and the geographic and national conditions, traditions, customs, and changes they underwent, which determined the everyday life of the times. Here it has proven very fruitful to study actual original sources, for example ones quite close at hand, such as our parents' or grandparents' family albums and genealogical registers of the times, in which traces of the prevailing racial hygiene laws may be found. In this way we younger therapists in particular could take in the dread which is part and parcel of the total impact of a totalitarian system. Such an approach fosters a climate of mutual empathy, which is necessary since the level of individual accusations and guilt so quickly becomes relativized or transcended.

The therapeutic work should consist either in making the question of collective guilt palpable in these families, by beginning with the individual-familial and then generalizing from that level, or else by freeing up the systematically rigidified question of guilt so as to open the horizon for a broader approach within the fabric of political and individual involvement. Here, the denazification* laws and their application to the entire population up to 1951 played a decisive role.

If I have selected only a few examples here, there are others from our therapeutic work that might have been named: refugee histories, ongoing Nazi ideals, the raising of grief itself to the level of ideology, racial prejudice against Jews or Gypsies, the consequences for families arising out of the denazification process, and much more.

Let me point out, under three provocative headings, possible present-day aftereffects of National Socialist worldviews in the areas of social Darwinism, racism, and "racial hygiene" which pose challenges to our own responsibility:

1. *Social Darwinism.* Hitler, 1940: "After so many centuries of drivel about protecting the poor and the suffering, the time has come to think about protecting the strong from the inferior." In the *Lebensbornheimen,** which were set up to breed a Nazi elite, handpicked young Aryan women, with the help of SS members, "gave"

the Führer some 100,000 children. The leading "racial hygienist," Lenz, lamented at the time, "Certainly mountains of prejudice and bad instincts still stand in the way of supporting the propagation of a minority which possesses outstanding capacities."

In the late 1970s, in private sperm banks in California, the sperm from Nobel prizewinners was being frozen, to be given to "intelligent" women for artificial insemination.

2. *"Racial Hygiene."* 1934: "It promotes precious racial kinship and defends against the foreign or racially destructive stock. The necessity of preventing any further penetration of Jewish blood stems from the danger which Judaism poses, through the admixture of blood and foreign spiritual influence, to the racial foundations of our people and thereby to its Germanic Teutonic character."

In a pro and con program on television in 1986, 75 percent of viewers were opposed to the admission of political refugees seeking asylum. Political refugees as undesirables? Exploited ideologically by politicians to stir up public opinion about worthy and unworthy human life?

3. *Hereditary Health Code.* In 1933 the Law for the Prevention of Hereditary Disease was promulgated. In 1939 euthanasia was introduced. Beginning in 1941 anthropological experiments were performed on living human beings of different races.

In 1953 Watson and Crick published the three-dimensional model of the genetic material DNA, which had been discovered in 1944. A turbulent new phase in genetics began. Intentionally altered genetic material can be introduced into the chromosomes. The production of human beings under laboratory conditions is no longer a utopian idea, but a future which has already begun. With an unexamined mixture of fascination and horror, the public is amazed by embryos conceived in test tubes, the birth of babies after months of embryonic freezing, and children from host mothers. In the view of Amendt (1986), the scientific-medical motive is not so much the treatment of individual childlessness, but rather the exercise of a new technology of control over people. It strikes at the very *conditio humana* and destroys the living connection between conception and sexuality in order to bring forth life by technological means (sexuality understood as the expression of human connection).

Have we learned from the inhumanity of the National Socialist epoch, or will it be repeated worldwide in even more ghastly dimensions, and indeed by a science created by humans, and a medicine which does not allow its own ethics to be questioned?

Are we allowed to hope, as the title of Peukert and Reulecke's book

(1981) has it, that the ranks are really only *almost* closed tight?[3] In the therapeutic sessions described here, we were strongly confronted, together with the families themselves, with the ideals of Nazism, which held human life in contempt. Our work lay in allowing these ideals to come to life at a feeling level and then working them through with the goal of developing a critical consciousness for socioeconomic conditions and threats to humanity in the present day. Human misery in the form of neurotic symptoms—as the expression of a powerful, indeed a *healthy contradiction*—will lead us inevitably, let us hope, to a *completely integrated vision* of individual and cultural suffering at last.

---

3. The title referred to, *Die Reihen* fast *geschlossen* (The ranks *almost* closed), is itself a reference to the Nazi "Horst Wessel Lied" mentioned earlier ("*Die Reihen* fest *geschlossen*"—The ranks closed tight.) See Glossary, "Horst Wessel Lied." —Trans.

7

HOW CAN I DEVELOP ON A MOUNTAIN OF CORPSES?
Observations from a Theme-Centered Interaction Seminar with Isaac Zieman[1]

Wolfgang Bornebusch

"The Third Reich and Jewry, a Chapter in Our History: How Can I Further My Own Growth in Confronting This Theme?" This was the title of a Theme-Centered Interaction (TCI) seminar offered in August 1987 at the Klausenhof Academy on the lower Rhine. The announcement read:

> Third Reich, National Socialism, Jewry—these terms awaken the memory of a part of our history which still torments us today—in our dreams and nightmares, in the scarred and open wounds which we carried from it. Repress, keep silent: that is the way that many went, and still go, in the effort to deal with this past. It becomes more and more clear that the only thing that helps is to face the past—or better still, to take on the past and transform it in the attempt to comprehend it.

The announcement also described how, at least at the beginning, this facing of the past, taking it on and transforming it, might happen:

> Building on the basis of Theme-Centered Interaction together with elements of Gestalt therapy, we hope to create a process in which to address such questions as: How do we continue to be affected by this past which is handed on to us yet remains only guessed at, unspoken? What do my own past and the past of my parents mean for my own present? How can I live with this past . . .

---

1. Isaac Zieman is a psychoanalyst and Gestalt group psychotherapist; he is a faculty member of W.I.L.L. International, Institute for Mental Health in New York City and of The New York Institute for Gestalt Therapy. Theme-Centered Interaction is a form of group work founded and developed by Ruth C. Cohn. —Trans.

in the confrontation with the older generation . . . in the encounter
with Jewry? Where in all this do I need a more profound understanding of the culture and religion of the Jewish people in history
and in the present? What can I do?

The seminar was led by Isaac Ziemen and myself, Wolfgang
Bornebusch. Isaac Zieman, born in Riga, Latvia, lives today in New
York, where he practices psychoanalysis and Gestalt therapy. He
graduated from W.I.L.L.[2] and has been leading TCI courses in the
Federal Republic of Germany, in Switzerland, and in Israel since
1973. Before and after World War II, he was involved in the Zionist
Socialist youth movement. His family was murdered by the Nazis.

I was born in 1945. Today I am a Protestant minister in
Schermbeck, a rural community on the lower Rhine, which, until the
middle of the Nazi period, abutted a neighboring Jewish community.
Exploring the history of this Jewish group in the context of my
parish work, making new contacts with Jews who formerly lived in
Schermbeck and who survived—all this, together with the attendant
personal experiences, made up the background for my working in
the seminar. I am familiar with the methods of TCI; in addition I am
trained in family therapy.

Even the phase prior to the seminar itself seems worth men-
tioning. The Klausenhof Academy had sent out its year's program,
including our seminar, to about 10,000 people. All the Jewish communities were on the list; all church leaders charged with promoting
Jewish-Christian dialogue were urged to support attendance at the
seminar; all members of the group Friends of Nes Amim, a Christian
settlement in Israel, were invited; all daily papers along the lower
Rhine had announced the seminar—with hardly a response. By the
end of May 1987 a mere three applications had come in. One last
attempt: an extensive announcement of the seminar was published
in a nationwide church newspaper and in the *Jewish Weekly Times.*
(West German Radio had no interest in drawing attention to this
seminar.)

The seminar did take place. Many of those who ultimately participated had been alerted by reading the *Jewish Weekly Times*—
non-Jews who were interested in exploring the life of Jewish communities within West Germany. For a while it seemed as if there
would even be a long waiting list, but in the last four or five days,
one after the other withdrew. It may be coincidence, but it is nevertheless striking: the majority of those who withdrew were people

---

2. W.I.L.L. is the Workshop Institute for Living-Learning. —Trans.

who lived close to the Klausenhof Academy. The "closer" the en-counter with such a delicate chapter of one's own history came, the greater one's anxiety—and the greater the temptation to avoid the confrontation. In this connection, perhaps it should also be men-tioned that a second co-leader, who had originally been expected, became ill shortly before the seminar and said she could not take part.

I also would like to mention briefly my own personal experience prior to the seminar. The closer the seminar came, the more I felt that I was not sufficiently prepared. I read and read. At the same time, the pressure within me grew to get down at last to the conversations with my father that I had so long intended but thus far had always avoided. My father was a junior surgeon in Poland until the end of 1944. At the end of the war he was in Krakow, not far from Auschwitz. Must he not have known what was happening in Auschwitz? But when I put this question to him, the answer was, "No, I knew nothing!" I remained mistrustful. But apparently this question set something in motion within my father. A few days later he told me about his train trip back from Krakow to the West. On the way, the train had to stop. On the next track stood a train going in the opposite direction, with many regular passenger cars, but there was one car with boarded-up windows. There were people in this car, presumably Jews. He told, too, about Munich, where he had studied. There he saw the results of the Kristallnacht.* He found it ghastly. But what should he have done?

Then, two days before the beginning of the seminar, my father telephoned me. He wanted to share something with me which he had not been able to talk about: before the seminar began, every-thing should be talked about and made clear between us. So he talked—the distance afforded by the telephone surely helped—about his student days in Munich. The fraternity to which he belonged was supposed (like all the others) to join the National Socialist Student Union. They refused. Thereupon each fraternity member was required to join a National Socialist organization as an individual. Since my father and his friend loved to ride motorcycles, they became candidates for the motorized SS. But they were never accepted. Then he and his friend went to Königsberg to continue their studies. Entry into the Party was a requirement for matricula-tion. He went along with this requirement. Here again, he never got beyond candidate status. While in Munich his fraternity had been

---

* See Glossary, here and wherever an asterisk appears. —Trans.

ordered to rid itself of Jewish members, which it had refused to do at first. But then when he studied in Königsberg, the fraternity did go along with this requirement. One of his best friends thereupon announced his resignation from the fraternity. My father himself did not take this step. In both of these cases he could have made a different decision. Presumably the consequences would not even have been that dire. Now he knows that he could and should have made other decisions. Up to now he had not been able to say these things to me. When I heard that, I wanted to burst into tears, but I was happy, too. I had always hoped that my father could talk to me as he just had. I was no longer left to my fantasies about him and his actions. With this gift I went to the seminar.

The group, including the leader, consisted of the following 20 people: five participants had experienced the Third Reich as young persons and as adults; for two others (born in 1935 and 1936), this time was connected with important, formative childhood memories; there were two young participants whom Hitler would have called "half Jews" and two whom he would have called "full Jews," who both had had to leave their homeland during the Nazi time—among them Isaac Zieman; the remaining nine members were in their twenties, thirties, and forties. The youngest participant was 20 years old, the oldest 76: three generations talked with each other in this seminar. It should be added that about half of the participants had already attended similar seminars and were at home with TCI, with self-experience, or with methods of Gestalt therapy. For all the others the experience was a new world.

The introductions at the very start showed how much each person still carried, in the present, his or her own past—as well as the pasts of her or his father and mother. I'll call one of the participants Edda Herz: a "Germanic" given name, a Jewish family name. Her name reflects her inner torment and dividedness. Her loyalty to one part of her name, her origin, makes her deny the other part of her name. Try as she will, she cannot bring both parts of her name together and integrate them. Another participant had put aside his name in his early youth and taken on a new one. His father had been a warden in Dachau. He didn't want to carry his father's name or to become like him. Later on he took back his family name—a sign of his having again grown closer to his family, and no doubt also a sign that he could not so easily leave the family heritage behind. To be sure, he did not take back his given name, which is also his father's name. He continues to bear the first name which he chose for himself and which he forced his father to call him.

In the first two sessions of the seminar everything went very fast. Everyone seemed to be happy that the seminar, which they had anticipated with much inner tension, had finally begun. Most seemed quite willing to engage themselves and to open up. But soon the red lights went on: Watch out! I must control myself! I can't let myself go! After all, I have to know what I'm getting into. Each proposed exercise became a problem. I have never taken part in a seminar where so many reservations were expressed, where so much caution was to be felt. Always, there was the fear of being led astray, of running after a new Führer. In the evening, Günther had danced with some other members of the group. He had felt good, had fun, loved the movement and the music. But the following day he felt bad because he had experienced the buoyant songs and the stirring marches from the Nazi time as a hidden seduction.

Never follow a leader again! Don't trust the authorities! Isaac had said, in response to a particular remark, that impatience had also been a part of the foundation on which the Nazis had built. People had not had enough patience either *in* or *with* the Weimar Republic.* The Nazis had responded to this impatience very effectively, and in a short time they had achieved a great deal, which had fascinated many people. Democracy is hard, often clumsy, slow. A light went on for Annemarie: Yes, that was it! But in the next moment came defense: No, I mustn't accept that either. If I accept that, then I've already submitted to a leader. And I know that's what I must not do! Isaac hadn't really said anything new to her; Annemarie had only gotten clear about something she had always felt and known. But her inability to accept what she had heard from Isaac parallels her inability to trust her own perceptions and feelings. This ability has been destroyed, although there had been a time when she did trust her own feelings.

Power is bad! Again and again there is opposition to Isaac, who obviously takes his function as leader seriously:

"Manipulation! You are forcing your themes on us!"

"Then go ahead; fight for your themes. I fight for mine. That's why I'm here."

"I mustn't do that. Power is bad! I mustn't use my power! If I use my power, I become guilty."

"If you make yourself powerless, you're guilty too. You can't keep your hands clean! Those who refuse to get involved are guilty too!"

It became clear that "refusing to get involved" was a widespread strategy in the group: hardly a single person was a member of a political party. Nobody belonged to any organized group. The church seemed to be an exception. A profound mistrust existed about being taken in by something which, ultimately, one cannot stand behind.

One of the participants related in tears how she belonged for a time to a leftist student group. She joined because she wanted to get involved in creating a better Germany. But then, following some demonstrations, she was interrogated by the police in a way that was humiliating to her. The representatives of the state to which she had wanted to devote herself hadn't understood her at all, hadn't even wanted to understand her. No one had even been interested in her motives. She began to feel she could not continue to live in West Germany. She thought of emigrating. Nor was she the only one. This thought occurred again and again for several people in the group, depending on how oppressive the individual had found the political situation at a particular time.

For many, the relationship with the Jews in our country and the quality of that relationship provided the measure for judging the political climate. A young woman said, "Now I have more anxiety than I used to have. Maybe it's because I now have four children. But anxiety has been my lifelong companion. If I went into the Jewish community, my parents always used to say, 'Don't tell anybody.' Today when I come into a new city and want to stay for some time, the first thing I always do is open the phone book to see whether or not there is a Jewish congregation. Then I go there to see if everything is in order. Only then do I attend to my work."

The feeling of living on very shaky ground here in West Germany is shared by many in the group. To connect the word *homeland* or *fatherland* with West Germany is impossible for most of the people. The word *home* does not cross their lips, particularly in the case of the younger members. When Isaac, of all people, maintains that the Germans need to develop a new sense of peoplehood, he is met with massive resistance. But Isaac doesn't budge: it's important for psychological reasons, he says. All human beings have a deep need to feel good about the social group, the people, the nation, and the culture to which they belong, and to feel pride in its achievements. Naturally, that doesn't preclude the possibility of criticism. A new national feeling is important for political reasons as well. Otherwise it can happen only too easily that this human need for identification with one's people, one's nation, will once again be usurped and exploited by criminals.

Everybody was confused and had difficulty accepting this line of thought. The daughter of an SD* officer protested: "We are without honor. We lost our honor when the murderers among us annihilated the Jews." The older people in the group had once known this feeling of wanting to belong, of being proud of one's own people and its achievements, and yet it was uncomfortable for them now. One of them still remembered the theme of a school essay: "You Are Nothing, Your People Are Everything." Some felt relieved when David said, "When Hitler marched into the Sudetenland, everybody stood beside the road and waved and cheered. I would have loved to be part of it. But I wasn't allowed to cheer. I felt very alone."

Marches, Nazi songs, Hitler's speeches—with these I associate force, violence, indoctrination. Yet one thing became clear to me: their content and bias are one thing, but the connection of these with their context is something else entirely. Context means family, childhood, a beaming father, a proud mother, security, warmth, a homelike atmosphere, treasured memories. Günther mused, "I think I have finally understood what the Third Reich really was. And yet when I hear the old songs, all my understanding is gone and I'm back in the old days again, I'm at home again. That's where I can still be seduced." Günther shields himself against this seduction, but in so doing, he blinds himself to very important childhood memories.

Isaac lightens his burden: "Go ahead and sing one of your old Nazi songs some morning when you're alone under the shower. That doesn't automatically make you a Nazi again. And if later on you greet your fellows in a more friendly and relaxed fashion, then that's OK." I could hardly say the same thing, although I do say— hesitantly, I notice—that I agree.

It was Günther, too, who from time to time said he was afraid microphones were hidden in our meeting room and that we were being listened in on. "I know it's dumb, but this fear is just simply there." He sees conspiracies at work everywhere. He knows precisely, it seems, just which old friends from the time of his studies swept Mayor Diepgen[3] into the Berlin Senate, who it was who used his position to enrich himself illegally, and so forth. His perception of this part of reality is enormously acute and sensitive. And thus, in the final analysis, all politicians are corrupt and can be bought, and are intent on taking care of their own. You can't trust any of them.

Isaac inquired what role the idea of the "Jewish World Conspiracy"* had played in Gunther's home. And it became clear: the patterns stay the same; it is only their contents that change! With all its distortions and limitations forged through upbringing, education, and experiences in the time of the Third Reich, this way of

---

3. A conservative mayor of West Berlin during the 1980s and 1990s.

perceiving the world had hardly changed. Only the objects of the perception have changed. It is no longer the Jews who conspire against the German people: now it is those accountable to them, their own politicians and functionaries.

Peter Mosler, one of the participants, looking back on the seminar, wrote, "Germans born after the Third Reich like to see themselves as victims. . . . The thing that struck me most deeply was the realization that in me, also, there lies a part which is victim and a part which is perpetrator."[4] Certainly many had the same experience. For some it was horrifying and shocking to discover in themselves the same harshness and brutality against which they struggle so vigorously. Often this harshness is fiercely directed against one's own person in the form of rigid demands on one's behavior and morality—and often also against fathers and mothers.

Walter tells how as a child he was beaten by his father, often for no reason. The father jammed the son's head between his knees and whipped him with a leather cobbler's strap. When he was beaten like this he would mock his father, demanding, "Is this how you handled the prisoners in Dachau? Go ahead! Show us how you did it!" Later he brought his Jewish friends home with him, and after his father had greeted them, he would say, "These are the sons of the people you killed."

Annemarie, too, told about her hatred of her father and her rage at him. During the Third Reich he was an enthusiastic Nazi; right up until the very end he believed in the final victory. For her, as a little girl, he was the shining hero. She admired him and loved him. After the war he disappeared for some years into a denazification* camp. "That's where he belonged. I'm glad he had to go through that." An old, broken, silent man came home from the camp. She had a similar experience with her mother. At times she had the fantasy: those are not my parents at all, they adopted me. She was unable to put together her various parental images. She said that she felt split, schizophrenic.

These are the most important impressions and realizations that the seminar brought me. I would like only to add the following: It was particularly important that—because of the group's composition—three generations talked with one another. Several of the older

---

4. Peter Mosler in "A Painful Gift," an article which appeared Sept. 20, 1987, in *Die Tageszeitung*, Berlin, a leftist daily newspaper with national circulation. Several other direct quotations used here are also taken from this article.

participants said that this was the first time younger people had really listened to them. And in their turn, quite a number of the younger participants noted that this was the first time they had had any success in gaining an empathic understanding of the older generation's history. They were grateful to the older people for standing up to the younger participants' attacks and accusations.

Also important was the presence of the Jewish participants. Sometimes they were able to lighten the burden of the older members in a way that was impossible for any of the non-Jews. They contributed centrally to the process by which several people were able to be open to the ambivalence of their own feelings, their oscillation between disgust and fascination. They were also able—without becoming suspect themselves—to challenge others to take a look at their own "positive" experiences during National Socialism.

It is also worthy of mention that the members' confrontation with their own histories was made richer by examining the origins of anti-Semitism as well as by coming to know Judaism more profoundly. Important elements in this encounter were Yiddish poems, rabbinical stories, Klezmer music (the folk music of eastern European Jewry), an Oneg Shabbat (a celebration on Friday evening of the arrival of the Sabbath), and an author's reading of a fragment dealing with rural Jews in Hesse at the beginning of this century.

Peter Mosler had asked himself before the beginning of the seminar, Is it not arrogant of me to imagine that I can develop and grow on a mountain of corpses? Is not my suffering at the murder of millions a grain of dust compared to the granite mountain of the agony of the murdered? He—and with him all of us—received an answer at the seminar: "You not only have the right, you have the duty to come to know yourself, your wounds, your aggression. Only in that way can you help to prevent something like the Holocaust from happening again."

8

UNWILLING TO ADMIT, UNABLE TO SEE
Therapeutic Experiences with the National Socialist "Complex"

Waltraud Silke Behrendt

From our present historical standpoint in Germany, concrete bio-graphical reality, comprising in turn both individual and collective history, includes the relationship to National Socialism (hereafter, Nazism). Even the youngest therapists among us were brought up by an elder generation which spent a long slice of life in one of the most inhumane reigns of terror ever known. Granted, the oldest among our elders were still young at that time; nevertheless, they shared and bore the experiences of the time. Now as therapists, dealing profes-sionally with those often unconscious powers from the past which affect the present, we cannot do this work cut adrift from our own consciousness and our own knowledge. After all, it is precisely values and norms which emerge from a particular common background; this background can itself undergo vivid changes and emerge differently, not only among the generations but also among dif-ferent social or educational classes. In the course of arguments, corresponding misunderstandings can thus arise. Above all, our *unconscious* values and beliefs can cause us to reduce political, eco-nomic, or social conflicts simply to their *individual* significance. Massing and Beushausen (1986) even go so far as to defend the thesis that when working with the Nazi complex,[1] the person of the therapist comes into the foreground more prominently than usual. They relate this in part to the insufficient working through of the past by their own professional group, but also to the individual countertransference feelings of disbelief and denial.

In talking with each other, we can attempt to seek out the gaps

---

1. The concept of "complex" was chosen because of its double connotation of massiveness/many-layeredness on the one hand, and the psychic results of the repression of affect on the other.

in a collective defense—gaps which are much more difficult to find than those in the individual's defenses and their manifestations. I would like to speak of *collective historical gestalts* which become taboo and thus become rigid to a greater or lesser degree and which then keep us incapable of dealing with new dangers. The (good-)evil categorization of everything that has to do with Nazism is one such moral-historical gestalt which calls out for the exercise of greater differentiation. Precisely because this discussion is filled with emotion and with attributions of guilt, we must insist that it take place not intrapsychically but rather interpersonally, in the space between people.

My Personal Approach and Several Examples of Encounters with Patients

Here I wish to limit my own personal approach to the Nazi theme to my therapeutic or therapeutic-educational role. This limitation is of course artificial inasmuch as I have always, more or less consciously, experienced my own family home and the homes of my playmates, boyfriends, girlfriends, and, not least, in-laws, as all marked by Nazism in quite varying ways. When I say "us" I refer to the generation which, even if born during the war, still has no conscious memories of it.

The war itself (as the unavoidable consequence of the Nazi regime) left vestiges behind in us which I will only hint at with a personal example: at a group session, working on our self-experience by using gongs, a certain frequency evoked instantaneous anxiety, panic, and feelings of terror in me. Others in the group confirmed that this was precisely the frequency of the dive-bombers during the war. At that time, at the end of the war, I was not yet 14 months old. It is superfluous to emphasize what kind of an appraisal of the war I developed, just out of my own experience.

FIRST EXAMPLE: WAR

With this I come to one of my first relevant therapeutic experiences. It already lies a number of years back. I was in my mid thirties when a patient, who was about twice as old as I was, began to tell about his war experiences. Different kinds of weapons were mentioned, and places that I at best knew about only from history books.

A military language forced itself into my ears and I found myself unable to shut it out. I felt only the wish that the session would soon be over. Mainly I felt myself threatened, and I froze despite my irritation with this man, who sat there in front of me and told me I could not possibly understand him, but that he wanted only to make clear to me that for him, friendships simply cannot be compared with the comradeship which he had experienced in the war.

At that moment I wasn't sure that I didn't *want* to understand him, but I grasped my dilemma as a therapist very clearly: my own anxieties and my own defenses would determine the radius of my therapeutic possibilities. The idealization of comradeship in the war, which sounded to me like an idealization of the war itself, made our conversation stagnate. Through my own defenses it was impossible to assist the patient in gaining an awareness of his defenses, which might have led to sorrow and to a reawakening of his old feelings. Thus, either I had to come to know my own anxiety and work it through or I would remain stuck in the mechanism of not-wanting-to-be-aware and also of not-being-able-to-be-aware.

SECOND EXAMPLE: NAPOLA*

Later on I encountered a still stronger defense theme. My dilemma, caught as I was between my own therapeutic understanding and my feelings of condemnation, was even more clearly delineated.

A patient, who was born in 1929, was sent to me by his speech therapist because he was suspected of drug and alcohol dependency. Not knowing his way in the complex clinic grounds, he was late to our first meeting and greeted me saying, "I could just cry, that I got here late." I took up his sentence as a question and, laughing, he played down its meaning. Instead, he tried to make clear to me that he—on the contrary—never cries, but that he suffers because in his youth he could do *everything* by himself, whereas today he can no longer control himself and fears the worst for his future. After his first meeting with the speech therapist he tried to get along without pills. He then noticed that he was continually under stress, that he couldn't restrain himself, and that he really had to find out what was the matter with him. I let him describe what he was suffering from and then returned to his earlier remark about the "other times that were completely different," a remark that clearly referred to a very different feeling of positive self-confidence. He sighed resignedly

---

* See Glossary, here and wherever an asterisk appears. —Trans.

and told me that I wouldn't be able to understand, adding, "Or do you know what NAPOLA is?" As I deciphered the acronym for him, to his obvious astonishment, a torrent of words poured out of him, and then he said, "You know, one single time in my life I *did* cry. I don't know anymore whether it was for one or two or three hours. A world collapsed within me . . . when we were 16, standing in the trench . . . and suddenly someone called out: 'The Führer is dead!'"

My reaction to this revelation was as ambivalent as my dilemma itself. I derived a clearly malicious pleasure from the fact that I stood on the side of "good" and could now witness the punishment of "evil." The difficult fate of drug addiction was all too well deserved by this politically disturbed person. But I also sensed this man's despair beneath his facade, and I understood how basically lonely he had been as he tried to find his way after the war. From one minute to the next, everything living and strong, everything with which he had identified, was lost. I reminded myself that in 1933, when the Nazis seized power, this man was four years old. I was touched by his suddenly rising hope that someone might know about his lost past and thus be able to understand him. And all the while my "knowledge" rested on something which, on account of my literary interests, I had read quite accidentally —Michel Tournier's *The Ogre.*

Third Example: Obedience

In the meantime I have learned to recognize more easily when and how to ask about the implications and consequences of the Nazi period. In the process it became clear that the gravity of this entire problem area often comes to light only in the course of therapeutic work.

A patient, born in 1940 with a congenital hip dislocation, said without hesitation, when I asked her about it, that this birth defect, which was definitely regarded by the Nazis as hereditary and therefore as a defect to be "persecuted," hadn't mattered at all to her. She could not remember even a single insinuation—much less anything worse. Her parents must have succeeded in keeping the full truth from her. My hypothesis, that she thus had not been harmed by the Nazi regime, turned out to have been too hasty. In one session when we were examining the patient's present life and she was bemoaning the withdrawal of her adolescent, anorectic daughter, we stumbled directly on another Nazi story out of this woman's life. Prompted by my question, she recalled how she had argued with her parents in hours-long if unsatisfying debates. Until she had finally become completely resigned about it, the patient had wanted to find out what her father, who had meanwhile died, had done during the Nazi time. She remembered well that he was released from American captivity rather late and that he then slept with a knife in his bed. The parents' version of this threatening fact was that the father had been mistaken for a Nazi. At this point the debates with the parents regularly broke off and the patient was left with a feeling of resignation and helplessness. Later on she studied history and so was able to clarify for herself some of the collective lies and taboos. But the dark feeling about her family remained.

Now, as a mother, she again encounters the old fury when her daughter withdraws from her, which certainly strengthens the daughter's withdrawal. As a teacher, the patient had intended to trace the Nazi history of her school, but here again she became resigned and ended up in insurmountable anxiety states when she experienced the reaction of the principal of the school and a few colleagues. Later, her voice failed her as the school principal—despite her function as the teachers' confidante—demanded loyalty from her (my patient even called it "obedience"). In both examples she recognized that her vocal symptomatology, which up until then had been thought to be of organic origin, was related to a feeling of resignation and fear deeply rooted in her own history.

FOURTH EXAMPLE: A FATHER FAILS

I wish to add a more recent experience, first to point to the indirect connection between present experience and Nazi themes, but also because this example conveys what a relief it can be to find someone to talk to about the long years of self-denial, the years of taboo.

The patient, born soon after the war, had already told me in many therapy sessions that he had never been able to talk with his parents about "the topic." His mother would soon become terribly nervous, leave the room, and return with statements like, "It was bad enough, we can be glad that it's over with," or "Does this have to be?" His father would sigh and remain silent. My patient also remembered well that in his childhood the whole family was full of admiration for a certain "big shot" in their circle of acquaintances who had a lot of influence and prestige and who "had already been somebody under the Nazis." My patient didn't get the connection and first found out at his father's deathbed, where he "risked everything" to find out—alone with his father and without his mother's presence—

about his father's attitude and point of view during the time between 1933 and the end of the war. His father could have made quite a career as one of Freisler's* staff members, but he didn't feel up to this and took refuge in a safe but mediocre bureaucratic post.

At a comparable juncture in the son's life, the father had urged a similar safe step. The son followed the path unhappily and without enthusiasm but never felt the choice had been really his; he remained convinced, at an idealized level, that he could have accomplished something much more ambitious.

As I now carefully offered him the connection between his own historical heritage and that of his father, his eyes filled with tears. When I asked what made him sad, he answered, "I'm not sad. I'm happy that finally there's somebody I can talk to about it."

THE COURSE OF A THERAPY: THE "WATCH OUT!" POSTURE AND LOSS OF ORIENTATION

As a final example I would like to report in some detail about a patient whose expressive language touched me greatly, although his voice and his articulation often could not carry the content of what he had to say. This discrepancy was the expression of a series of ambivalences, which became more and more clear to me as our conversations progressed. In the course of his working through of the Nazi past, it became apparent that his specific resistance was derived from this issue. A bodily stance and a bodily tension had developed from a life posture. This stance kept alive the symptom which caused him to be sent to me.

The official speech and language diagnosis was "mixed form of a hyper-/hypofunctional dysphonia with asymmetry of adduction; rule out incomplete mutation." The 59-year-old patient made an "impression of premature aging" on the speech therapist. He was said to have championed the 1960s ideology and he was therefore, as a teacher within the school system, constantly being transferred. He had made indirect accusations against the speech therapist, telling him that he asked the wrong questions, but he drew back when the speech therapist asked him concretely what he meant.

Since his vocation as a teacher meant chiefly speaking, he was assigned to six weeks of intensive speech therapy and given sick leave. But for bureaucratic reasons the intensive speech therapy could only begin a half-year later—or possibly this was because of the patient's "bad conscience," since he felt his students wouldn't get proper attention without him. So until he could begin his speech therapy, he was referred to me for counseling or psychotherapeutic sessions, should I find these indicated and be able to motivate him.

In our first session he seemed on the one hand alert and engaged, but on the other hand hardly understandable, mumbling and giving monologues. His movements and gestures seemed inhibited, as if he were disoriented, lost. At the same time, he was perfectly willing to deal with me—he kept almost no distance—and seemed to be feeling his way in the dark, childishly playing up to me. When I asked him about his own view of his voice disturbance and its possible psychic causes, he immediately offered me several: constant tension in confrontations with colleagues; the aggressiveness in his classes; the bad care by doctors, who, 20 years earlier, had surgically destroyed his wife's ability to become pregnant;(suddenly sobbing) the guilt feelings he had had since he was 17 when his mother was trampled to death in a mob during a wartime fire as she was on her way to visit him when he was a young soldier. Altogether, the war and Nazism in general were the exclusive belief systems in which he had been brought up; his father had been "away at work," his mother was a cleaning woman, he himself was placed with the Hitler Youth* and found his home there. Hatred, despair, and cynicism filled his voice as he spoke about all this. His metaphor remains stuck in my ear: "Just imagine, somebody tells you, Jesus ate baby puppies! . . . Except that Hitler probably meant much more to us than Jesus means to you."

In this and later sessions I got the impression that he urgently needed psychological help in order to work with his loss of orientation. He himself brought up the fact that he felt well understood by me even though usually he was a very suspicious person; he connected this to my interest in his Nazi childhood. I had the impression that positive transference had occurred. Nevertheless, he kept asking if he had to keep coming.

In light of this question, we worked on his attitude toward professionals and authority figures. This discussion provoked his energetic criticism and resistance. Even his previously mentioned feeling of duty was not consonant with his secret wish for someone who could see how incapable and weak he felt in his role as teacher. At the end of the treatment, traces of this discrepancy still remained to be seen, as he—despite being symptom-free—scolded his speech therapist for signing the form which said he was now healthy again.

For a number of sessions we began with his acute problems and conflicts with colleagues, and in so doing we came up against connections with Nazism. He emphasized that, even if it was only toward the end, he still had risked speaking up instead of just blindly obeying. As I asked for concrete details about why he had done this, he said, "Otherwise I could go back to the Nazis right now!"

In order to convey to the reader the full flavor of this patient's ambivalence, I have transcribed rather long passages taken from a therapy session. At the start, the patient is relating that he has studied the books of the Mitscherlichs with great interest but that he doesn't quite know how he can make use of them for himself. I then bring up the question of whether his disappointing experiences in the Third Reich had perhaps resulted in his giving himself too little permission to rest even now.

> Patient: Yes, ever since I've known what was happening—I still don't really know it all, I always keep studying further. I consider it an enormous risk, to handle things the way we did then, my mother and my family. In those days we just swallowed every-thing. And that's something that people are practicing now again, that's coming again: only paying attention to oneself.
> Therapist: Is that the thing that prevents you from relaxing?
> P.: Sure, and something new can always come up, and then it might happen that one could get hurt somewhere, really deep, and that's when one assumes the "watch-out!" stance—so it can never happen again.

I try to let him keep his picture of himself and his wish to take over some higher responsibility, but at the same time I try to clarify what it costs him to do that. In this process he attempts to convince me that the only choice is between a watch-out stance and total passivity.

> P.: I want to say it once in my language: instead of passivity I could also say "desertion," meaning "after me the deluge," or "do your shit all by yourself." And I mean that very concretely. You see lots of people all over the place who have a Nazi attitude, who now are just totally self-centered, who don't say anything except "Well, what does my beer cost?" or "Where to on the next vacation?" If I put all this together, then we can easily start up and go crazy again with this fine country. I lived through this in such a grisly way—I don't want to see that again, and I wouldn't wish it on anybody. And that's why there have to be a few people who stand up to it.
> T.: "Watch-out!" stance—that sounds very bodily.
> P.: Yes, it is; it's bodily weaknesses that I don't like.

Then he goes on to tell about a tree that fell down in his neigh-borhood, which at first no one cleared away, and then they did, but only after he drew attention to it. The sawed-off branches, however, then stopped up the drain which is supposed to protect against flooding. He is furious that nobody pays any attention "when the trees fall down or when the Nazis come."

> P.: If I notice nobody else does it, am I supposed to let the tree lie there and take it easy myself? I can't do that!
> T. (laughing): No, naturally, despite your bodily pains and illnesses, you should drag that tree away all by yourself.
> P.: Yes, yes, I'd like to, too, and only because that other schmuck doesn't do it! Who even notices? If I had somebody who'd do it, I'd step aside. That's really the point. If I had somebody, I'd gladly pass the torch to the next one and then sit down in the grass myself and get well. And that's the way it is with everything that I see. I say to myself, there comes my replacement—but he or she doesn't come, even though the younger ones are supposed to be better!
> T.: How far do you want to go, then, in sacrificing yourself?
> P.: Yeah, you're digging around in me. But I'm digging around into the question, the question of whether you can just let things take their course, of whether you should just coolly let a Third Reich come again. . . . It's hard to say. Can one go that far?
> T.: But let us look very carefully at the connections. Is the blocked drain the same thing for you as the Third Reich?
> P.: Yes. Of course, just as a beginning. Preparatory. Because if a person doesn't see that tree, he won't see the marching boots either. Nor will he see anybody killing Jews.

In the course of our talk, we move from his fear of repetitions to the positive things he has lost. Totally different class distinctions had prevailed before Hitler than do today. He had felt very alone at the high school, with his poor and uneducated parents.

> T.: Maybe two themes converge here: in his program, Hitler broke down the social barriers, and he offered a collective *we*-feeling that then built on that.
> P.: I know what you're trying to say: for sure, it's the warm nest that was a help back then! I was looking for the warm stall again with Kurt Schumacher*, as a reversion to barbarism with a new look. Everybody said, "Kurti, Kurti," and I still remember it as if it were today: at the corner of the Ernst-Merck Building, I forgot everything except this warm nest and Kurti and "Hello, come along, chum." I found that so comforting that I joined the party. It's exactly the same thing as when I was a Hitler Youth: warm, too, politics, too. It helps you. But later on I got frustrated, if you really look closely . . . You do it a few more times. I was also in the CDU.* I wandered through it, got disappointed. In the Catholic church, too.
> T.: So you tried to find this supportive feeling of a collective again?

P.: But in a decent club, I mean . . . in one that's the opposite of the one before. But there's always something frustrating about it because the *ideals* aren't followed, the yardsticks.

T.: You had attached yourself to a particular type; is that someone with high ideals?

P.: Yes, and he can be very objective, precisely because he is also cold, cold to all feeling.

T.: What would happen if he permitted more feelings?

P.: Everything you just tied together occurs to me again: I became a Nazi with emotion, with emotion a Socialist, and with emotion I joined the CDU, and then always the cold shower, the horror, that even *this* is nothing either—it's all totally in vain. I'm looking for something where ideals are followed, something that corresponds to the yardsticks.

He tells still another complicated story, in which he felt tricked, although he had selflessly invested a lot of work.

P.: And I ask you, what is there about me that's so diabolic? There must be something that's bad or anti-social (*volksschädlich**) or something like that. Because otherwise things can't happen the way they do. I want the best and then get nothing out of it for myself.

T.: I don't experience anything diabolic about you. But if I take a look at my own feeling about you, either you seem to turn your back, or you demand a great deal from yourself and from others. Since you were injured in your youth by the breakdown of your sense of security, you built up something like ideals, which permit you to experience yourself as completely insignificant. To put it another way: the contents, the values, the goals are very important for you, but maybe you don't take your *own* feeling about those things seriously enough. Maybe you don't even notice little hints or insults because for you the only thing that matters is the good cause—is sticking to the yardsticks.

P.: That's so, yes, that's so, because other people are always saying to me, "Didn't you notice that?"

T.: "Yes, didn't you notice that?"

P.: Yes, I'm not dumb, I did notice that, but I didn't want to pay attention to it in view of what was *more* important to me.

T.: I'd like very much to learn a lot more about your struggles, more about your way of struggling. There have been a lot of struggles in your life, you've told me that already.

P.: I haven't told everything, but there are all kinds of things, that's true. On the topic of "struggle": there again there's something that's connected to the Nazi time, it's a continuum; in fact, it's the literal translation of my name.

T.: Namely?

P.: The word comes from Old German: *Gunt* is "the struggle" and *Hari* is "the master"; Gunt-Hari—Gunther.

T.: You found that out during the Nazi time?

P.: Yeah, we had to find out about the origins of our names, take a look at the Niebelung saga.

T.: Clearly this is a central theme.

P.: Yeah, struggle and watch out! I have a horror of turning into a laggard!

We end the hour with the usual question, whether and when he wants to come again. He twists and turns and would like to leave the decision up to me, but then decides to go on with the therapy.

In the next hours he works with the "God-figure," Hitler, for whose sake he wanted "to be consumed in bloody flames." Hitler and truth had been one and the same for him. And other guilt feelings appear besides that over the death of his mother: he hasn't been able to forgive himself for testifying against a comrade who had been charged with sedition against the armed forces. His hurt and his fury begin to come out. Often he notices he still seeks a substitute for his old allegiance, and he continues to notice his disappointments in the time after the war. He senses how much this constant effort and constant disappointment have cost him but realizes too what exaggerated demands he has made of others.

Then present-day problems with pupils and colleagues come into the foreground again. In several role plays the *realist* and the *idealist* become differentiated. He realizes how his "idealist" quickly breaks to pieces over his disappointments, that he avoids his sadness over it, that he isn't so important as he would like to be, considering his ideal. In his orientation as a realist, he perceives his own limits but feels himself closer to others, with whose experience he is now better able to empathize. The search for meaning and then the search for his *own* meaning lead him more and more to listen within himself. With me he knows better what he would like and no longer asks what is "objectively" right for him. After about nine months he at last takes his leave with the statement, "I'm finding my way. I'm a little sad, and the 'idealist' would have kept me from leaving, but now I can go."

Since then he has also completed his speech therapy. His voice and articulation have become normal.

Defenses and Working Through in
Ourselves as Therapists

PERSPECTIVES

In the first part of this contribution I concentrated on partial aspects of the effects of Nazism on several of my patients. Now, in the second part, I turn to ourselves as therapists. Of course, the case presentations did contain my own perspectives as therapist as well as the perspectives of the patients. For instance, in the first, short example the theme for the patient is comradeship: he wants to tell me where he learned what "true friendship" is. I address *his* psychopathology by forming the hypothesis that by idealizing, he holds himself back from dealing with his own life. My own real perspective is a very different one: in a certain part of the therapy I experience an overwhelming fear at a very profound bodily level; I have to defend against this threatening introject. The consequence: I do not permit real contact with the patient, although that is my therapeutic task so that I may support him in his own healing process. The patient, moreover, then indicates that he never expected anyone to understand him anyway. The example with the theme "watch out!" showed me how subjective and how governed by our own perspective is our interpretation of reality, yet how it is also simultaneously influenced by the perspective of the other person. At the start, my emphasis lay in the wish to help the patient by working with his symptoms: I wanted to show him that *now* his burdensome life story no longer had to put him under such pressure. But after this simple beginning of mine, I began to vacillate when he urgently set before my eyes the way irresponsible politics can imperil the most basic conditions of our lives. At that point, my own quite personal "bad conscience" began to throb.

Looking more closely, I see into the sad eyes of my parents, particularly of my father, who, to my early questions about his experience of Nazism, softly and believably admitted that he hadn't thought much about resistance because it left no room for him to get ahead. And then, a week after he had refused a second summons to join the Nazi party, the notice came ordering him to the Russian front. For me that means that honorable political action, even simple resignation, will be punished and will be paid for at a price which includes the risk of death.

The Mitscherlichs (1970) helped me to understand that my more or less unconscious attitude toward politics was really a collective reaction: they describe it as "the German way of loving the unattainable so uncompromisingly that the attainable is lost (p. 18)." They even talk about "being oriented toward the unreal" and argue further that since most citizens of this country agreed with Nazi racism and with the Nazi ideology of domination, when the regime fell they lost their orientation. This denial and defense against guilt left traces in the German character. "Where we could expect the greatest attention to be paid, we meet with indifference. There is relatively little thoughtful participation in all those activities which should be of heartfelt concern for any enlightened public (p. 18)." The authors emphasize how we are developing ourselves into an apolitical, conservative nation, lacking *curiosity* when it comes to studying the motives which permitted the Germans to become followers of this Führer. The same lack of curiosity lessens the creativity with which we address the new form of our political life. They go on to describe how we don't reject the idea of a democratic state, but "we cannot do much with it because we don't understand, to put it psychologically, how to possess it libidinously."

These thoughts fit the interpretation of the above-mentioned patient particularly well, and at the same time I am becoming increasingly aware that these attitudes continue to affect me and also to affect the next generation. And I also am becoming increasingly aware of how little discussion has taken place to date within the professional group, which deals preeminently with the processes of bringing things to consciousness, namely among ourselves, the psychotherapists.

THE SPLIT BETWEEN INDIVIDUAL EXPERIENCE AND SOCIAL INVOLVEMENT

In continuing-education seminars for beginning psychotherapists, I meet with characteristic aspects of my own experience over and over again.[2] The learning goal of one of the training units is to use self-experience—to become aware of the influence of concrete social conditions, and then to express this influence in role plays developed on both a feeling and an action level. This training unit seeks to bring into consciousness the way individual psychological experience is conditioned by collective background material. We also seek to work out the possibility of individual influences on collective outcomes. We work with a simulation in which various social

---

2. I refer to the Theory I Seminar held at the Fritz Perls Institute. The chief emphasis is on the premises of Gestalt psychotherapy.

groups are represented by participants in the seminar. In addition, at the starting point, a concrete conflict is introduced, which is supposed to be resolved by the various groups in the process of the game. Despite variations in the form of the games and although, at the beginning, we report on our experiences in former simulations and urge the participants to seek solutions, the simulation regularly escalates into a rigid constellation in which the following two (oversimplified) positions appear: One group has the power, but they are experienced as being unjust and guilt-ridden; the others try to free themselves from their feeling of impotence by frenzied action, devoid of any real contact (unless they simply become resigned).

At the beginning of the simulation, all the groups (except for a few individuals) experience a fairly unenthusiastic attitude, which turns out to be, as work continues, resignation in the face of political confrontation. Many emphasize that they have met with failure in actual political encounters and that they no longer want to suffer the deceit that goes on in political debate. A few do recognize how important it would be to move beyond a change model that starts simply with the individual, but they regard attempts at political solutions as hopeless.

FURTHER DEVELOPMENT THROUGH EXCHANGE

When I was supervising a thesis, it became clear to me how very much our confrontations with authority and with power have their roots in the Nazi period.[3] This colleague became interested in the theme of the loss of identity brought on in several of her patients by the collapse of the Third Reich. She experienced patients of a particular age group as strikingly spineless and without any identity. It turned out that these patients in their childhood and youth had suffered particularly intensive training in the National Political Educational Institutions (NAPOLA). She felt they were playing up to her and deferring to her therapeutic authority in a mechanical and unfeeling way. Only when she suddenly and almost accidentally grasped the quality of the defense mechanism of one of her patients, and recognized it from her own history with authority figures, was the spell broken and did understanding begin to be possible.

Ultimately the method used in the thesis embraced four clearly differentiated levels, which could be seen to be in a process of reciprocally influencing each other: (1) that part of the patient's history

---

3. A scientific contribution from the area of integrative individual or group therapy is part of the curriculum of the Fritz Perls Institute. In this case the thesis is an unpublished work by Jutta Erhardt.

that had to be defended against as long as (2) that history itself hadn't been worked through; and beyond that (3) the information which was lacking for the patient to understand specific historical phenomena; and (4) the search for clarifying theories and models out of sociology, psychology, psychoanalysis,and psychopathology.

The encounter with this thesis taught me a great deal. The author had gathered a richness of historical material I had never heard of during my school days and, along with the description of altered family structures, she gives a picture of the fiendishly elaborate school and teacher-training systems of the Nazi time. Not only in the NAPOLA but also in the teaching materials of "normal" schools, the Nazi ideology had taken a firm hold. Even mathematics textbooks were full of macabre problems in which, for example, the economic "exploitation" by Jewish families was used as the material to learn the rule of three! This work also describes how alongside the school as a realm of public influence, the work of the youth groups was structured (in the *Jungvolk* and the Hitler Youth) and how a fine-meshed net of training drills was thrown over the young people from the very beginning.

The fact that all this was cleverly linked to the genuine needs of children and adolescents does not make it any easier to confront the realities of the Nazi regime today. Rather, it requires creating a theory which deals with what needs are genuine and what needs are invented, what healthy needs are and what injurious needs are. And such thinking leads logically to the question of values in social groups. The author describes the close connection between ideology and organization through which a sense of identity is constituted and a structure of meaning is created. In the course of her discussion she works out the ambivalent function of hierarchical structures and shows what was "gained" back then from orders and from obeying them, and also how these same dynamics can function in present-day organizations (for instance, in athletic groups). The individual is nothing but a part of the whole; he has no concept of himself as an individual. This ideology gives him clear attributes as man, woman, Aryan. So when the system collapses, a corresponding loss of identity occurs.

THE TIP OF THE ICEBERG: A SHORT WORKSHOP

Out of these early experiences grew the idea of talking with people who perhaps were also dealing with a similar consciousness of conflict. The framework of a congress on the theme of ethics and psychotherapy offered itself. My co-worker, Rik Van den Bussche, and I announced the topic in the program with an invitation to therapists who work with "patients hurt or supported by National Socialism." In the text of the program, we posed such questions as, "What are my goals with former 'perpetrators'? Is understanding an appropriate approach? Are my needs for revenge and punishment compatible with my therapeutic identity?"

The congress organization gave us a "working group" consisting of two sessions, each one-and-a-half hours long. As it happened, the rather theory-oriented form of a working group turned out to be inappropriate, since a heavy emotional atmosphere soon developed and the participants spoke very personally. After the announcement, only a few people said they were interested, but those few apparently really wanted to take part. The intensity of personal involvement even led to categorical exclusion of new people who wanted to attend the second session. (The atmosphere forced a personal association on me: when, in spite of our protestations, curious people kept coming into the room, the group had the idea of actually barricading itself in; I felt as if I were in an illegal underground society. Other participants had this same sense of it.)

There was a surprise at the beginning of the session as people introduced themselves: not one participant actually "fit" our opening announcement. The closest thing to an exception was the single remark by a participant that he skirts the National Socialist theme as soon as it surfaces in therapy. But the other therapists in the group did not mention having worked with either "perpetrators" or "victims"—at least this theme didn't come up during the workshop. Far more did they all have in the foreground the relevance of the theme to themselves personally, and that in very different ways: as children many of these therapists had seen their parents openly identified with National Socialism and hadn't yet found a way to come to terms with the issue. For example, in the case of one participant who had become involved in extreme leftist activities, one could clearly feel a painful cynicism as he told how in his home village once, a peasant woman, with only the best intentions, drew parallels between his own "political gifts" and those of his father and uncle.

A few "only" suffered from the taboos which ruled the household at home, and these clearly expressed their sadness over the lack of contact and the lack of discussion in their own families. Beyond these, there were several who remained very ambivalent about the values and ideology of the Nazi time. One participant wept over her lost childhood, saying that she felt, after the regime collapsed, that she had had to deprecate good, important memories of the community spirit of the League of German Girls* and its rituals. With a sort of brave defiance, she told how she still doesn't know if she's prepared to do that. After all, every person—and thus she, too—has the right to a childhood.

Alongside these statements it was, above all, another participant's contribution that had a great impact in the group. He was born in the fifties and had involved himself in a neo-Nazi group. He had now distanced himself from the group *verbally,* but with us he ended up making a vehement plea for a source of values, such as he had gotten from the neo-Nazis and which he now still sorely missed in his family home, which was empty of meaning and geared only to consumption.

On the emotional level there was much sadness and anger in the group, as well as fear and shame. We fought repeatedly against the oversimplified split into good and evil and in the process we split ourselves: as we tried to discover who, then, really had been a "genuine" Nazi, one group tried to argue along social psychological lines (for example, aggressions arose from personal frustrations such as unemployment and were then discharged on weaker persons), whereas another group tried to objectify events historically, so that the extent of the horrendous events and deeds could not be diminished by putting them in the background while shifting attention to possible motives. We determined that the black-white division into good and evil represents a primitive form of defense, the splitting off of incomprehensible inhumanity.

Looking for books or articles that could help us further, we discussed Alice Miller's theses in her commentary on Hitler's autobiography (1983). She develops the idea that "persecution" derives from "the defense against being a victim." She goes on to say "that our conscious experience of being a victim protects us more from sadism—that is to say, the compulsion to torture and humiliate others—than does our denial of being victims (p. 230)." Thereby she creates an understanding of connections through several generations, which could help us to avoid simple reaction formations. Her discussions seem to me to be particularly relevant for our therapeutic posture when she develops the distinction between "acting out a hatred in contrast to experiencing a hatred (p. 231)." She describes experiencing as being an intrapsychic activity, whereas acting out takes place on the plane of reality and "can cost other people their lives."

Naturally there wasn't enough time for more thorough analyses, and above all there wasn't time for reaching some emotional resolution. That showed itself symptomatically in the heated remarks of one participant in response to statements made during the closing session. Several people had expressed sadness that one legacy left from the Nazi regime had been the loss of so many good memories and traditions, as well as pride in belonging to a group. Her response went something like, "All right, I participated here because I know how important it is to overcome the past, but I will have nothing to do with the idea that there is even a tiny positive spark about the Nazi time or about the Nazi ideology. I never want to attend a group that comes to *that* conclusion."

THE COURAGE TO GO DEEPER: AN INTERVIEW

Finally, I want to tell about contact with a colleague who, when I told her about the workshop discussed above, expressed interest in talking with me about her own story as a person who had been affected. She was affected in her double identity of being, on the one hand, a patient (in the original meaning of "one who suffers") and, on the other hand, of being, as she was well aware, "privileged," in the sense that through her long and multifaceted training to become a therapist, she had had opportunities to work through her problems—both in her training analysis and in her theoretical training. She felt herself to have been affected as the daughter of a high official in the civil government of a part of the *Generalgouvernement.**

My conversation with her touched me on several levels. It was easy to see in her face that she had to struggle in order to expose herself to my questions and thus to the opening up—and possibly even publication—of her profoundest feelings of shame and anxiety. But her interest and her willingness won out precisely because she had noticed, in the process of coming to grips with herself, how important it is to understand and admit one's own suffering. Later she described at length how she was afraid "to call the things by their right names, because I always heard very quickly from friends: 'Thank God *my* father wasn't . . .' If you get into those things on the present-day level, you're immediately threatened by other people's defensiveness. They don't mean that at all like it sounds . . . nobody means it in a bad way!" Later on she met friends in a work group who "knew in their hearts what I was talking about." She grew closer to these people and found out "what a witches' brew they had found themselves in, as they worked through these issues." She said that that was the second such experience she had had with people whom she had known for years. "Now I slowly begin to seem courageous to myself. Only because *I* present something do the others come forward and say, 'My father was such and such.' It's so important that we mutually protect and encourage each other."

The story of her searching reaches far back. She can remember her time at school, when she came home from history class with questions to which she received only incomplete answers. Since 1973, because of her therapeutic training, the struggle has taken on a new quality. In the course of various kinds of therapeutic work she experiences, even at the present time, massive bodily reactions and feelings which she knows "do not lie! My body doesn't make mistakes!" She experiences conditions of panic and the fear of death, often an atmosphere of cold and ice. She can vividly describe the conflict between her anxiety and the hope of being able to externalize everything.

It is important to her that the therapists went with her beyond her limits but at the same time kept their own boundaries. "They gave me the feeling that they could accompany me into my confusions because they themselves had more space. I could cry out loudly in my fear; when I drifted away into magical thinking, they could always manage to bring back reality. . . . I was afraid of flipping out. But that's not what happened: instead of flipping out I was allowed in. . . . He [a therapist] simply protected me, he himself is stable and has no fear. He knows death and life, and his own boundaries are so certain that no confluence occurred. He simply gave warmth, held nothing back, and stayed completely grounded, completely concrete. There was never any kind of ideology."

Once, in some body therapy work, she felt, through the contact with her therapist, a thick outer layer of certainty ("maybe 10 centimeters thick"), which inwardly turned into ever more unbearable fright. But she could always come back to the protective layer of certainty. Sometimes images appeared (in her preconscious, as she says); for example, of partisans, officers. It isn't so important to her to know whether she actually saw these things (she was born in 1940) or whether they came to her through the media during the postwar period.

Just as her body did not err in its sense of fear, she was able to feel the resistances in her body in the same way, even when she was motivated to progress further. She knew how much she always needed to go at her own pace in order to allow herself to confront her own history. Repeatedly in the course of her analysis she had to test out her own suspicions; repeatedly her therapist showed her the reliability of his presence; repeatedly she experienced that she could trust her own perceptions. For herein lies the most frightening and deepest injury in her own history: frequently she was not allowed to trust her own reality; often she had been given explanations which simply couldn't be true. She remembers herself as a lively and difficult child who was full of questions and delighted in asking them. At the same time she experienced depression because of the absence of answers. "That makes you crazy—and at the time the present, in which I lived, *was* crazy. People with the background of the Prussian code of honor maimed and murdered hundreds of people. And in such a situation, the child is not crazy who asks, 'Why is that man hanging on the lamppost?'" In this discrepancy between what was seen and the answers given lay the seeds of insanity. "For a long time that was one of my profoundest fears."

Each parent gave her different responses. As she (reliving her past in therapy) shared her fears of death with her mother and told her of her deep need, her mother "said in answer to my direct question, 'what could have caused all that?'—at the same time turning to ice and becoming absolutely unapproachable: 'I never left you unattended!' That was her only comment, and naturally that caused an inner hell to break loose! I won't show her a second time how things are going with me. If I open myself to her, I get ice poured in. . . . Even today my mother gets an angry look in her eyes when she mentions my curiosity. She feels threatened by my need to know. She cannot delight in the intelligence of her child and the child's joy in questioning. Maybe I can understand that she protected us children back then, but the very idea that now, today, she still blocks any hint of a question! And then after that there comes a sort of power play, and at that point one is supposed to be *obedient* to her. Then she can't get beyond the generation barrier. She retreats behind her authority. Then she can no longer talk woman to woman with me—something she can do very well about other subjects. She simply switches to power. Naturally that serves her defense, and I ask myself 'What's she defending against?' I have a thousand ghosts in my head . . . (which ones?). Naturally she knows the facts . . . but what are they? Damn this mess!"

Through my colleague's excited and despairing utterances it became clear that she had found her way beyond the therapeutic working through of her situation and has arrived at another means of working through, namely by *getting into the facts themselves*. Recently she began bitterly to work on all the historical data that she could find in order to get closer to the truth—and to her own uncrazy self. "I can't find what I need as a child, I can only find it as

an historian." She reconstructs, for example, her mother's movements and social duties and then says, "She had little time for us
children. Let somebody explain that to me!" Or she figures out, by
retracing her mother's travels, what she must have known about contacts with partisans. Above all, she would like to comprehend the
ambience in which she grew up, which was marked both by her
familial space and by the political space. In doing this, she seeks real
points of departure—dates, names, descriptions of landscapes and
houses. She wants to find out what wasn't talked about.

Working through her relationship to her father (who died in the
mid 1980s) and dealing with her memories of him takes a different
form. Here, too, she's still in the dark about many things, but her
defense against a real confrontation with this relationship is motivated by her experience of her father's entirely positive and
supportive attention to her, which she cannot reconcile with his pre-
sumed activities during the Nazi period. She assumes that as a jurist
he had to carry out orders coming from Hans Frank and his Gou-
verneurs. In her talks with me, she told me twice, in connection with
her father, how much she felt like sobbing without knowing the
reason. Then later she said, "Now I can put it in words: I simply love
him. He was such a warm man. Up to the very end we had a close
heart-to-heart relationship. That makes it even harder to face these
shadows."

She described how deeply she was identified with him, how he
wanted to answer all her questions and how after the war he invited
her and her siblings to discuss the Nazi time with him in order "to
learn from history." These were almost philosophical talks which
were very important for her. But when questions arose about his own
concrete historical experience and about a specific time period, he
decompensated. "He stood there weeping and shaking from head to
foot, and we couldn't find out any more. Sometimes he said, 'I just
do not know anymore what I saw back then.' After 1945 he decompensated often, altogether some 32 manic-depressive episodes. . . . I
think that he must have seen the barbarity of the SS. Half the city
was massacred, the Jewish half, of course. I have a need to get into
all this; I know I'm very identified with Father. I loved him a great
deal and I was his favorite daughter. It's like a sound barrier. Only I
cannot break through it, I have to force my way. I don't want to fly
to pieces myself in the process. I'm just beginning to make my own
safety net. I need time. I have to be careful with the dosage, with how
much I can bear at once. Father suffered an amnesia of images, but
not a bodily amnesia, otherwise he wouldn't have wept so."

In her own process, she was facing these final "revelations," which then had to be organized in a more complex way. At one point during our talks I experienced her as particularly blocked and confused. She had made some critical and distancing statements about her father. She remembered the scene when she, as a student, had helped correct a black friend's paper and her father shoved himself vehemently away from her table. And then she became upset over his idealizing description of the "building up" of the Generalgouvernement,* without apparently noticing that war and destruction had necessarily preceded it.

Then suddenly images came up from his time as a prisoner of war, about his internment, about the depressing time when he was not yet "denazified." She could hardly mention her critical attitude without feeling a lack of solidarity with her beloved, sick father. She had experienced him in the time after the war "as if purged, as someone who was doing everything to find his bearings again. . . . The hardest part is to come to terms with all the contradictions." Then she described how she came to realize that "there's some truth to the fairy tale that tells how the lord of the castle continues to haunt it for centuries as a ghost! And there always has to be someone who finds the key to free him. Then something happens and he has his peace and can really die."

I was fascinated by this image, and as I was quietly asking myself how long her way would continue in disquiet and fear; and how many haunted castles still remained in our country, she said, "Very slowly I'm reaching a kind of knowledge: I cannot mourn for everybody; there are too many and I am too small."

When in the course of writing this article I called my colleague to ask if she approved of my presentation of these excerpts, she told me that the very night after our interview, using all her courage, she had found the strength to reconstruct the precise historical data surrounding a specific point in time. She put onto the screen of her self-made biography the thing which hadn't been possible for her before, the most extreme taboo in her family: she determined that during her father's first tour of duty in the Polish city, 10,000 Jews had been murdered in a cemetery and that further pogroms had followed. Now that she could grasp the extent of his impotence and stupefaction, she even thought that through his psychological decompensation he had protected his family. A kind of quiet peace settled on her, which will, for some time at least, give her the strength to pursue her way further.

FINAL THOUGHTS

Why try to understand what I cannot accept? In my role as a therapist—in which empathic understanding is a given—and in my role as a citizen, shocked by the war and the other consequences of the ghastly Nazi regime, I find myself in a conflict that so far has been little considered: are we supposed to *understand* yesterday's perpetrators when they become today's "patients"?

I now can clearly feel my fear of being misunderstood or of saying thoughtless words, should I overstep the bounds of the associated taboo. Maybe this fear corresponds with the fear of the perpetrators who "so far as is known . . . have never . . . presented themselves to an analyst" ("National Socialist Heritage . . . ," 1987). It is true that several of the aforementioned patients were not simply "volunteers" who came in with the idea of working through issues from Nazi times. Nevertheless, above and beyond the medical symptoms, in many places the tip of an iceberg is becoming visible. Its hidden bulk includes the menacingly unresolved Nazi past and touches not only perpetrators of radical crimes but almost an entire people. Nor is it just a question about the past; it is a question of the present and future as well. Sichrovsky (1987) notes that today the perpetrators' grandchildren are studying at the universities. He goes on to say that their parents missed the opportunity of "learning from the perpetrators' history. The perpetrators' silence can become a sort of time bomb."

Whether understanding produces change may still be a question; but the desire to produce change without understanding historical connections—and the people involved in them—can lead to blind and destructive actions. The psychoanalyst Simenauer (1982) thus sees "in some terrorists a sort of return of the persecutors of the past."

The massive problems of the perpetrators' children are the chief subjects of this article. Many themes which belong among the consequences of Nazism have not been addressed. It is when I am confronted with the victims of Nazism or their descendants that I feel a great shyness about showing understanding of the perpetrators, even though the victims and their descendants are the decisive reasons for dealing with this complex of themes.

If I nevertheless plead for attempting to understand the perpetrators, it may be because I read an article by H. Klein, late professor at the former Eytanem Hospital in Jerusalem, who studied the consequences of the Holocaust and the mechanisms by which they might be overcome. He describes not only the time of the Holocaust but also the time afterward: "We found that the needs of the Holocaust survivors for love and reintegration were often ignored, since society, because of overwhelming guilt feelings, denied their very existence, avoided them, and shunned them. The victims had to recognize that the general public was incapable of addressing their needs. Their utopian dreams came up against a society which was itself powerless and which lived in terror and fear of its own self-destruction—because that society saw itself confronted with its own aggressive impulses" (1986, p. 161).

I understood: the pseudo-strength of the powerful collapsed and turned out to be a poor basis for the surviving victims to build on in their attempt to surmount what had happened to them. Only through understanding and working with the disturbances in the perpetrators, and in the society which produced them, would the victims perhaps find fitting consideration and regard.

9

THE DIALOGUE BETWEEN THE GENERATIONS ABOUT THE NAZI ERA

Helm Stierlin

Why the Dialogue?

It is difficult to find historical truth. The further we go back in time, the more the sources dry up and memory pales. The facts we are working on often do not fit our overall concept and can be variously interpreted according to our perspective and our frame of reference. But our frame of reference and our perspectives change as our concerns and interests change. Thus we must tolerate uncertainty and ambiguity if we are to bring into harmony the contradictory goals of seeking out the historical facts *and* evaluating them, of confronting our own history *and* accepting *and* embracing it—indeed a complex task of reconciliation.

Is this task necessary? I believe it is. We can think of it as part of a search for meaning which we must undertake if we wish to maintain our mental and spiritual health. In the process, following Kant, we can delineate three questions: (1) What can I know? (2) What must I do? (3) What may I hope? With all three questions our eyes turn to the past.

The first question can be broadened as follows: What are my sources, my roots? What made me into what I am? What formed my present identity? Into what conflicts—intrapsychic, interpersonal, and social—was I born? In the light of Kant's second question one can ask: What essential goals, expectations, values, loyalties, and tasks determine my life? What are their sources? How were they transmitted? What sources of strength and integrity do I find in my

Note: This chapter appeared originally in *Familiendynamik* 1 (1982), pp. 31–48. Reprinted here and in the German text with the kind permission of the author.

parents, my relatives, my forebears, my people? And finally, turning to the past, I can ask: Is there a continuity to be seen in all this, a necessary sequence of events, a basis for historical justice? What can be learned from all that, what can be hoped for?

To find the answers, a dialogue between the generations is required. Above all, such dialogue makes it possible to separate the facts from the myths, to dissolve ambiguities and to create the basis for necessary evaluations and decisions. It allows the partners to demand and to give an accounting. Then it becomes possible to discover the necessary continuum of tasks, rights, and duties, and to insure that they are attended to.

Experience with family therapy has shown that this dialogue takes place in all families whose members feel close to one another. Usually even the very young children share in these discussions. The dialogue intensifies when the children become adolescents and young adults; by that time their cognitive and linguistic tools are fully developed. They are capable of complex, formal thought processes or, in the words of Jean Piaget (1926), of "reversible operations"; and perhaps most important of all, they now often exhibit, as Lawrence Kohlberg (1969) and other authors have described, a finely tuned ethical sensibility, a strong sense of justice and fairness. Therefore they are in a position to reflect critically on the goals, values, and tasks which their parents, in part as society's "representatives," set before them. But at the same time they are able to call these parents to account for their share in achieving and transmitting these goals, values, and tasks. The children's question then becomes, What did you, our parents, contribute to the past that now structures our present and our future?

In times of rapid social change and political transformation, such dialogue between the generations becomes more difficult and at the same time more urgent than ever. "Larger-than-life" historical events now reach into the life cycle of the families, into the work of the parents in caring for and educating the children, as well as into the children's search for meaning. At such times both the essence and the possible pitfalls of such dialogue become particularly clear. We see how one generation creates "facts" which fatefully influence following generations—facts which require a still more intensive dialogue in order to be understood and mastered. This is particularly true for the dialogue between German parents who knew and participated in the Nazi Reich—often as active Nazis themselves—and their children, who have meanwhile become adolescents or adults.

Two Perspectives on the Political Past

As a psychoanalyst and family therapist I was, as it were, strategically placed to gain insight into this dialogue, into its forms, its ups and downs, its risks. After I returned to Germany from the United States[1] my colleagues and I together saw a great number of families with adolescent or young adult children whose parents had been adults during the Nazi time. Many of these parents had participated in shaping this era in one way or another: not a few had belonged to the Nazi party (some also to the SS) and had fought—frequently as officers—in Hitler's Wehrmacht and had in one way or another assented to Hitler's policies. Although the family conversations were not originally directed at illuminating the Nazi past of the parents, this past came up repeatedly.

The Nazi past revealed itself in various ways. Today—some 35 years after the end of the Nazi time—individual age groups have varying relationships to it. Those who now[2] are 54 years old or older were already adults when the war ended. The children born during the Nazi time are today 35 to 47 years old. Some of *their* children have already grown up to be older adolescents or young adults. Among their contemporaries there are some older adolescents and young adults whose parents were already adults during the Nazi time.

These constellations of the generations make it possible to investigate how the Nazi past of those involved affected various generations of participants and nonparticipants, and how these effects are still continuing. Still, I did not make a special point of asking about this past but rather noted the resonance or echo of it from time to time. The following observations and conclusions are to be taken with caution. Nonetheless, they do permit us to reflect and to ask, In what way and how much, in the dialogue between the generations, was the parents' Nazi past brought up?

I first came closer to an answer, however, as I began to distinguish seriously between two perspectives, or two attitudes, which can be assumed when facing this past. Within the first perspective we remain focused on larger-than-life events. These events recede from

---

1. The author left Germany in 1955, working and studying in the United States and elsewhere. He returned to Germany in 1974. —Trans.

2. In 1980, that is. —Trans.

the control of individuals, overwhelming us, reaching fatefully into our lives, and permitting us to appear as victims, sufferers, or survivors in an historic drama which took place without our willing it and without any responsibility on our part. Within the second perspective we emphasize, by contrast, the active role played in the past by both individuals and families. We ask about the personal point of view and the personal stand taken at the time, about the personal contribution, about personal responsibility. With this the interpersonal causal process appears variously highlighted, depending on our own viewpoint. In one case, people reveal themselves as passive sufferers; in the other, as active shapers of their own past life.

Usually the study of our past requires both perspectives. The first perspective addresses primarily Kant's first question (as elaborated by us): What can I know about my history—the history of my family, my community, my people? What caused the fact that today I find myself as this person in this time, at this place, in this community, and in this social and political situation? The other perspective addresses particularly Kant's second question—put by us into the past tense: Which values, loyalties, and tasks determined my life and formed my identity? What sources of strength and identity do I find in my parents and forebears?

Our family conversations revealed that it was usually easier for parents and children to adopt the first perspective. Many parents were relieved and grateful when they could tell their children how the political and military events of the Nazi time had influenced their personal and family life. They were able to talk about these events, even when the memory of them was painful. What they told in this way helped their children and grandchildren to understand what the parents had gone through in the days when they themselves were young parents trying to bring up their children to the best of their abilities.

The Effects of Nazi Events on Parental Tasks

To be able to fulfill their parental tasks properly, both parents have to be physically and emotionally available to their children. In their own relationship as marriage partners, they need to fulfill their individual vital needs and resolve their own conflicts without involving their children as allies, confidants, or scapegoats.

Psychological boundaries reflecting differences in age, sexual maturity, and responsibility should exist between the generations. Home life should be relatively stable, so that the children can develop lasting and trusting relationships to their parents, to the rest of their family, to their contemporaries, and to their teachers, as well as to the other parts of their human and nonhuman environment.

Our conversations with families showed repeatedly that the political and military events of the Nazi time undermined the conditions essential for the fulfillment of parental tasks.

Most of the fathers of today's young adult patients were away from home fighting in Hitler's armies during their children's formative years. Many of these fathers died, leaving behind widows and orphans. Many others were wounded or came home after years of captivity. Often on their return they were shadows of their former selves: the once-proud landowner, businessman, or officer had aged prematurely, had become poverty-stricken and then lived on, a lasting and bitter disappointment to himself and to his family. A patient said it in these words: "One day—it was four or five years after the end of the war and I was 10 years old—a shabby, haggard, unshaven, ugly man stood before our door. I felt uncomfortable, I got frightened and called my mother. My mother came and said to me, 'This is your father.'"

During the wartime absence of their husbands, many women had to take over additional responsibilities, for example running the family farm or business, and they thereby suffered even more loneliness, uncertainty, and sexual frustration. As time went on and the war shifted more and more back into the geographic area of Germany itself, the situation worsened for many women and children as they endured air raids or fled before Russian troops. Millions lost their homes and suffered hunger and sickness and the death of close relatives. In order to be able to survive psychologically, many mothers turned to their children; they recruited them—openly or covertly—as intimates, and, if they were boys, as quasi-lovers and as substitute husbands. In this process the boundaries between the generations were erased. Above and beyond all this, many children were expected to fulfill their mothers' hopes and expectations, which had been obliterated by the war and the absence of their husbands— hopes perhaps for a stable home, for social success and status, for fulfilled sexuality and partnership.

Such children were often recruited as "committed delegates" as I have described elsewhere: they remained inwardly tied to their mothers, they were exploited by the excessive demands made on them by tasks out of proportion to their age, and yet they often enjoyed the consciousness that they were irreplaceably important to their mothers. By contrast, many other children were neglected or cast out. In order to be able to survive psychologically, they had to assume a precocious autonomy. In either case, however, whether these children remained overly tied to their mothers or were cast out too early, their emotional development suffered damage.

This first perspective brings into our field of vision the suffering, traumas, and privations of one generation, which in one way or another continued to weigh upon following generations. We see tales of suffering comparable to those of other victims of Hitler's policies, even to the stories of former concentration camp inmates. (Studies by J. Sigal [1971] and other authors showed that the children and grandchildren of former concentration camp inmates, for example, were more disturbed than children whose parents had not suffered such horrendous trauma.)

But the comparison with other victims becomes difficult as soon as we turn to our second perspective and ask: What active role did the parents play in the political drama of that time? Typically, in our talks with families, this perspective was difficult to get hold of. And it was precisely this perspective which was important for the dialogue between the generations. Here, it was a question of the parents' deeds and derelictions, of their participation in the Nazi crimes. Were they ready and able to recognize their own contribution and to accept responsibility for it, to grieve over what they had helped to cause, and as far as possible to make reparation and to learn from past mistakes? And to what extent did the children try to help their parents in such attempts to master the past? The answers to these questions determined whether and how the children could experience their parents as models and as sources for their own inner strength and integrity, whether they esteemed or scorned their parents, whether they trusted or didn't trust them, and to what extent they, the children, were able to accept themselves as members of a chain of generations.

The Role of Parents in Nazi Germany

If we turn to the role of parents in Nazi Germany and to how this role appears within our second perspective, we must remember the following: when Hitler came to power, a large number of opponents of his regime were forced to emigrate, were thrown into prison or into concentration camps, were overwhelmingly threatened or killed. But the vast majority of Germans needed neither threat nor force. They followed Hitler voluntarily—drawn by his successes and his magnetic personality. According to the historian Rudolph Binion (1976), after assuming power Hitler was surprised at how willingly most Germans accepted him and at how little terror he needed to use.

The Germans who followed Hitler shut their eyes to the brutalities and injustices which he and his followers committed at the start. In 1934, a scant year after assuming power, Hitler had his old friend Röhm* and several hundred other (real or imagined) opponents of his regime executed without trial. With this he showed himself to be a murderer who despised government by law. Only a short time later the Nuremberg Laws were put in force without evoking much opposition. They provided the legal basis for the discrimination against and persecution of the German Jewish minority. In 1938—before World War II—Hitler staged the *"Reichskristallnacht"** in which, within sight of every German, their fellow Jewish citizens, in all the larger towns and cities, were attacked, arrested, and in some cases killed, while their synagogues and property were destroyed or confiscated. At about the same time the euthanasia program was introduced, with the goal of killing all those "unworthy of life"—the mentally ill and the mentally retarded. In the end this program cost some 80,000 to 100,000 people their lives. Today it can be documented that many respected members of the healing professions, among them numerous psychiatrists and university professors, collaborated in this program. Thus the genocide, which was carried out in the occupied eastern territories in the war that followed, was begun and built up on a foundation of political programs that the Germans, still in peacetime, were prepared to tolerate and to participate in, in their own country.

But although it is true that the crimes and injustices of the Nazis were visible to everyone who wanted to see, it is also true that the regime (Hitler and his closest collaborators) came to the help of those who *didn't* want to see. In the first place, the regime offered myths and a worldview which defined the prevailing interpersonal and political realities in a new way. In my book (1975) about Hitler I explored this. Many Germans, by accepting Hitler's definition of reality, were able to immunize themselves against guilt feelings. They could believe their own cause to be just, the enemy's unjust (in particular the Jewish enemy's)—and therefore his fate well deserved.

---

* See Glossary, here and wherever an asterisk appears. —Trans.

Indeed, there was no longer any basis on which Jews might hope to find recognition. They were regarded as vermin and parasites who were to be mercilessly eradicated in cold blood.

In the second place, the regime glorified the virtue of absolute obedience: the Führer commanded, the Germans followed. Inasmuch as the regime suppressed any critical reaction as well as personal autonomy, any sense of responsibility for the crimes committed faded away. If one accepted the premise that Hitler alone could command and that all other Germans had to obey, then no longer was anyone responsible for his own deeds. The Germans were just doing their duty when they passed on orders to murder, fabricated the machinery of annihilation, organized death transports, or without questioning fought in a war which made Hitler's genocide possible and inevitable. Finally, whenever possible, the regime practiced secrecy and deceit.

Therefore, the question is not merely were the parents aware or were they not aware of the crimes? The question, rather, is did the parents take advantage of—do they still today take advantage of— the ideological escapes provided by the Nazis, escapes by which perception can be narrowed, guilt feelings deadened, and crimes made to seem innocuous? Were they (and are they today) willing to tackle secrecy and deceit actively? And lastly, were they and are they willing to activate their memory so that the Nazi past and their part in it can be spoken about in the dialogue between the generations?

Our family talks made it clear that most parents were not ready for that. Instead of activating their memory they manipulated or clouded it and thus rendered innocuous their roles as former Nazi activists, sympathizers, or supporters. They behaved in accordance with Nietzsche's words: "'I did that' says my memory. 'I can't have done *that*!' says my pride, and won't give in. Finally—memory yields." (*Beyond Good and Evil*, Aphorism 68.)

Not infrequently an unintended hint revealed the historical truth. A father, for instance, denied that he had ever felt any sympathy for the Nazi regime. Later on, however, his life story revealed that in 1940 he had christened his oldest son Adolf—"out of gratitude and enthusiasm for Hitler as Führer and his role as Germany's savior." In other cases parents were not able to admit former Nazi ties until a trusting therapeutic relationship had developed.

Yet even when parents were prepared to activate their memory, they frequently activated only the aforementioned subterfuges and—in updated form—discharge mechanisms. They pointed to Germany's heroic war against a world of enemies, played down the

murder of the Jews, and countered every report of German male-
faction with a story of Allied crimes, like the expulsion of millions
of Germans from the eastern areas, the rape of German women by
Russian troops, or the bombardment of Dresden.[3]

Many parents stressed the first perspective on the past—the one
which emphasizes the larger-than-life events—at the expense of the
second perspective, which highlights personal responsibility. These
parents emotionally painted themselves as bearers of the sufferings
of the Nazi time, as the playthings of uncontrollable social, political,
and military events. With that, questions about their own active participation seemed beside the point. When they emphasized the first
perspective at the cost of the second, it was as if they construed the
past to their own benefit. They unburdened themselves and could
at the same time appeal to some higher justice. As victims of larger-
than-life events, their share of misery and suffering had fallen to
them, just as it had to other victims—the Jews, for instance. Only
God or fate was responsible. Questions about accountability and
historical justice could thus (seemingly) be answered and avoided
simultaneously.

The attitudes toward the past described above (clouding of
memory, distortion of perception, grasping at ideological excuses,
avoidance of accountability) were to be found in most of the parents
who had been Nazis or who had been in sympathy with them. Such
a posture was understandable: it served as a defense against shame
and guilt. But it did not help to win the trust and respect of their children, and it prevented or made more difficult the long-overdue
dialogue with them.

How the Children Need the Dialogue

If we turn to the children, it is hard to say whether they or their
parents needed and need this dialogue more. If the dialogue doesn't
take place, the parents risk estrangement, if not contempt, in their
relationship to their children. But the children, it seems to me, risk
even more. These children, we saw, need parents who provide them
with tasks and duties which give meaning to the children's lives, and

---

3. Dresden, a cultural center without military or industrial significance, was destroyed late in the
war in a single night of Allied fire-bombing. An estimated 60,000 civilians died in the raid.
—Trans.)

which make trust possible as well as demonstrating justice, fairness, and integrity. Dialogue alone cannot fulfill all these needs. Nor can it transform people, or make up for all that was lacking, or recreate something that never existed. Nevertheless, dialogue offers the children their best possible chance of discovering qualities in their parents heretofore not seen or suspected. Further, it offers them the chance of understanding their parents better, of developing empathy for the conflicts in which their parents found themselves at the time, and of asking themselves whether they, had they been in their parents' place, would have behaved differently. And this, in turn, offers them the chance, finally, of differentiating themselves from their parents and at the same time of being reconciled with them. The example of one family can show how such a chance can be useful.[4]

In this family the father was already in his mid-seventies. For many years he had spoken with his son only about superficial things and had not mentioned his Nazi past. In the eyes of the son, he had remained a Nazi. Partly as a result of the family meetings—initiated because of other problems—the son finally took a new approach to bringing up his father's Nazi past: he asked him why he had joined the Nazi party well before the outbreak of the Second World War. The father was at first disconcerted and dismissive. But his discomfort lessened as he sensed his son's empathy and real desire to understand him. And so he was able to tell his son how, as the manager of his factory, he had found himself in a desperate situation at the time when Hitler came to power. The worldwide economic crisis had forced him to let more and more workers and employees go and had thrown the continued existence of his factory in doubt. Like countless other Germans, he saw Hitler as the savior. He credited Hitler with leading his employees and with them the entire German people out of misery and despair. In recognition of this service, the father gave Hitler credit on account, as it were: he extended him his loyalty—unearned and ultimately ruinous. His decision to enter the Nazi party stemmed from this loyalty, and he fought, without questioning it, as an officer in Hitler's armed forces. Although more and more doubts arose about Hitler, he loyally fought on up to the very end. But now, as he reflected with his son on his behavior at the time, he admitted his mistakes and his failure to take a stand about Nazi policies. Paradoxically, it was exactly this admission which enabled

---

4. In this, as in the examples that follow, I have changed a number of details or have constructed an "ideal case" out of several examples. I did this so as to prevent the identification of individual patients, as well as to bring out typical and essential issues.

the son to discover an integrity and humanness in his father of which he previously had been unaware. In facing his mistakes, his failure, his shame, and his guilt, the father did not lose but rather gained respect and authority in the eyes of his son. The dialogue between the generations developed in the sense of a positive mutuality as I have described elsewhere—a movement of mutual self-revelation and confirmation, carried out on an ever more meaningful and existential level. In the process it became clear that the son's active questioning helped the father to master his own past, as far as this appeared possible. Moreover, by helping his father, the son had also helped himself. In standing by him as his father sought to discover or perhaps rediscover his own self-esteem, the son's self-esteem grew also.

In most situations which I came to know more closely, however, such a positively developing dialogue about the parents' Nazi past was not the rule. Far more often, all real dialogue remained blocked. This is shown, for example, in the following exchange between a mother, in her late fifties, and her daughter, in her mid thirties, during a family session.

The daughter asked her mother in this session about the circumstances surrounding her father's death. The father had fallen on the eastern front in 1943. The daughter had never known him and had grown up with a stepfather from the age of six. Stimulated by what she had learned in the previous family sessions, the daughter tried again to get a clearer picture of her father. What kind of person, what kind of husband had he been, what goals had he sought to achieve, how had he died? To find out these things she had looked through old letters and papers and in the process found a newspaper clipping about her father's death. The black-edged announcement ended with the expression "In proud grief," followed by her mother's name and the names of several other close relatives. (Many German war widows, we must remember, signed the obituaries of their fallen husbands in this way, but it was not required.) In connection with the obituary, the daughter now asked her mother, "Why did you write 'in proud grief'? What does that mean? What was there to be proud of?" The mother was silent, then very hurt and reproachful. Despair and reproach were mirrored in the daughter's face. The daughter asked nothing further and from then on let her parents' political past rest. Nor did any additional dialogue take place later on.

Had the dialogue gone further, the mother would have had to confess to herself that her husband had fallen in a criminal war, and that his—and her—sacrifice had no meaning. This was impossible for her. But neither was the daughter able to give up the ethical sensibility and political conviction which led her to judge the war and with it her mother's attitude.

But although their real conversation collapsed, a strong bond continued to connect mother and daughter. Following the early death of her husband, a close tie had formed between them, which continued to exist despite the breakdown of the dialogue. The question is, What happens in situations like this when the dialogue ceases but the partners, through their mutual needs, obligations, and a shared heritage, remain closely connected?

Delegating Once More

With this question before us I wish to return once more to some aspects of the dynamic of *delegation* which I have described elsewhere. The Latin word *delegare* has the double meaning of "send out" and "entrust with a mission or task." Children who serve their parents as delegates gain a feeling of self-respect, importance, and integrity by loyally carrying out the tasks given them by their parents. In cases that are positive for the children, such assignments correspond to their age-appropriate talents and needs and can be more or less openly negotiated or adjusted. The children also receive recognition for what they do for their parents. In cases that are negative for the children, their missions are too taxing for them, or they may be exposed to massive conflict. In these cases it is nearly impossible for the assignment to be renegotiated or modified, or for the conflicts to be resolved. Furthermore, these children receive no recognition for what they have done and continue to do for their parents. But this causes a vicious circle: the children, who feel themselves exploited, betrayed, and unrecognized, "fail" sooner or later in one way or another. Some fail in school, others become delinquent, still others show symptoms of a schizophrenic break. Finally, they turn in despair and fury against their parents, who have actually or presumably exploited them by means of the task delegated to them. Typically, they can now use precisely this failure as a weapon in the battle against their parents: while they blunder about in school, developing into delinquents or schizophrenics, they are in a strategic position to push their parents' guilt buttons. They now provide these parents with living proof of their own badness or incapacity as parents. The expression and result of this is often a tragic, malignant deadlock, a power struggle which is both stuck and escalating and in which, in the long run, there can be only losers—the opposite of a positive reciprocity.

In other writings—in particular in *Delegation und Familie (Delegation and Family,* 1978)—I have explored these connections and illustrated them using examples from the area of clinical psychopathology. In what follows I would like to show how clinical psychopathology can dovetail with political psychopathology in a way which reveals a further dimension of the dynamic of delegation. In order to present this I wish to discuss more closely a family whom I shall call the Mehnerts.

The Mehnert Family

This family consisted of the 58-year-old father, the 45-year-old mother, the 24-year-old son, Claus and his 12-year-old sister, Margot. Claus, who was studying philosophy, sociology, and political science, was the reason for a counseling session in our institute. During the previous half-year he seemed ever more frantically driven. He had signed up for seminars on philosophy and modern German history as well as other topics. But he had repeatedly broken off the seminar work and turned to other things. Thus he had rather suddenly decided to take a trip to Poland, where he visited the manor on his parents' former estate as well as the concentration camp at Auschwitz. After his return to West Germany he broke off his relationship with his girlfriend and joined a students' communal living group. Here he tried to persuade his fellow students to demonstrate against the undemocratic practices of the university faculty. Suddenly, however, he moved out of the commune, gave up his philosophy and sociology studies and instead turned to the study of business. Sociological theories were nonsense and a waste of time, he declared; the only important thing was to earn money. He had expressed the wish to speculate on the stock market in order to be able to pocket a lot of money and then to buy his father a farm. But such plans took on an increasingly grandiose and delusional air, while Claus' behavior became ever more restless and driven. He felt himself pursued by the most various persons and forces. When one of his professors once failed to respond to his greeting on a busy street, he took this as proof that the man was planning a conspiracy against him. At the same time, he reached the conviction that terrorists intended an attack on him. (While he was living in the student commune he also had had contact with students who were said to be active sympathizers, if not collaborators, with several known West German terrorists.) Finally, in a state of panic, he demolished a windowpane, and it became necessary to have him admitted to a psychiatric institution. Here, an acute paranoid schizophrenia was diagnosed and treatment was begun with massive doses of tranquilizers.

When we saw him some time after his discharge from the psychiatric clinic, no traces of insanity were to be found. He talked reasonably and coherently, but he did seem somewhat flat. He said he wanted to take up his seminars in philosophy and sociology again. Neither he nor the rest of the family seemed ready or willing to revive and explore what could have led to Claus's breakdown. Since the Christmas holidays were soon coming, we recommended a second family session about six weeks later, to see where we were and to plan possible further therapeutic steps.

The session took place—but without Claus: Claus had hanged himself in his parents' house several days after Christmas, without any warning. The bewildered family members—all were dressed in black—asked themselves and us the same question over and over: why had Claus killed himself? In what follows we will concern ourselves with this question also.

Within the framework of this study, in which we are dealing with the mastering of the German past, I would like to limit myself to one aspect: Did the parents' Nazi past (or better, their incapacity to master this past) possibly contribute to Claus' suicide? More precisely, did this unmastered Nazi past contribute to delegating to Claus exploitative tasks and conflictual duties which finally caused him to break down and drove him to suicide? In limiting myself to this question, I necessarily neglect other features which could make Claus' and his family's tragic fate more understandable.

Turning to the Nazi past of the Mehnert parents, we must again distinguish between the two perspectives mentioned above: the one which focuses on larger-than-life events and the one which permits us to see how the individual either confronts these events or subjugates himself or herself to them.

When our family sessions took place, it was plain to see how these past larger-than-life events had overwhelmed and marked the parents. Both were prematurely old. Their faces seemed still to mirror the blows of fate and the privations they had suffered during the war and during the postwar years. The father had been a well-to-do farmer in East Prussia, close to the Polish border. At the end of the war he had lost everything and had had to make do as a day laborer, first in the eastern occupied zone and then in West Germany. He had lost his parents because of the war—they had died as they were fleeing—as well as his younger brother, who fell on the eastern front. He himself had fought for five years in Hitler's armed forces, had been wounded a number of times, and was decorated for bravery in action.

The mother, 13 years younger than her husband, had been born out of wedlock in the final years of the war. Her illegitimate birth could also be ascribed to the larger-than-life events of that time: her own mother, emotionally and sexually starved after years of separation from her husband in the battlefields, had finally had an affair with a soldier who was passing through and who thus became the biological father of Claus's mother. As a result of this, Claus's mother grew up in various foster homes. She experienced herself as unloved, as always passed on to someone else as quickly as possible, as an extra mouth to feed.

The mother had married Claus's father in the (unconscious) hope of finding in him the father she had never had—in vain, as it happened. Bitter himself and exhausted by a life filled with privation, he was not in a position to give her what she wanted. Soon after the marriage, he withdrew from her emotionally and lived his life alongside of her but not with her. Both partners sought to keep their growing rage, bitterness, and frustration from their consciousness. They did not speak about their conflicts and frustrations but instead presented, to themselves as well as to others, a picture of marital harmony. Claus, however, was not deceived by this facade. He remained attuned to his parents' misery and offered himself as a delegate for the task of relieving this misery. But in the end this burden proved too heavy for him.

His mother entrusted him above all with the job of caring for her emotional needs, making up for what she had never had. His task was to give her that feeling of importance, that warm love and affirmation which she, an unwanted child, shoved around among foster families, had never received. He fulfilled this mission not only by direct and active giving from his own side, he also offered himself as the object for *her* boundless and attentive giving; as she identified with his (supposed) childlike neediness, she was able to give him what she had wished for, from her own parents, but never received. (This mechanism, the transformation of earlier passive privations into later active giving and controlling, is well known from psychoanalytic experience.)

The consequences of such behavior were, however, that Claus, as the recipient of an excessively regressive spoiling, remained symbiotically tied to his mother, and that each attempt to loosen that tie aroused in him massive "separation guilt"—one reason among others why in the end his attempt to separate himself from her and from the rest of the family always failed. But whereas Claus, as the overly protected and tied down "baby" was symbiotically held fast in the web of maternal tensions, he had also to provide his mother, thirsting as she was for experiences, with something of the excitements of youth—of (apparently) carefree student life, a social life, and the sexual adventures which she herself had had to miss. That meant, however, that Claus not only remained tied down but also, although within limits, had to move out actively beyond the parental precincts.

The assignments which the father gave to Claus seemed quite different by comparison. For him, Claus had to achieve everything and succeed at everything which had not been granted to the father himself. Further, Claus seemed to be charged with making more bearable the (unmourned) loss of home, house, land, prosperity, and social status by developing himself into a shrewd businessman and capitalist who could replace the father's losses and possibly even buy him a new farm.

All the assignments and missions which we have mentioned as serving the needs of the father and mother bear the stamp of those political and historical events opened up by our first perspective. But if we turn to the second perspective, which emphasizes active participation as opposed to passive suffering, still additional assignments can be recognized. These assignments reflect the fact that the parents had not simply borne the larger-than-life historical events but as active Nazis had also helped to produce them.

There was no doubt about the Nazism of the parents, particularly of the father. Everything that he said—with which the mother usually silently identified herself—pointed to his affirmation and support of Hitler's policies at the time; even today, he remained convinced that he fought for a good cause. He found words only for the injustices and brutalities wrought by the enemy on the Germans, but not for those wrought by the Germans on others (Jews, Poles, Russians, opponents of the regime). Although he had lived for a long time on the Polish border and in Poland itself, he had managed so far to shield himself from all evidence of repressive German policies in the East. He continued to speak proudly of the time when he followed the flag of the Führer to defend the German fatherland. Even today, more than 30 years after the tragic events, one could still easily imagine him as an active member of the fanatic masses of German soldiers which overran and terrorized Europe.

Elsewhere I have described how certain young Germans conceived of themselves as delegates who sought to make reparation for the crimes that their parents, as active adults in Hitler's Germany, had either committed or tolerated, but for which they had not taken responsibility. There were, for example, the students who, within the framework of *Aktion "Sühnezeichen"** volunteered for work on Israeli kibbutzim.

Although Claus didn't volunteer for that kind of reparations work, he could be counted, it seemed to me, among such young Germans. His almost obsessive preoccupation (apparently unnoticed by his parents) with the Nazi crimes, his attacks against the antidemocratic practices of the university administration, even his wish to live in a democratic living commune rather than in a regimented youth group—all these things could be seen as an attempt to perform a work of understanding, mourning, and reparation, which his parents, as the ones actually concerned, stubbornly resisted. In the family meetings, the father repeatedly let it be known that he was not prepared to let the Nazi past come alive again nor to discuss it, even though he seemed to be heavily burdened by it. He didn't want to be exposed to these painful things, he said. But the more unyielding he became, the more desperately his son seemed to try to bring this past to life again, and even to make reparations, in spite of everything.

As we heard, his efforts were in vain. In the face of still other burdens and conflict-laden assignments which I cannot go into here, Claus seemed to have reached a point where he felt exhausted, where he despaired of accomplishing his tasks, and where he gave up hope of receiving recognition from his parents for what he did do for them. With that, we may assume, he came to the decision to commit suicide. At the same time, he intended the suicide—as is typical for such derailings in the dynamic of delegation—as much to free himself from the burden of his assignments and to punish himself for his failure as to take revenge upon the exploitative parental delegators of these tasks. (By killing himself he made them feel that they had failed as parents, and at the same time he deprived them of any chance of making good their failure and silencing their feelings of guilt.)

Closing Remarks

Claus's story reminds us of other German terrorists whose family dynamics I have investigated. But there are differences: in contrast to such terrorists, Claus was not able, for example, to distort his perception and to rigidify his conviction in such a way as to justify the killing of others. Still, like many of these terrorists, he turns out to be an exploited, despairing delegate of parents with whom no further dialogue was possible. And most important in our context, like many terrorists, he saw himself burdened by a past which his parents helped to create but for which they are not prepared to take responsibility. (The man murdered by terrorists several years ago, Schleyer, the chairman of the German Employers Association, was a symbol of Germany's unmastered past: as a convinced Nazi and SS officer, he had been centrally responsible for the integration of the Czech armament industry into Hitler's war effort.)

At the same time, the reactions of Claus and of young terrorists seem extreme and not typical of the majority of young Germans whose parents had been Nazis or Nazi sympathizers. Our daily experiences and our observations of many families suggest that most of these Germans in one way or another learned to live with their parents' Nazi past, or, perhaps more correctly, learned to leave it alone. The final question is, At what price?—for themselves, for coming generations, and for society.

I believe this price will be high. Without a continuing dialogue about their political history, these Germans, as we sketched at the beginning, risk coming to grief in their search for meaning. Only with the greatest difficulty, if at all, can they approach their own origins and historical roots, determine and understand their own tasks and legacies, see what family and societal conflicts they have received with their heritage, and really learn from history. It is also unlikely that they will find in their parents and forebears sources of that strength and integrity which they will require if they are to analyze exploitative, conflict-laden assignments, and, if necessary, shake them off. And in the end they may despair in the attempt to find and to shape a meaningful continuity between the generations, or, perhaps better, a continuity which creates meaning.

Are these considerations applicable to other nations besides Germany? I believe so, although no other civilized people seems as starkly affected. We can think of a political past which included slavery, colonialist oppression of "lesser races," collaboration with

totalitarian regimes, participation in imperialist wars, and silent tol-
eration of persecution and torture (as these were practiced, for
example, by the French in Algeria and are still today practiced by
many regimes in South America and other parts of the world). In all
these cases the capability and willingness of the generations to
engage in dialogue are challenged. To the extent that cultural and
social transformations speed up and the values, expectations, and
experiences of the older and younger generations diverge, meeting
this challenge becomes more difficult as well as more important.
Thus more and more will depend on that trusting dialogue which
gives the partners strength, which permits them to learn from each
other, and which directs their intellectual and moral resources into
common channels. For only together can we hope to deal with the
dangers—the spreading of nuclear weapons, environmental pollution, overpopulation, the hunger that threatens millions of human
beings—which today threaten to destroy our planet.

10

THE WORK OF REMEMBERING
A Psychodynamic View of the Nazi Past
as It Exists in Germany Today

Barbara Heimannsberg

Since Alexander and Margarete Mitscherlich diagnosed the inner resistance against working through a piece of our history 25 years ago, the dissociation and the isolation of the Nazi time from the rest of our past have developed markedly. In our collective consciousness that time is ever less "our" history, its meaning disconnected from our "national identity." It was "Hitler's army" which crushed our neighbors, it was "Hitler's sick mind" which ordered crimes "in the name of Germany," and it was the "Nazis'" reign of terror which sealed Germany's fate. Thus we obviously tend to play off the side of pride against the side of historical responsibility. The parts of the past that detract from a sense of pride are toned down and ignored.

The question of national identity comes to us again and is cast anew after the reunification of Germany. There seems to be a widespread longing to reach back to a traditional historical image of nationhood, and this longing receives stronger and stronger political articulation. In western Germany the pride in the technical and economic potency of the Federal Republic has remained, but suspicion and anxiety exist that the basis of this pride could weaken or that it no longer suffices to "provide meaning." In eastern Germany the insecurity caused by the complete ideological change, the new political order, and the economic transformation is so massive that the search for "new" ideals which might help create solidarity is only too understandable. In this climate conservatism and nationalism flourish. The return to old ways of thinking during the search for certainty of identity and the aggressive emphasis on boundaries are reminiscent of an individual's regressive defense against anxiety.

This turning back to anachronistic models of identification could be a reaction to the extreme demands of rapid social change; aggressive self-assertion could reflect existential insecurity. "Fury in the gut and authoritarian politics in the head"—this explosive mixture moves many young people in the new German provinces. In those eastern lands, now possessing a wider, but more diffuse, horizon, lands where well-known boundaries have disappeared, and where political arrangements which had been stable for decades suddenly dissolved in rapid succession, a collective need and search for identity is to be expected. This need is to be taken seriously and, in fact, requires a common, collective effort if we wish to assume responsibility for our historical identity.

Since the search for a true identity requires both self-acceptance and self-construction, the answer to the question of who we are, where we come from, and where we are going must be based on a critical ownership of our own history. We cannot reinterpret Auschwitz or put it out of sight without deceiving ourselves. Jürgen Habermas hit the mark when he formulated our situation in this way (1986a): "Our life's form is tied to that of our parents and grandparents through a web of familial, local, political, and also intellectual traditions which can hardly be untangled—thus through an historical milieu which has made us into what we are today. No one can steal away out of this milieu, because our identity as Germans, as well as as individuals, is indissolubly enmeshed in it."

"National identity" is an ambiguous, emotionally charged concept. It manifests itself in a feeling of "we" and supports itself via membership in a nationality. It is questionable whether the psychological feeling of "we" leads automatically to a special valuation of one's own nation and the simultaneous disdain of other nations. I believe that that depends, among other things, on what function national membership plays in the self-esteem of a person, and what other sources of self-esteem are available to him or her. National pride refers to the meaning which is attributed, individually or collectively, to being a member of that nation. Thus concern with, and thought about, national identity should not be confused with its nationalistic use. Nationalism is a specific form of exaggerated national feeling and, if we make a distinction between archaic identifications and more mature ways of stabilizing our sense of self-worth, nationalism belongs among the former.

When our self-esteem is threatened, we can seek stability through aggressive identifications which, hopefully, will guarantee our own superiority. The stabilization of our self-esteem through identification with an idol is fostered through authoritarian psychological structures. A more mature way of forging our identity should not depend, it seems to me, on pathos and power fantasies nor on narcissistic possibilities introduced from the surrounding environment;

rather, a more mature search for identity would reflect our common, collective development and would not seek to avoid painful truths. Leftovers of archaic identifications remain, but they merge into the background in contrast with the more dominant, riper forms. Self-esteem is supported by mutuality, ambivalences are tolerated, responsibility becomes a part of the self-design, and relatedness becomes possible because independence has been experienced.

In a comparable way one can construe the collective relationship of one's own country to its history. History can serve as the legitimation of the most various political interests, conservative as well as emancipatory. Looking backward and identifying oneself with a particular view of history or with a particular "narrative modelling" (White, 1991) is one thing; reflecting on our historical past from an enlightened, analytical point of view provides us with a critical relationship to the past and is something quite different. "The public use of history" to establish meaning, which is the political exploitations of a history transfigured by nostalgia, which Habermas criticized (1986a), does not differ much from the individual use of identification in stabilizing self-esteem, as described above. The corresponding psychodynamic processes have been penetratingly described by Alexander and Margarete Mitscherlich.

Indeed, with the reunification of Germany the myth of the "nation" has been actualized and the temptation is large to hide social contradictions behind nationalistic ideology and national symbols. In the metaphor of "standing tall," conservative politicians in the Federal Republic have long called for national pride as a part of normalization. Nationalistic tones are finding more and more political echo, and not only among extreme rightist groups. The conservative call for a regained national consciousness which would secure the inner continuity of western Germany as well as its reliability in foreign policy (Stürmer, 1986) corresponded to a general trend in the public consciousness. "Self-exculpatory tendencies in the writing of German contemporary history" (Habermas, 1986b) were considered an indicator of just this change in consciousness. In public discourse at that time, historians and publicists used the slogan "national identity" to refer to a conservative nation-state concept and to the creation of meaning through a narcissistically tinted picture of history.

In opposition to this conservative view I wish to propose a concept of collective identity which is derived from critical analysis and reflection. This consideration of the "we" feeling as a reflexive source of identity growing out of historical roots corresponds more to the mature person's searching of conscience than to the immature developmental form of identification with an idol. Identity is at once something which has developed out of the past and something which points to the future. The historical dimension of identity is obvious. A reflexive identity supports a sort of self-assurance which contains doubt; such an identity makes use of historical facts as well as related determinants. Even the choice of whether to accept or reject a particular tradition assumes that one can recognize them as such. Reflexive identity begins at the point where unconscious identification and fixation cease.

Probably a *knowledge* of history in and of itself makes up a comparatively small part of one's sense of identity. More relevant is one's *relationship* to history and especially to that part of history which one recognizes as one's own. Historical knowledge must be psychodynamically integrable, and from the individual's point of view that is a question of emotional maturity and the ability to tolerate ambivalence. If such maturity and tolerance are not sufficiently developed, there remains an unconscious search for idealized identification objects promising strength and security. Such objects could be, for instance, the power of the state, the greater whole of the nation, a stylized picture of history or all of these together. A community which supports its identity through such identifications may behave regressively for reasons other than the emotional immaturity of its individual citizens. Lying beyond the conscious working through of individual experience, we find the structures of our social unconscious.

An idea that belongs to the basic assumptions of psychotherapy is that the work of remembering is healing, and that in the course of such remembering archaic meanings become conscious and are shifted about in our minds. The collective work of remembering also contains integrative and emancipatory potential. Looking back over our collective history we can become aware of the chronology of events, we can perceive and reflect on goals and effects, patterns of thought and motives, and not least of all on moral valuation. A past which is not remembered, which is denied or repressed, continues to act as an unconscious template within us.

In a united Germany the Nazi past common to us all would have to become the central theme of our critical retrospection, upon which a common identity could be based—an identity true to reality, remembering that the division of Germany was one of the results of National Socialism. Some individual Germans may have succeeded in handling their country's past in this way, but it is not anchored in the collective consciousness.

In the other, conservative perspective, true, the crimes themselves are not denied, but the responsibility for them is reduced and dissociated, the perpetrators were "other people." Many of these characterizations have a polarized nature: for instance, many people make the distinction between the German people and the "SS state," the responsible elite leadership. The emphasis on the totalitarian and terroristic character of the Nazi dictatorship has a similar unburdening function, as does the appeal to the fact that one was commanded and had to obey. Another method of dissociation is the attempt to remove the Nazi period from the continuity of history, leaving only the time before 1933 and after 1945. The Nazi period is set apart as an exceptional situation in order to veil its connections to the "normality" which preceded and followed it (continuities in industry, science, politics, in the executive branch, and so on). Probably this continuity is true not only for the power centers of the Federal Republic: there were also careers in East Germany which began in Nazi Germany.

In the memories of both German states the trauma of having participated in the crimes of National Socialism was avoided. In the west the past was painted over and minimized, in eastern Germany it was dealt with through projection, which succeeded through massive identification with the antifascist struggle and the opposition to Hitler. The Nazi heritage was cut off and glued onto the other German state. The economic rebuilding and the reconstituted conservatism of the Federal Republic during the 1950s fit nicely into this eastern projection. In the West, anti-Communism became the basis of the new identity. The citizens of the Federal Republic identified themselves less with the democratic political order than with the marvel of the German mark and the rebuilding of western Germany. Later on, the Federal Republic, as a respectable partner in the western alliance, sought to shrug off the shadows of the past through a reconciliation over the graves of Bitburg. In both German states the search for narcotizing identifications and the warding off of mortification and painful truth won out. In the consciousness of many people in Germany, National Socialism narrows itself down to the person of Hitler. Then, in exaggeration, the following two self-images result: the citizens of the Federal Republic are made into seduced accomplices and faithful patriots, the citizens of eastern Germany are made into stalwart fighters resisting Hitler.

Since the reunification, both parties are primarily occupied with the past of only one side, with the Stasi-past, the crimes of the East German Secret Police. And the "Wessis," as the West Germans are called in the East, demand self-righteously that this past be dealt with. With supercilious accusations they fend off the heritage of guilt from the Nazi time. For the integration of the West German mind the picture of the enemy, of Communism, was important, but the most important support of West German identity was the triumphant economic rebuilding of the country. The identification with economic potency is also the main source for the current feeling of superiority which we West Germans feel in contrast with the East Germans. Both point to an increased sensitivity concerning self-esteem. In this case an economic recession would have psychosocial consequences which might seek ventilation in chauvinist aggression. But this danger cannot be confronted by simply looking ahead. Future German politics cannot avoid facing the experience of National Socialism. But at the present point in time the Nazi experience has retreated behind that other guilt of the Stasi-past; National Socialism is relativized through a leveling theory of totalitarianism.

And thus it happens that, disconnected and dissociated in many ways, National Socialism seems endlessly far away, belonging to another world and another time. Despite collective experiences and impressions from that time, the tie back to it can no longer be felt. This is particularly true of the traces of National Socialist upbringing; leftovers, continuities, which are the least conscious but which affect the largest number of people in both parts of Germany. The origins of attitudes, personal behaviors, and educational principles which were taken out of the Nazi time are no longer recognized—even to inquire into those origins is taboo.

Historical knowledge about the extermination policies of National Socialism is cleanly separated from the recollections of that time within German families themselves. The historical facts remain abstract, dissociated from the coherence of personal life. Similar behavior occurs around the celebrations of anniversaries of firms and clubs, even of historical exhibits: there may have been dark points in the past but they were long ago and are far distant from bourgeois normality. That normality which helps forge identity, that which is easy and familiar, seems fully separated from the daily disappearance of people, from gains one's family may have had by being "Aryanized" and by the removal of entire competing populations, from the bureaucratic policies and practices which supported and led to the genocide. Our historical memory is fragmented. Further, the images coming through the media remain superficial and marginal, "historical moments" in the great stream of images. Although one can be deeply touched by a life story, can feel one's way into images and narrations, can identify oneself with the victims, and can pity, nonetheless the connection to one's own real world cannot be established; they remain the stories of other people.

How can these various fragmentations be overcome? Are they symptoms of a collective diffusion of identity? I think that psychopathological categories have but a minor heuristic value here. But insofar as individual and collective development interpenetrate, the tie to collective experience and its integration through the work of remembering seem to me possible. For this to happen the family memories must be put in relation to the chronology of historical facts; traditional meanings must be newly explored with Auschwitz as the central point of departure. The goal of this work of remembering is not to veil the contradictions harmoniously nor to level out the differences, but rather to achieve a dialogue between them.

This work of remembering is an integrative process in which senses, thoughts, and feelings work together. The perception of various perspectives, feeling one's way into the attitudes of victims and of wartime enemies—all these belong to perceiving the facts and their consequences. Integrative work of remembering embraces the perceptions of events and the perceptions of their emotional meanings; further, it embraces empathy with the perceptions, meanings, and feelings of alien persons. One must stick with the tension of opposites which arises out of this process. A part of successful work of remembering is also repeating the experience of overcoming ambivalent conflicts over and over again.

The reconstruction of a life history in psychotherapy or in a family therapy setting is the best-known institutionalized form of confrontation with an individual past or with a family history. But in these settings contemporary history goes relatively unnoticed. Historical knowledge is generally not used in a confronting manner, and the fear of moralizing prevents many a therapist from making ethical questions into central themes. The following example should serve to remind us of how questionable such abstinence is. In his work with the children of Holocaust perpetrators, Dan Bar-On (1990) learned much in this connection. He had the impression that most of his interview partners (all were over 40 years old) had only recently begun to concern themselves with the atrocities committed by their parents; for some of them the interviews which he had with them gave the first push in that direction or awoke an interest for further searchings. They did not become freer or less burdened by the past of their parents through not knowing of the atrocities perpetrated by their fathers or by the fact that nothing at all about those deeds was mentioned in their surroundings as they were growing up. On the contrary, they were further traumatized by the silence of their parents. In some cases, through the half-structured interviews, a process of working through developed which Bar-On describes as containing 5 steps:

1. Recognition of the facts
2. Understanding of the moral meaning
3. Emotional participation and reaction
4. Emotional conflict
5. The integration of knowledge, meaning, and varied emotional reactions.

With this example it becomes strikingly clear—as also in many contributions in this volume—how important it is to bring historical facts into psychotherapy. This is only a single aspect of the collective work of remembering.

It is a clear step forward when, for example, school classes reconstruct the Nazi topography of their city and interview witnesses. If they relate this knowledge to their knowledge about the mass crimes and do not block out divergent perspectives, this is one way of doing some integrative work of remembering. Without such multifarious perspectives, the reconstruction of the normal, daily German life in the Third Reich can bring with it the danger of fragmentation (Diner, 1987). The narrations and memories which are colored with the brush of Nazism must be broadened through the memory and experience of those into whose world annihilation broke. Their world was also our world, and their world is also a part of our identity.

Connecting with the questions of guilt and responsibility is the most difficult part of reflecting on the Third Reich. Here the ambivalent tension is particularly strong as is the danger of blinding oneself to certain realities. But the ethical perspective is not only indispensable to the collective work of remembering; it is also the point of convergence of the partial perspectives in the dialogical process. I proceed from an ethic which is based in the immediacy of interpersonal exchange, and thus oriented by the question: what are the consequences for others of my own deeds? Without the recognition of mutuality and connectedness, an identity anchored in reality is not possible. Such an identity is threatened by crises and conflict, and it always has doubt within it. The collective work of remembering does not insure against doubt, but it honors questioning and it follows the healing concept of dialogue and integration.

11

THE DIFFICULTY OF SPEAKING THE UNSPEAKABLE
How an Article Entitled "The Nazi Past in Psychotherapy" Was Never Written

Irene Wielpütz

EARLY JUNE 1987

The telephone rings. I've grown accustomed to the sympathy calls that keep slowly coming in. My mother died suddenly and the cards[1] have just been sent out. But this is no such call. I am asked if I would be interested in collaborating on a book. Spontaneously I answer yes, the topic has always interested me. But I caution the caller that I am neither a writer nor a scientist. My doubts are dispelled; help will be forthcoming. It is ideas that are important, and I have plenty of those, even if in some disorder. Still, I have to ask, why me? Through a colleague whom I hold in high esteem. Immediately there comes to mind the memory of a train ride together returning from a strenuous conference: we begin to talk about ourselves, our fathers, our origins, about the burden of being the children of parents who carry around so much that is undigested on "both sides." I am content for the moment to let the vague term "both sides" stand without further differentiation between those referred to as victims (the Jews) and those referred to as perpetrators (the Nazis). We talk about therapies, about how we might be able to view the whole from a systems perspective. The atmosphere is very heavy. He hadn't forgotten our discussion either.

I want to write the eulogy for my mother. I think about her life. The central kernel, and pole of her being, determinative for the rest of her life, as the daughter of a Jewish father, was the period 1933 to

---

1. It is customary in Germany to send bereavement announcements after a death in the family. —Trans.

1939. In 1938, when she was 17, immigration to South America. From the eulogy: "Then came the great tragedy of her life—and I know of no one who has succeeded in working it through—namely the Nazi time. For my mother and my family it meant fear, persecution, degradation to the status of third-class human beings, humiliation, uprooting, the loss of all rights, going away to a totally unknown country which they did not choose, and finally, the murder of family members. Christa Wolf (1979) once wrote, 'Exile, that means one is saved, yet connected to nothing.'"

After the funeral, relatives from her family come forward to thank me. My words, they said, had been words for all those in the family who had been persecuted and killed. I ask myself silently how things can be going for the others from her circle of friends who in those days belonged, even if not actively, to the "other side." A taboo theme that I can't easily bring up, either. The taboo is on "our side" as well. Since 1957 we have been living in Germany again, and one simply doesn't reflect on the past or work it through; one looks ahead.

My mother was German; she loved her homeland and left involuntarily. She imparted her love of Germany to us, and as for what had happened in the meantime, it was best left undisturbed. In the face of her death, I have to talk about it. Suddenly I experience a great uneasiness. I don't want to be conciliatory anymore. Once again I am thinking a great deal about my Jewish roots.

JULY 1987

I run into Mrs. X. at the theater. The article immediately occurs to me again. I want to write about the therapeutic work we did together. Her father was a member of the SS. It was a hard burden for her to bear. I tell her about the article. She is diffident, or better said, mistrusting. We had wanted to make a film on this theme at one time, but to come out so openly . . . I have the feeling that she is still afraid of the reality of it, as it really was. I suggest that I can write something at some future time and send it to her; she can then add her view, and so forth. We part; I have the feeling that it will never come to pass, as the film never did.

AUGUST 1987

I take the typewriter with me on vacation. There, in quiet and at leisure, I want to write my thoughts on the subject. It need not be a formal case description after all. Although the weather is very bad—ideal for writing—not one line emerges.

After the very moving and shocking death of my mother, and my obsessive concern with the past, I am fed up. I have no more interest in writing. I want at last to be able to take leave of earlier times, particularly from those things out of that undigested time which our parents silently passed on to us. Above all, I have no desire to occupy myself with the past of the "other side." Back from vacation, the typewriter goes in the corner, the article is forgotten.

SEPTEMBER/OCTOBER 1987

It suddenly strikes me that so many films about the Nazi period are again being shown. Once again the article comes to mind. Why do they want to write about that just now? I forgot to ask. I thought that theme had disappeared forever. But it is true, people have scarcely paid attention to the aftereffects, to the things that can't be seen. Just as it was after the atom bombs. The events themselves are too horrifying for one to have to pay attention to the later consequences as well. What is to become, then, of the children of that time and the children's children? They would certainly all be better off if everything were really over.

I notice that the theme has gripped me again. Not the content of the article itself, but rather why this book just now? It strikes me that most of those who are making films or writing books now were either children during the Nazi time or were born during that period. The next generation had no further interest, and the older ones who had lived through it all probably cannot break the silence. They want nothing more to do with it, they want to forget. Somehow, that's at times understandable. Are they delegating the talking, the writing, the filming, the rage, the fear, the mourning to the children? I suspect so. Is everything flaring up once again so that it can die down for good? I don't know; so much is going through my head, I can't sort it out. In any case I can't write anything in this state of mind. The typewriter remains in the corner.

Maybe I should simply write down a few thoughts anyway. I can always decide later if it isn't fit for publication, but I should at least put my thoughts in order. Maybe I could get involved with family reconstructions,[2] as I did often enough during my training. For that, people need family trees and as much information as possible about the past, from as far back as possible.

It occurred to me over and over that the background of the family

---

2. Family reconstruction is a group psychotherapeutic technique. For a more detailed explanation of the technique and several interesting examples of its use, see Margarete Hecker's essay in this book. —Trans.

histories was usually not available. I don't know how often the question, "Do you know what your father did in the war?" elicited large, unknowing eyes, shoulder shrugs, irritation, embarrassment, sometimes fright, and occasionally the memory that their father did talk about the war and they couldn't stand to hear it anymore. To the question, "Do you know if he was a member of the Party, what he thought about the regime?" the frequently stereotypical answer was, "If at all, then only because he had to; at the most, he just did what everybody else did," and so on.

Another curious thing occurs to me: actually, every German family has a quite complete family tree. But now, somehow, the data are laboriously sought out, parents can no longer remember when this or that person was born or died. Had they destroyed all this data, or was it too embarrassing to use it? After all, all the information was contained in the Aryan Certificate.* I have never known children to ask their parents about it. Or was I the only one who knew that such a thing existed? Sometimes it seemed that way to me.

I have encouraged many people to be sensitive to the sufferings, the fears, the destruction of families, as well as to the consequences of the Nazi period and the war. I have personally understood a great deal about the many things that must have happened, including tragedies.

Sometimes I have wondered whether the period is as important to my colleagues who do the same work I do and whether they ever think about it, or whether they feel forbidden to see it because then they would have to see themselves and their families. We have never talked about that subject.

Did I so very much need to throw light on this time in Germany in order to be able to understand it myself? Alice Miller, who has tried to understand Hitler, comes to mind. I believe she is also a Jew, but I am not sure.

Thoughts upon thoughts. Not really properly thought through, nothing researched. No documents, no data, no records. It is my memory of my work. I should have collected everything in writing, then maybe I could have developed something out of it. I don't read much; maybe it all exists in writing already, maybe someone has already done the research.

How did I ever get the idea that I wanted to write something? I am neither a researcher nor an author—though perhaps a thinker with a good memory.

---

* See Glossary, here and wherever an asterisk appears. —Trans.

NOVEMBER 1987

A notice comes from the editors. I am shocked; I had forgotten all about it and had also thought I was out of the whole thing, since I hadn't given any sign of life, not a single line. Nothing of the sort: I am listed among the authors.

Something peculiar happens. I sense a great resistance. It seems that I have lined up more with "my side." I feel only prejudices. I don't trust anyone who comes from the "other side" to write something really open. I ask myself what past the other authors might have had, from which "side" they might have come. How can *anyone* find the necessary distance to write a scientific treatment of the subject?

The letter lies on my desk with the to-be-answered mail. I want to withdraw my name, give notice that I will no longer write.

My feelings are in a tumult. I sense a diffuse anger with the title, so black on white: *Collective Silence*. Somehow that anger is not allowed. Was I brought up too much on reconciliation? With us there was no hatred of Germany; and yet sometimes I felt anger, strong and undirected, particularly toward certain older people. It could be on the street or anywhere else.

I remember how at my nephew's confirmation, in the church full of people, an almost uncontrollable fury suddenly overcame me and I wanted to scream, "You are all nothing but hypocrites, sitting here, talking about God and love and you have killed hordes of people, or at least condoned it." I myself was shocked by the vehemence of my feelings and the clarity of the sentences. Naturally I didn't scream, but I felt sick, I had to cry. Nobody noticed.

DECEMBER 1987

My mother has been dead for half a year. My father, who always bounces back, now becomes seriously ill. He has never been sick. But that isn't quite right either. Once he had severe "manic-depressive episodes." At the time, that was, of course, "nerves," which naturally had nothing to do with his past.

Now he has a tumor in his lung. It is incomprehensible. The doctors were unsure at first since nothing in his life-style would point to that. He never smoked, he never had any contact with dust or any other such substance, he had always lived healthily. I have a horrifying thought which I quickly tell myself must be totally false: my father is a "full Jew," as it was so nicely termed. He emigrated and thus saved himself from being gassed to death. Choking and coughing are his symptoms now.

I am filled with dread. I can hardly bear these coughing attacks. My father wanted to go to Israel to visit his sister and brother-in-law. We learn that both of them are also sick, both have cancer. But not in the lungs. I can't stop thinking about why it should strike all of them in precisely this year? Fifty years ago they were strewn in every direction and they saved themselves from certain death. Is their strength gone now? I simply don't know. Whom can I ask, with whom can I talk? Certainly not with them. They would say once and for all that I was crazy. They have repressed everything, after all. I should simply believe the version which most people offer me: "They are just old. So many people get cancer. Everybody has to die some-time." But why all of them at once? My uncle dies at the end of December. I never knew him. My aunt met him in what was then Palestine. He came from Poland. I was never in Israel, he was never in Germany. Maybe I should write a family chronicle. I have decided for certain not to write about the Nazi past, not about the family dramas of Nazi children. If I write at all, then it will be about the dramas in our own family.

JANUARY 1988

I am having a termination session with a client. It has been a long road. I talk about myself, which I sometimes do in therapy. I tell about my father and about the impossibility of writing this article. A very moving conversation. She insists vehemently that I must write an article on this theme. She says she has never met anyone who has such a clear understanding of the interconnectedness of things from that time, and that may well be due to my heritage. I think about the mishmash of my heritage. Maybe she's right.

She tells me one more time how useful it has been to her to see her present problems in the context of the history of her family, who were uprooted because of their flight from the east at the end of the war. Again she tells about her embittered fight against her father's denial, about her own radicalism and how hard she was on herself in order always to distance herself from his opportunism.

Then I tell her how much my father's denial has shocked me. He doesn't want to admit the truth about his illness. He clings to the idea of an operation (a lobe of his lung is to be removed). I can hardly bear his denial and repression of disease and death.

Now she is the one who makes me aware that my father had, after all, already once saved his life and built a new one, looking only ahead. And she can well imagine that if one has escaped the Holocaust, one does not want anything more to do with death—it would be too horrible.

And there we sit, she, the child of a "Nazi collaborator," and I a "Jewish child." And laughing and crying we acknowledge that we have to contend with the same behavior in our parents, namely with the repression, the denial, the "I-don't-remember anymore" on the one side, and the "I-don't-want-to-hear-about-it-anymore" on the other; with the unlived mourning, with the unlived rage, with the unlived fear. And we don't know where to go with it all.

I am so moved that I immediately decide to write. I write a foreword in which I try to thank her and which I dedicate to her, and then I begin with my origins and a sort of life chronicle. I have the idea that I must explain where I come from. I begin, "I was born in 1947 in Bogota, Colombia, as the second child. . . ." And there it begins to get complicated. How do I write it? In the terminology of that time? That would be, ". . . of a fully Jewish father and a second-degree Jewish mother." Does anyone here actually still know what that meant? With my father it was clearly written in his Aryan Certificate*: nothing but Jews for generations past. With my mother it was complicated. Her mother—my grandmother—was Protestant, and until her marriage to my grandfather, the entire family on that side had been "racially pure." My grandpa was a Jew of the first degree, his mother half Jewish, his father three-quarters Jewish, and so on.

My grandma was advised to divorce her husband and to marry an Aryan; that might rehabilitate her and her children. Actually, grandpa would have gone to a concentration camp and grandma maybe not. But they went to South America with their three children. The oldest one, my mother, was 17, the youngest just 10 years old.

I feel the desire to write it all down sometime, but not here. What does it have to do with this subject?

I move forward in the text. "My parents met each other in Bogota. I myself was not baptized—not baptized in a Catholic country, with a pagan-Catholic governess and a family background which I only found out about much later on."

At this point I stop writing. I am supposed to be writing about Nazi children, not about myself.

I make a note, handwritten: "Hypothesis: There is no such thing as a 'psychotherapy with the children of Nazis. *All* children of Nazis, collaborators, deniers—plainly put, all children of people who participated in those times—must bear the burden today if their parents haven't taken it upon themselves, which is to say, haven't themselves come to terms with that burden. So I believe that there is at least one whole generation who, if they were to enter therapy, would be confronted with their parents' issues: guilt, fear, rage, grief, and so forth. The contents and the weight of the imprint will vary, as will the extent of the denial. The revolt of '68[4] was certainly an attempt to master the Nazi past. But how can one free oneself from something whose roots one cannot or may not name?"

Everything goes into a little folder which I have acquired in the meanwhile, and there it waits on the desk, ignored until further notice. On top is the telephone number of the editors. I want to let them know that I can't get anything suitable down on paper.

February 1988

There are more and more films and exhibits about the first atom bombs. That too is already quite awhile ago. Is the preoccupation with the Nazi horror over? Is the next one coming now? Must such things always rest for such a long time, without being worked through? Is the Nazi time our past and the atom bomb our future? Gruesome to see it this way. No wonder that once again so much attention is being paid to the esoteric. Somehow it is comforting to find a comprehensive explanation. But are we done with the shock, terror, fear, rage, and grief? Probably not. All these things seek their own paths.

March 1988

I meet the colleague through whom I became involved with the article in the first place. The editor sends greetings. Mushrooming guilt feelings. They haven't yet stricken me from the list. Nor have I been in touch with them. I tell my colleague, whom I consider to be a good writer, about my difficulties; everything is confused and all of it so personal. I know it from dance, where I find it awful when others present something and I feel like a voyeur. Then when I dance, I am always afraid of being either too banal or too personal, too private. I don't want this in my writing either. My colleague reassures me. He thinks that what he has read up to now is good precisely because it is personal. At first I believe him, resolve once again to look over everything, make various stabs at it, find no proper entree.

---

4. A reference to the wave of student protests and demonstrations that swept Europe, particularly France and West Germany, in the spring of 1968. —Trans.

I lie on my bed, staring blankly into the distance, letting the slowly rising sun warm me, thinking of nothing. Suddenly, a title for the article comes to me, out of the clear blue sky. Again and again I had wondered why the whole thing didn't just come to me all at once. Surely the title could be, "How an Article Was Never Written," with all the hurdles and barriers. Immediately thoughts are flowing; never before have I had so many coherent thoughts on this theme.

I decide to write, regardless of whether what I write fits the book. Just to write seems to me important for myself. I can tell by the sudden pounding of my heart.

At this very moment my breath stops. As if by magic, the editor calls wanting to know how things are going. I report, somewhat bewildered, about the ideas that have just hit me. He'd like to have it just as I've described it. I sit down at the machine, this time for several hours. My writing flows, something has been freed up in me. I am free to write about how I really think and feel without letting myself be intimidated by the fear of possible corrections. But the fear keeps resurfacing when the text seems too intimate to me. I am not, after all, writing under a pseudonym. What difference does it make, what do I have to lose anyway? It's true that I'm a little nervous about the interpretations and commentaries. That's the risk when one reveals oneself. That I know from dance, the fear of going on stage, out into the footlights.

We drive into the country. I'd like to recuperate and write some more. I sense profound connections between what I want to write and what is happening in my family. I find the words not right. Everything is too close. My entire energy goes to my father.

As the only possibility, they removed one lobe of his lung. A very difficult operation. Hardly anyone thought he would live through it. We had already taken our leave of him. He lives, he has saved himself; he says he has "jumped off Death's shovel."

My thoughts again go down strange paths. I want to push them away. It doesn't work. I make a comparison with the time of some 50 years ago. At that time my father saved his own life and helped others as well, and together they started a new life. They left suffering and death behind, they strode forward with strength and courage, they dared not look back. Now, too, he has "survived," but there is neither strength nor courage to forge ahead. Suffering and death have overtaken him again. He is not finished with them. He sinks into deep depression.

And I, to whom the struggle with suffering, grief, anxiety, and death has always been handed over, I who have taken a hard road trying to free myself from this past, I am there and would like nothing better than to relieve him of it once more. The helplessness of not being able to do anything is dreadful. I have a deeper understanding now of extreme repression: to have saved oneself but been unable to do anything for those who stayed behind—who wanted to stay behind, because they could not believe such barbarity existed—and who were then killed.

I don't want to write anymore. I have no more desire to look back. Will it all end only when they are all dead?

In order to think of other things, I read. I have looked forward to this book for a long time, to Isabel Allende's *Love and Shadows*. I start to read and I can't stop. And it's no different, it's the same subject. When both of the main characters have to leave their country for political reasons, the last shred of difference between us melts. I feel such deep pain, such sorrow. It cannot be only the memory of how I felt when I had to leave Colombia. It is also the pain of my parents, of my family, who, like the people in the book, had to leave their homeland in order to avoid being killed.

I again think about what I am writing. I understand that I mustn't write a theoretical treatise; then I could never say everything that I want to say. If only I could write like Allende, perhaps I could actually put words to the unspeakable. If only there actually were someone who could write about Germany with this same love for the land and the people, with this same sense of human frailty—not out of hate, not out of a need for self-vindication, not out of guilt, but out of love.

APRIL 1988

Time presses, the last and final deadline comes closer and closer. Again I am searching for clever thoughts, again I have great doubts about what I have written. Should I really send it off like this? For me it was good to write it, but does it have to appear in print?

Meanwhile, I am happy to be writing. But there comes another interruption. This time I would like to write in peace, find a good conclusion. But there is no conclusion, at least not in the family. My aunt from Israel says she is coming. She wants to see my father, her brother, once again. Both are extremely ill. It is my task to pick her up and bring her to him at his clinic. I can hardly face the whole thing. I get sick; naturally, it's my back. I, too, have learned very well not to show my fear or despair, to be strong and to persevere. Afterwards, I can weep and get everything clear. Before she departs, she is at our house again. I ask questions, and naturally I ask about earlier times; how was it before the Nazis? It is then that the conversation becomes lively and pleasant. She didn't give up the Jewish tradition as my father did. One could never really ask him about it. I feel a little melancholy that I received so little of it. Some things do fall into place: an interesting family from Cologne, witty and creative and at the same time very Jewish, as others are Catholic or Protestant.

Then again the break in continuity. Things which I had not known until then. My grandfather was already unemployed by 1933, when my aunt left high school. Although she was not yet legally forced to leave, the abuse of the Jews was already unbearable. I had always thought that it was in 1936, at the earliest, that things had gotten worse. Now it's even harder for me to imagine that the others never knew anything about it. I also hear for the first time that some of our family had died in the concentration camps. I had always lived under the impression that because father's family were all "full Jews," they had left in good time. Many, but not all.

I am very sad but no longer so shocked. I feel the desire to leave this time behind, no longer just because it is shocking, but also because I have pretty much "seen it all" and I will go on, knowing well that I have these roots and that they have determined my life. I think about my cousins in Israel whom I don't know, with whom I would have to speak English. They, too, have these roots and are perhaps living out another side of them. They hate, they go to war, they join the military with enthusiasm. How much do they really know about their roots? Do they see connections from yesterday to today and tomorrow?

My generation—what things do we still carry around within ourselves? After all my experiences of the last year, as painful as they were, it is good to know what happened, it is good to know what I carry with me and not to remain stuck or to flee from it as our parents did. But I believe they could do nothing else. It is like an inheritance; it belongs to you whether you accept it or not. You can then either accept or reject everything without looking at it, or you can take the trouble to accept it, examine it, and slowly sort out what you'd like to keep and what you'd like to leave behind.

It is the end of April. I have to finish. Maybe I could organize everything and write an article with more perspective, with more distance. Maybe, maybe not.

EPILOGUE (AUGUST 1988)

A year and a month to the day after the death of my mother, my father died. It was not a sudden death. I was prepared for it, I stayed with him until the end. We were able to share many things with each other, other things we couldn't. I always had the text with me in my bag. I wanted to read it to him but I didn't have the courage to do it. I was afraid that he would finally declare me crazy, or worse, that he could be so horrified that he would die on the spot.

Now, in retrospect, whenever I look at the text I am sad that I didn't do it. I would like to have known what he thought about it, and perhaps in the face of death he could have let go of his repression from those days. I simply do not know.

And did I not also fear, way down deep, barely perceptibly, that I really *could* reach him and that then a dam would give way and all the feelings of fear, rage, and grief would come to light, unvarnished and intense? Could I have endured it? I don't know.

Strength and control, mastering feelings such as fear and sorrow quickly and alone—these were always guiding principles in our family. Only once did he say that it pleased him very much that I would prefer it if he were buried in the Jewish cemetery. It would have meant a fight, since he wasn't in the congregation, but I would have done it. He didn't want it.

Thus a piece of this invisible wall between us, which allowed the unspeakable to remain unspoken, remained standing.

But roots also find their way under walls and can come together. There, underneath, they are and they remain knotted together. I can feel them more than ever.

I am proud to be one of the two daughters of this man, Jacques Meyer. I loved my father very much and I will carefully tend the roots which he imparted to me, and I will see to it that they will never be severed again.

AND AFTERWARDS . . . (APRIL 1992)

I had imagined that the "careful tending of roots," with which I had ended my article in mid 1988, would have been simpler. I had to recognize that I was far from being able to bring this matter to a conclusion: on the contrary, something very powerful had gotten going, something which pulled me along with it, which wouldn't let me go and which ultimately ripped me out of the apparent calm of my adjustment to Germany.

Again a folder came into being; it is yellow and bears the title, "Unfinished Thoughts on the German-German Past." Below it is painted a Star of David—and suddenly I am shocked by the accidental choice of the color yellow.

And the "German-German"? Anyone who saw it would surely think of the Federal Republic and eastern Germany, but I am referring to the Protestant and Catholic Germans and the other Germans who were Jewish.

November, 1988: fifty years since the *Reichskristallnacht*.* As if addicted I follow the event in press and television. Simply looking at the pictures and reports of that night, a flood of sorrow, rage, incomprehension, helplessness grips me. How must it have been for those who experienced it directly at the time.

Maybe the hypothesis is correct that when our feelings get too strong we must suppress or repress them, just in order to be able to go on living. If that is the case I would have to accept it for both "sides." For the first time that seems endlessly difficult to me. On the contrary, after such a long time outrage seizes me, now, when my parents, who experienced the tragic times, are no longer alive. Everything within me falters.

I am no longer outraged about what happened long ago, but about how it is handled now, fifty years later; it is handled so falsely, so awkwardly, everywhere I sense the repression and disrespect. For example, Jenninger. Phillipp Jenninger, at the time president of the Bundestag, delivered a speech before that body in November 1988, which commemorated the 50th anniversary of *Reichskristallnacht*, the Night of Broken Glass. In his attempt to do justice to the mentality of that time, Jenninger quoted extensively from contemporary Nazi politicians. Thereupon many representatives from all parties were appalled, and accused him of utilizing Nazi language! He was forced to step down immediately. What complacency and self-righteousness lay behind the demand that he step down, merely because he used words which everyone still knew so well, but which no one was supposed to know? Nobody understood that I was on his side: he seemed to me the most honest and honorable of all!

I don't want to go on loving everything that is German. And what about those who, unlike me, were brought up to *hate* Germany? Perhaps they could begin to love Germany. Indeed, what would happen if the children of formerly German parents began to love Germany? Maybe that would be the biggest awkwardness of all. With hate one can defend and justify oneself; but with love?

In April, 1989, I've been given the task of saying something at a family therapy conference on the occasion of the death of Virginia

Satir, the well-known American family therapist and a famous therapeutic personality as well. I cannot and will not speak any longer without the historical context within which I live. I think, that can't be just *my* theme, where is the other side? How does my generation think and feel on the "other side"?

I am determined to make this my theme: psychotherapy and family therapy *in* the German *and particularly in* the *historical context.* Why do we turn our eyes so strongly to America? It's hardly on account of the Jewish emigrants, or, as we would say today, asylum seekers. Who knows, or wants to know, where they came from, once upon a time? And I want to deal with how I developed into a therapist, against my own background and the background of my family.

The talk that I finally gave was brief. My yellow folder with the unfinished texts contains lots of sheets of paper, covered with sentences about fear, doubt, being lost.

For example:

"The past is here again, if simply because, despite some moments of anxiety, I give out copies of the article in this book. I heard about someone who loves to hand out the book because his article is in it. A person has to ask me at least three times and even then it isn't certain that I will pass it along. I fear the reactions, too, and the longer I deal with the whole theme, the more helpless and perplexed I become about how a dialogue can take place at all."

"I write something for the conference that I experience as belonging deeply and profoundly to myself and I'm only afraid that I'll lose the ground under my feet. I ask myself if it's not totally crazy to step up to the podium with such a subject in mind. When I listen around, the topic interests no one. Am I then the only one with a broken past? How did the others resolve it? Or is it just my own obsession, wanting to resolve something about all this?"

"Feelings that shock me: I go through the streets and I feel hatred and scorn. With every older person I pass, the question comes to me: what did he or she do after 1933? What did they think, how did they deal with the times in their own family and among their own friends? I can hardly find any excuses for why they seek to make everything look so innocent, so innocuous: I don't believe them any more when they imply that they didn't know anything. I don't believe anyone from that generation. . . . But then I am silent and feel utterly helpless and anguished. I would like to be able to make excuses for them. . . ."

"How can I explain to anybody that the past which is overtaking me now is not my own past but rather that of my parents and my unknown relatives? Ralph Giordano dedicated his book *The Second Guilt* to the burdened guiltless sons and daughters and grandchildren. What should we be called, the children and grandchildren on the other side: perhaps the sacrificial victims who weren't sacrificed, or the sadly raging artists of life, or 'those who are supposed to thrive without roots'?"

"What right, then, do I have on my side? My parents didn't come out of the concentration camps, they weren't hidden away by anybody, they simply left. And then I am ashamed about my feelings and about my despair. . . ."

I could refer to my lecture at the convention as a brief appearance with long and lingering aftereffects. The words were short, a little compromised, censored (by me) for security's sake. The aftereffects began with the immediate reactions: there were very moving, utterly unexpected responses from people who knew the Nazi time out of their own experience. One man, with tears in his eyes, embraced me and, whispering into my ear, thanked me and expressed his admiration for my courage in daring, in this setting, to place myself in the context of the history of my family. Suddenly we are allies, bearers of a secret. He was hidden as a child and so survived.

And there were the ice-cold reactions, too, and the ignorant people who chalked it all up to my neurosis—and the many, many silent ones. The children are silent just as the parents were silent. Just why did they have to be silent? Why couldn't we reach out, seeking some kind of understanding? I wanted especially to talk with them, and I wanted to find out from them how they live with their history.

Feeling a mixture of sadness and anger, I resolved not to try to build bridges any longer, and for the first time in my life I visited Israel and my family there (I had hardly known any of them, besides my father's sister and his cousin).

There is so much to say and to write about that trip. The pages that I wrote after my return, which were a sort of afterword to my talk at the conference, give the essentials:

"I believe that I will never be able to say that Germany is my home. But I know that I belong here, among all those things which oppress me and delight me. It had never been so clear to me before, as it was in Israel, that my family, my parents, were German above everything else. Germany was their home and had been my family's home for many generations. They were Jewish, just as others happen to be Catholic or Protestant. It wasn't "Jews" who had been massacred, but rather fellow countrymen. Wouldn't that be called fratricide?. . . . So Germany is also the land of my forbears. What schizophrenia, that I believed for so long that I had to make myself as invisible as possible here, because of my history. Or that I must almost excuse myself if I remind people here of their past or of their parents' past, and so evoke in them guilt or other feelings.

"I belong here, I have the right to live here—that right which was taken away from my family. And I have the right to be infinitely furious about what happened to my own family and to other people. And if apologies are necessary, then not from my side.

"I hope I will have the courage to continue to be furious."

Alas, my courage didn't continue. Fear and insecurity came upon me again. I thought a lot about my grandfather. When I was a child, he had been a very important person for me; we felt great love for each other and he always remained a trusted figure for me, even long after his death. In the family history he was seen more as the tragic figure. He was the Jewish half of a mixed marriage, a fact which had no meaning up until 1933. Later on his entire family of origin (his parents and three siblings) failed to survive the Holocaust.

And so I began to write letters to him.

November 3, 1989
Dear Grandfather!

It will surprise you that I write to you, since for a long time you haven't existed. But I have the feeling that you are the one who will have the easiest time understanding me.

There are so many things that I'd like to talk about with you, for instance about "Jewishness." I don't even know what to call it. What did it mean for you, before the Nazi time? . . . But how could knowing that help me now? Could it help me get out of the ever-returning, awful insecurity? I keep seeking identity again and again, seeking belongingness, home.

I am often ashamed about this insecurity, about this awful fear which continues to haunt me. There is no real basis for it: my life runs its normally secure course, I have achieved a great deal and built up a great deal, but it is as if on sand. I call myself to order again and again, and that works too, but it is as if I never reached the real basis of this fear. All of you, your family, your children, father's family etc., had real reasons to be anxious. Your very lives were in reality in danger. Mine never seriously.

Can it then actually be that your fear continues to live on within me? Do you think such a thing is possible? I think it sometimes, and there are people who claim it's true. But somehow I never think it out to its logical conclusion. Then I go looking for new theories; in my profession I certainly have choice enough. And seen from the viewpoint of my profession I am still just not yet adequately "therapized," just a little bit sick and neurotic, coming from such a difficult family system (each "school" would call it something different). And I, too, often see it like that, but something within me struggles ever more forcefully against such a perspective. I can also already give interesting talks about all this, but in my heart and my stomach I am filled with a terrible fear. And not only that; sometimes I get angry too, but only a little, and to show it . . . I get terribly frightened again. . . .

Dear Grandfather, how nice it would be if I could, like a little child, be based in your security, if you held me protectively on your lap and gave me the courage to go after my own things, to let myself loose and to fight where I hold it to be the right thing to do, and not adjust myself or lower my voice or betray myself. And if I could then come back to you again and know that here is refuge, here I can rest, here are the roots which nourish and support me.

It's not easy to live in Germany. But you knew that, nor did you want to return.

And after the Nazi time you would certainly—even if with rage, impotence, and sorrow—have had no doubt that you are German. And you were, when you had to go, exactly the age I am now, barely 43.

They should have prepared me better for Germany. They didn't prepare us children at all. When you were dead they all wanted to go back, "your people," everybody except Papi. You knew that too and it broke your heart. You believed that you had brought suffering over your wife and children just because you were a Jew. And at first it looked as if things wouldn't be that dire for your brother and his family—they weren't honest. When you then heard how all your siblings, including your brother and his "Aryan" wife, had perished (your parents were believed to have died of natural causes in a nursing home), did you perhaps wish to be dead, too? They hadn't done anything to your brother's family, and therefore they wouldn't have done anything to your wife and the children, who were so unhappy and discontented in this foreign land. (The German doesn't make any sense here either.)

Maybe you left so early and so suddenly because you wanted to open up the way back. Back. Unfortunately, though, your family didn't come back in anger, they came as if nothing had happened, as if one could extinguish that time. That is why we children were not prepared. Your two big grandsons boycotted the whole move, refused any exertion; I adjusted myself with frightful effort.

You know, Grandfather, in Germany at the moment there is a lot of talk about the fatherland. And isn't Germany your fatherland, your family's fatherland? Your family was an old Hamburg family, Papi's an old Cologne family.

If I knew that you, despite everything, held Germany to be your fatherland, your home, I think I could do it too.

Don't you think that's funny? When I talk about fear I always end up at the issue of "home" again. If I could accept Germany as home, would my fear go away? Maybe it would get even bigger. Maybe I should simply look somewhere else, or stop seeking altogether and just live with the fact that I do have quite a bit of fear. Maybe that's the best. And then I flee, like a child, simply to you, and then things are better until the next time.

Dear Grandfather, you'll hear from me again.

Besos y abrazos, your Granddaughter.

December, 1989
Dear Grandfather!

It's rainy and overcast here in Germany, almost winter.

Did you miss the seasons? In the country where I was born, your land of exile, there were no seasons and you never came back again to Germany or to Europe.

I marvel when I think that, seen from my point of view, you were neither an immigrant nor an emigrant, but a seeker of asylum! Your life was threatened because of the political conditions. When I think that today in the Federal Republic the refugees are the poorest pigs—and my beloved Grandfather also a refugee! Frightful, no wonder, that after the fact those seeking asylum, those refugees, are declared emigrants or migrants, that's not so terribly shameful. But I mustn't think about that any longer, I'll be overcome by cold fury or immense sorrow.

But the fury and the sorrow got to me anyway. And somehow there is a connection. It is this *living-in-Germany*, that I already wrote you about, to live in Germany with *your* past. Sometimes I have the feeling, if I don't deny myself and if I don't deny my roots, that my very existence will be unpleasant for some people, embarrassing to them. Somehow I remind them in a peculiar way of something that doesn't want to be remembered: if I were really "Jewish," I mean if I were in a congregation, had Judaism as faith, as religion, then that would be less unpleasant. It would be easier to classify me, then I would be one of the Jews in Germany, one of the few, but among those who are organized, have their own language; but in my presence what actually happened becomes clear: this was not simply a religious war. It was one's own countrymen who were exiled and murdered. And all this gets clearest in the case of your family. You didn't live in a Jewish community, you were at the time more like citizens of the world—and world citizens aren't only Jews, right? In your family there had long been so-called mixed marriages, but they weren't called that simply because this kind of thinking didn't exist.

I miss you terribly.

Besos y abrazos, your Granddaughter

February 11, 1990
Dear Grandfather!

I've been meaning to write you again for a long time, but I didn't know how. I am so confused and I want to be clear when I talk with you. I have a counter-thought for every thought I have—how can I reach clarity? Can you imagine that your granddaughter, who outwardly appears to live a clear, regulated, "normal" life, of which one would say she has everything that a person needs—so can you imagine that I am mostly confused and restless and sad and angry and anxious about the things which are out of your life, out of your years 1933 until . . . ? Was there really an end? Is it just that I haven't noticed that everything really *is* over? Are you thinking you can give me no answer to this?

Naturally we live here in a relatively free country, naturally we're doing wonderfully, naturally my life is no longer threatened, as your life and the lives of your family were; but the fear, the fear Grandfather, doesn't leave me. It won't leave me until I have understood the whole, and I understand it now less than ever. All my theories aren't enough. Even my profession, which I chose in order to understand things that are ununderstandable, gives me no real answer, none that could take away my fear. For a long time I thought that it is your fear, yours and your family's, which I carry within myself. Surely it is that, too, but if it were only yours, it could have been resolved. I cannot say that nothing here would have changed, but no one dares to look for the turtle in the well, the toad which repeatedly poisons the water. And the idea that Hitler alone was the toad cannot be defended. And I'm not thinking here of the people of the new radical right; they make up rather a neighboring theater of war which serves again to divert our attention. It is a posture toward other people that is repressed, a posture of envy, jealousy, lack of respect, all repressed. I, too, know these feelings well, know my own struggle with them. So its not the feelings themselves, but rather their repression. But maybe it's also something completely different. Nobody speaks of all this, at least not honestly, neither the parents, nor the children either, at least very seldom. Aren't they plagued with doubt, anger, fear?

It's all so useless, I keep going around in circles. Should I try to stop thinking about it? What then about the feelings? They can't be turned off so quickly. A vicious circle. Despair, impotent fury, longing for rest, joy, lightness. . . .

Besos y abrazos, your sad Granddaughter.

February 23, 1990
Dear Grandfather:

I must write you again about Germany. I would like so much to leave all that behind me, to forget it, bury it, but it always overtakes me again, and sometimes I think I'm going crazy. The feelings are overpowering, much too strong for the real situation, hardly understandable, and when I try to express them, people often look at me with pity or astonishment. So I write to you.

When you still lived in Germany, when you were still a German, there was only one Germany. I have no idea whether you, in your emigration, were aware of the division of Germany—in the last analysis this was a consequence of the war, something which, even today, many people here don't want to believe true. In a certain sense it was an answer to the immense destructiveness which emanated from Germany. Somehow it really is funny: people here just love to see themselves as victims; they never took part in anything. As you already see, I'm getting angry again—and doubtless unjust to many, but they will surely forgive me.

As to what concerns these two states, now, all of a sudden, everything is different. The wall in Berlin, which was a symbol of the split, was torn down, the people from East Germany achieved that. Great joy everywhere, in me, too, although I never had much connection to East Germany; when I came to Germany (to be correct I have to say "to the Federal Republic") I knew only this one Germany. Now I suddenly had the feeling there could again be a Germany like the old one, a Germany where we or, better said, you, were at home. Now I imagined that we could go back again to the place where everything once began, to the terror, and people could talk with each other, we would work it through together so that finally we could lay aside the burden of the past. Now I believed that I had found a way to connect myself with your roots, with the roots of all my forebears, openly and without fear. But somehow, and I can't describe accurately how it happened, this connection became its opposite. Our old theme: I have more fear than ever, fear of not belonging, fear of being shut out. . . . Here they simply have another history. I don't mean the big history, I mean history as it is written in small things. There is nobody among my friends or colleagues who has anything resembling a similar history, with emigration out and emigration back. They were born during the war or after the war and still experienced hunger and times of need. Or they began their lives in the still better times and were brought up by people who had experienced the Nazi time and the war here, and somehow or other bore it and then wanted to hear nothing further about it—and thereby they brought this country to great wealth. Maybe I should now stop wanting to make myself understandable. Nor can I seek my belongingness or security among the Jews; I don't belong to them either, I didn't grow up at all in that tradition.

Dear Grandfather, can you imagine that sometimes I want to cry out loudly, to shout people's denial into their faces, to spare them no longer? I don't have the courage! And it wouldn't change much. So I can only write to you.

Besos y abrazos, your Granddaughter

October 3, 1990
Dear Grandfather!

I have to write you again. I don't know where I should begin. I wanted to stop thinking so much about our old theme, I wanted to try, as everybody says, to look ahead. But I can't do it anymore. Today is an historic day, everybody says, a day of joy for the Germans. Whether I'm a German or not, I'm not rejoicing! I am sad, despairing, I feel myself shut out, slighted, and that means not only myself, but our entire families.

It is the day of German unity, Germany our united fatherland! The division of the two Germanys is finally ended. I can't join in the joy that now maybe a new epoch is beginning for Germany. They simply forgot us! The fears of the other countries confronting a strong Germany have been discussed over and over, promises and assurances were made, people have been reconciled. And what about the Germans who were scorned, driven out of the country, murdered? Why doesn't anybody mention those . . . ?

Our Chancellor Kohl talked to the nation yesterday. He said the sentence, "We owe our remembrance to the victims, we owe it to our children and grandchildren." A nice sentence, but it didn't refer to us. Rarely have I heard such a clear sentence from the mouth of any German or German politician. He was referring to the "victims of the regime" in eastern Germany; and to you I can admit it: I get furious when people talk about it the way they used to talk about Jews or Nazi victims, and what is so terrible is that nobody wants to remember *your* fate. They just erased us out of memory. So how can I rejoice and feel myself as a German today? You know: nobody here ever says that Germans murdered Germans; those were Jews, and German citizenship was taken away from them in good time. You don't belong anymore in the united fatherland. And today, do I belong here, am I a rehabilitated German? At the moment of my birth I was, according to the law, a child of Columbians, Mommy and Papi had gotten Columbian citizenship in the interim. And if it's not just wishful thinking on my part, possibly they were stateless, without nationality, and that would make me the child of stateless people. Maybe that would be a solution for me: "Nationality: none."

Besos y abrazos, your sadly furious Granddaughter

April 14, 1991
Dear Grandfather!

I haven't written for a long time. But I believe that I am slowly mastering our "theme"; I believe I am slowly finding my way. That surely has to do with my plunging myself so deeply into it. I have understood many things, and I believe that slowly, out of all those things that are simply part of my history, an identity is developing, a mixture of everything.

On this my way a couple of things have happened: the meeting together of a group of people, widely different in age and back-

ground, but all in very different ways occupied with the so-called
German past (1933–. . .), four of them from a so-called Jewish background (I'm still seeking another word—I hesitate to use the words
"persecuted" or "victim").

And we found a very beautiful title for our meetings, naturally
afterwards, after we had spent the first day together. The title is
"German Destinies." I like that. This day gave me a lot of courage
and took away some of my fear. I felt how oppressive it is to get
stuck in diffuse feelings of guilt on the "other side." It became very
clear to me that it is precisely the diffuse quality of these feelings
which makes up much of the lifeless, gray, somehow life-denying
quality of our existence here in Germany. I also understood that this
posture needs victims. The guilty and the victims nourish each
other mutually. In our little circle the whole thing somehow
couldn't hang together anymore. As a man, who had been in a concentration camp as an adolescent, told about himself in an
undramatic and non-instructional way, I had to cry the whole time.
But these weren't the stories of victims. Suddenly a kind of understanding became possible, the fog of guilt feelings began to lift,
everything became more alive but also more insecure. We all felt
ourselves to be pioneers on new paths to this old pain-ridden
theme. The feelings in the room became more angry, more painful
and lively, more gay. We all had indeed to give up some encrusted
ways of thinking and that isn't so easy; but there was again a lot of
air to breathe, an image of German history which reached from East
Prussia to South America and back, and no longer the question
about Jews and non-Jews. . . . A good beginning, and it will go on.

Now I have acquired an additional living "Grandfather" and a
couple of very interesting "relatives," from whose life-affirming
stance I can learn much, despite all the suffering which they really
have experienced.

The other event, about which I'd like to write you, is many sided
and I can't really write correctly about it, since many pieces won't
come clear, even within my inner self. I have strong feelings,
thoughts not spoken nor fully conceptualized. The event is the
war that broke out in the Persian Gulf, or better, was made there.
The war is supposed to be over but its consequences are surely not.

We are offered every conceivable possibility about how one
should think about it. But I can't get rid of the feeling that most of
the official, and also nonofficial, ways of thinking serve more to
cover up something than really to clarify it. Perhaps the cause is that
this war unloosed an immense insecurity all over the world and
churned up to the surface masses of unresolved, buried conflicts
that haven't yet been worked through. I'd like to tell you only
about the part that touches "my" theme, the part through which I
have come to understand a lot. It's a matter of these guilt feelings,
and how feeling guilty doesn't change anything. Rather, as I see it,

guilt feelings are used more to avoid dealing with things or to avoid taking responsibility for them.

Shockingly enough, German firms delivered poison gas to the so-called aggressor, who then threatened to attack Israel with it. The connections were obvious between the gassing of Jews by Germans in the Third Reich and the use of German gas against the Jewish state of Israel. These facts disturbed me less than the reactions to them. These reactions made it frightfully clear to me how little the German past has been worked through. To you I can say it a little more angrily: the German nation fell apart in a mixture of diffuse guilt feelings, and those guilt feelings degenerated into utterly exaggerated, sugary avowals of solidarity whose false tones hurt my ears—then into payments of money, into weird splits ("Those were just bad people again, whose victims we ourselves became"), into impotent peace demonstrations or unfocussed overactivity, and much more.

One thing I have really understood: these guilt feelings, repressed or open, help people not to be shocked and above all to accept no responsibility for errors, for failure to act, or whatever. And it nourishes the victims who again feel themselves slighted, betrayed, and in some sense sold. . . . What would happen if we went beyond guilt feelings and existence as victims? Do you know what I think would happen, dear Grandfather—and these thoughts make me feel so much better about myself and my/our history: I believe they would all attend to their history, on both sides, including all that was so ugly; they would have to go through fear, rage, and sorrow, and they would then have to enter upon a new road to their own identity, regardless of whether they were German-Jewish, non-Jewish, "Aryan," or "non-Aryan," regardless of whether they were born in '23, '35, '42, '49, '55, or much later.

I believe that for the very first time I'm not limping along but have advanced a piece of the way. The trip was well worth it.

You accompanied me and indeed gave me a very beautiful answer, when you recently visited me in a dream and told me it was now time for you to grieve for your dead, your own family, whose members were killed here in Germany. When I then told you that I had already tried to do that for you, you answered me that you deeply honor my effort and find it a good thing, but that you yourself must also mourn. And so we stood at the window and wept together, and felt a deep connectedness. A burden slowly lifted, and outside it gradually grew lighter, bright, and serene.

I thank you.

Besos y abrazos, your Granddaughter

12

HOLOCAUST PERPETRATORS
AND THEIR CHILDREN
A Paradoxical Morality

Dan Bar-On

It is true that we often translate our
egoistic motivations into more
"acceptable" utilitarian ones. It may
be that the process of developing
moral maturity is simultaneous with
overcoming such self-deception.
Boyce and Jensen (1978, p. 218)

Did Holocaust perpetrators, the participants in a mass murder of
new dimensions, bury their secrets? Or did they deceive themselves
into thinking they did not have any? Did they feel they had acted
morally? Or did they have inner conflicts of morality later?

According to Freud (1930), individuals who had committed such
atrocities as those of the Holocaust could not remain psychologically
intact for long. Guilt feelings of great intensity might drive them
crazy or kill them. After 1945, when German society no longer considered the atrocities legitimate, one would expect to find evidence
of suicide attempts or psychological breakdown among the perpetrators (Blasi, 1983). Little evidence was found of suicide attempts
among perpetrators after the war and no reports about psychological breakdown (Charny, 1986), though suicides can also be
motivated by reasons other than moral (Mitscherlich and Mitscherlich, 1967).

We tried to find out whether some Holocaust perpetrators, during
the last years of their lives, showed signs of an ongoing moral conflict that could be associated with their roles in the Holocaust. It has
been assumed that for many years, perpetrators tried to protect
themselves socially and legally by burying any conflicts of morality,

Note: A version of this chapter first appeared in *Journal of Humanistic Psychology, 29*(4), (Fall 1989),
424–443, © 1989 Sage Publications, Inc.

if these ever existed. We assumed that toward the end of their lives, perpetrators would have the need, as well as more opportunities, to let possible conflicts of morality "leak out," to use Spence's term (1983), if not emerge full-fledged. At least some would, toward the ends of their lives, need to prove to themselves and to others that they had moral consciences (Sereny, 1974). We assumed that if conflicts about these needs existed, they could surface even 40 years after the extermination process had taken place. In time, with less danger of legal procedures, one's demands to suppress the conflict might have let up and one's needs to bring it to the surface might have increased. For those who died, committed suicide, or were executed, the conflicts of morality were neatly resolved. But in those who lived for years after the war, sometimes without even being tried or sentenced, did a conflict of morality exist, and did it ever surface?

We also tried to find out how the perpetrators' children, who were not responsible and had no atrocious memories of their own, handled the knowledge of their parents' atrocities. We assumed that perpetrators' children would have difficulty sorting out the discrepancies between their own conflicts of morality and the suppressed conflicts in their parents. How did the parent's role during the Holocaust affect the development of the child's independent "moral" self (Nisan, 1986)?

Method

We assumed that very little first-hand information would surface at this late stage by interviewing perpetrators directly. Therefore, we chose two indirect settings in which we might detect a leakage of guilt feelings or evidence of an ongoing inner conflict of morality:

1. *Confessional settings.* Could priests, physicians, psychiatrists, or psychotherapists report about perpetrators who had turned to them in times of stress (Harris, Benson, and Hall, 1975)? We expected perpetrators to prefer medical professionals to priests or psychologists, because many perpetrators left the church during the Nazi regime and going to a psychologist would imply some weakness that they had been trained to overcome all these years.

2. *The family setting.* Could a leakage be reported by a son or daughter? Children are biased participant-observers and need to back their parents' defenses (Montessori, 1987), but they may also have an urgent need to find in their parents signs of regret and guilt

(Sichrovsky, 1987). We assumed that those perpetrators' children who struggled with the conflicting demands to remain intact psychologically and morally should come to terms more easily with a father who showed signs of a moral conflict due to his horrible deeds rather than with a father who had adopted the manner of "business as usual" (Boyce and Jensen, 1978). Because perpetrators' children were in their forties or fifties, the timing of this study seemed optimal (Bar-On and Charny, 1988; Ekman and Lundberg, 1971).

According to this, two groups of subjects throughout Germany were chosen: (1) *potential confessors* (Protestant and Catholic priests, physicians, nurses, psychotherapists, and psychiatrists, in total 56 persons); and (2) *children of perpetrators* (48 persons).

We contacted each potential confessor by letter, phone, or personal interview. About half the contacts were made by colleagues in Germany and the other half by myself.

We said that as part of wider research carried out by the universities of Wuppertal and Beer-Sheva, we wished to know whether at any stage in their professional careers they had been approached by a perpetrator who wanted to confess or tell about an atrocity he or she had committed or witnessed, or an emotional burden the person bore later on that account. We asked them for a detailed story of a person who had tried to confess, or whether they knew of such an attempt but wished to remain silent, and if they did know, why they wished to remain silent. We also asked them whether they had heard of similar confessions or stories from their colleagues and could recall any. If no stories were recalled, we drew attention to the potential confessor's own possible need to forget such stories, because "we all feel very uncomfortable in such encounters." We then asked them to let us know if, at a later date, they recalled a story.

I asked the children to recall whether their parents had ever discussed wartime experiences at home and had shown any signs of regret, a wish for expiation, or other expressions of emotional tension or outbursts that could be associated with that tension. I explained further the objectives of our research and asked their opinions on the question, How could people do or witness such terrible things and either never be bothered by them or hide their inner moral conflict from others so well? I interviewed 14 children two to four times and asked that question again and again. I also asked them whether they could recall any war-related dreams or nightmares their parents had had and any dreams of their own. I speak fluent German, and this probably reduced the interviewees' discomfort.

Most interviewees spoke openly and, except for one, were willing to be re-interviewed.

The situation was not always easy for them or for me. I could not have carried out this extensive and emotionally difficult program without the support of close colleagues and my family.

Results

Findings from the confessional settings were remarkably poor. Only one of the 25 priests could recall a single confession of a perpetrator—a person who, before dying, confessed that a pair of eyes had followed him all his life. These were the eyes of a six-year-old Jewish child who had come out of a bunker after the Warsaw ghetto uprising and had run over to him with a frightened look, her arms held out to hug him. According to his report, the commander ordered him to stab her with his bayonet, an order he had reluctantly carried out. The eyes of that girl dominated his life from then on, and he could never talk about them to anybody before this reported confession.

Out of 29 psychotherapists, psychiatrists, nurses, and physicians, only two recalled indirect reports of perpetrators who had talked "from the heart" before their imminent deaths. A psychiatrist and a physician heard the same story from colleagues, who have not yet been traced. An Auschwitz physician confessed directly to me, when I interviewed him before seeing his son. The physician—R. Lifton wrote about him as Ernst B. (1986, pp. 303–336)—was acquitted at the Polish Auschwitz trial because he had refused to carry out selections and had shown "a humane attitude to the inmates." At Auschwitz he had decided to keep away from selections, but nonetheless he had continued "to work there." (His boss asked to be moved and the request was granted.) It seemed he had a somewhat moral approach, compared to other Nazi physicians at Auschwitz. Yet he surprised me (and Lifton) by saying that Mengele was "the only intelligent person you could talk with in Auschwitz." When I asked him how he had been able to live all these years with his memories from Auschwitz, he spontaneously came up with two stories that had been preoccupying him (Bar-On, 1989). One was about a camp inmate who he thought had been a former schoolmate. He recognized him one morning in a parade and never saw him again. Ever since then he felt guilty that he hadn't tried to rescue his schoolmate. The second story had to do with his gardening. When he looked for snails in his vegetable garden and squashed them, he could never touch the last one because it reminded him of the selections in Auschwitz.

Some children (11 of the 48) could report only indirectly about their perpetrator-fathers, as the men either died, were executed, or committed suicide around the end of the war. Other children (5) could give direct reports of stress or other psychological impairment in their perpetrator-fathers, such as excessive drinking and general unrest, but those were exceptions and could be attributed to economic, family, or other difficulties. No words whatsoever were used. Parents didn't discuss the extermination process in the presence of their children at home, and the children couldn't report any signs of their parents' inner moral conflict (Bar-On and Charny, 1988). There were no reports of dreams, nightmares, screams at night. Children dealt with the problem of a lack of knowledge by repeatedly using one sentence: "We had a very *normal* family life (father, mother)." That children called their parents "normal" may have reflected their own and their parents' wishful thinking: "If we behave like normal human beings, maybe we won't have to relate what happened to how it affected us" (Ekman and Lundberg, 1971). The physician's son used the "reduction to normality" argument again and again. He also tried to play down what happened in Auschwitz: "Similar events have happened before and ever since" and his father's involvement in it: "All I know is that he tried to behave properly and was acquitted accordingly." But when asked to explain how people like his father moved back and forth for years between their own families and the extermination site and behaved "normally," the son reacted emotionally for the first time: he had never thought about it before; perhaps that had made him try to distance himself from his parents' home as soon as he could; he had never tried to confront his father with those issues (Bar-On, 1989).

Maybe the children of perpetrators or witnesses did not grasp what their fathers had talked about. One encounter between a perpetrator's son and me started with the statement that the father had been a train driver in East Prussia during the war but "only drove ammunition transports." I was surprised, hearing his apologetic tone, and asked how he knew. The man, himself a railway engineer, said promptly, "My father told me so, long ago." Again I was surprised. There had been many transports of Jews at that time in that area, but I hadn't heard of the organization of separate ammunition drivers. The man agreed and said, "I will ask my father next time I see him and will let you know."

We met again socially a few days later, and he drove me to a meeting. As I got into his car, he said, "I talked to my father and he again confirmed that he only took care of ammunition transports. He did not know anything about the transport of Jews."

> "How interesting," I said. "But they must have drunk beer together and heard from each other about their transports."
>
> "No, only Party members drove those transports," replied the son.
>
> "Didn't they ever get sick and have to be replaced?"
>
> "Yes, actually. I have an uncle who died, and he told my father that he had heard from a friend that he saw some transports of Jews, but he was warned not to disclose it to anyone." When we were about to get out of the car, he added calmly, "And this time my father told me of another matter. He was on duty when they took a big group of prisoners of war and shot them on the platform in front of his eyes. It was close to the end of the war; they drove everyone out, but he was on duty and so he saw the whole event."

I felt as if I had been hit by a hammer.

> "How terrible. He never told you about it before? It must have been very difficult to keep that hidden all these years."
>
> "This was the first time he spoke to me about it. He never told anyone about it."

Only two children reported about parents who had broken down psychologically. One report was of an 80-year-old father, whose beloved 40-year-old daughter came to him recently and said she found out that he had killed a Jew during the *Reichskristallnacht*.* In reaction, the father broke down emotionally and had to be hospitalized in a psychiatric clinic. The second report was of another railway worker, deeply religious, who had worked with Jewish forced labor brigades repairing railroads in Poland in 1942. Sensing hidden, imminent danger, he and the Jews prayed together for their lives every night. One morning the SS came, surrounded the camp, and killed all the Jews in front of his eyes. Afterwards, he broke down physically and psychologically, was released from service, and was sent home. His son, an enthusiastic Hitler Youth* member, remembers that he didn't believe his father's story and accused him of betraying the fatherland. The father never fully recovered, but he

---

* See Glossary, here and wherever an asterisk appears. —Trans.

wrote a detailed letter about the event in May 1945, which the son brought with him to the interview (Bar-On, 1989).

Only two children reported that their fathers had told at home what they had "accomplished" during the war. These reports included stories of burning villages and killing Jews and partisans. We couldn't verify the fathers' involvement in the *Einsatzgruppen* or similar units. From what we could find out, they might have been minor servicemen on the front and boasted at home in order to sound important. Paradoxical as this may sound, these children might have preferred to have real perpetrators rather than nonkillers for fathers. A new kind of psychopathy evolved out of that incomprehensible era.

Discussion

Several theories attempt to explain the nature of the morality of perpetrators and their children:

1. *Perpetrators did not have moral selves in the first place. They were recruited to the extermination process on the basis of their pathological sadism and immorality* (Gilbert, 1963). If this theory was true, some perpetrators would probably have exposed their pathological, sadistic behavior after the war, too. There is little prima facie evidence to support this theory (Charny, 1982), and research findings show that normal human beings can be drawn into activities and situations harmful to others (Milgram, 1975; Zimbardo, 1973). Hannah Arendt (1977) coined a phrase for this phenomenon after the Eichmann trial: "the banality of evil."

2. *Perpetrators excluded the extermination process from any moral dialogue.* Nazi ideology proclaimed that the mentally sick were a burden on the German economy and that Jews, Gypsies, and other minorities were "bacteria in the pure German blood." *Untermenschen* (inferior human beings) did not have to be considered in any moral dialogue with one's self or others. One could have a kind of conscience and at the same time exterminate all who threatened to give that "conscience" a twinge, especially during a war.

Even if we followed such "totalitarian logic" (Herbst, 1976) and agreed that consciences were clear before the end of the war, would we expect perpetrators to extol Nazi ideology afterwards? In postwar Germany, those who still adhered were liable to become a marginal group, hardly fitting the description of being "very normal"—and those who no longer adhered might later develop an inner conflict over their former activities (Ekman and Lundberg, 1971).

3. *Perpetrators' moral selves were destroyed during the extermination process.* Perpetrators were not only brainwashed by Nazi ideology, but by step-by-step exposure to the atrocities, by participation in them, and by a sense that there was no way out (Lifton,1986; Segev, 1989), their moral selves were destroyed as well. So successfully was the "extermination self" trained (Lifton, 1986), that nothing was left of the moral self, no human feelings toward the exterminated (Hardtmann, 1989). We could interpret our findings as support for this theory: Because their moral selves were destroyed long ago, perpetrators had nothing to report to our confessors.

Active involvement in the extermination process also led to a psychological defensiveness, which has been variously called *numbing, splitting, doubling, disavowal, blocking out, oblivion,* and *the inability to mourn* (Charny, 1982; Hartmann, 1984; Lifton, 1986; Mitscherlich and Mitscherlich, 1967). None of these terms sufficiently clarifies what actually happened *after* the war. If their moral selves were destroyed, how could perpetrators have functioned as "normal" human beings, raised their children, worked and participated in society? Just by maintaining the split? By always successfully denying or employing some other defense mechanism?

4. *The social context theory.* The social context during and after the war enabled perpetrators, as well as most other Germans, to distance themselves from taking direct responsibility and feeling shame and guilt (Hardtmann, 1989). This distancing developed out of a pseudo-morality, along with the punitive legal procedures and the financial reparations to victims. The personal suffering caused by the war, together with the passing of time and the evil perpetrated by Holocaust survivors on others (in Israel), "balance" the harm done the belief in this "just world" phenomenon (Lerner, 1970).

We could interpret our findings as evidence that perpetrators might have had a moral self deep down, but because the social context helped erect a massive wall between it and an "acceptable," utilitarian self, we did not find perpetrators who confessed publicly.

This theory is not refined enough to differentiate between individual perpetrators of the extermination process and certain bystanders and segments of German society who tried to resist the regime in different ways.

We would like to propose a fifth theory: *Some perpetrators had an ongoing inner conflict between their moral selves (superegos) and their existential selves (egos)* (Nisan, 1986). Acknowledging moral responsibility for all of one's former atrocious activities threatened a perpetrator's psychological integrity. Totally repressing all the atrocious memories could be evidence of not being moral at all. Therefore, only a *para-doxical morality* could resolve this conflict. By remembering a single vignette of an atrocious activity—and feeling guilty about it all those years—a self-perception (or deception) of morality could be maintained.

Only two confessors gave indirect reports that suggest this kind of paradoxical morality among perpetrators. The priest's story of the soldier and the eyes of the six-year-old Jewish girl suggests that already during the war the perpetrator had erected a psychological wall between his morality and his daily activities. The girl's eyes bored through the soldier's defenses already then, something other victims killed by that soldier had not done. Had his moral self been destroyed, he could not have recalled the eyes or made his confession. Yet had he confronted the whole scale of atrocities in which he had been involved, his psychological integrity might have been at stake. The girl's eyes alone had caused disquiet in his soul, enough to make him feel suffering and the need for expiation. The inner moral dialogue with those eyes helped suppress the other atrocious memories and convinced him of having been humane after all (Wisenthal, 1976).

The Auschwitz physician's story matches Sereny's account of Stangel seeing trainloads of cows on their way to the slaughterhouse (1974). Our physician did not, and probably could not, feel empathy for the millions of people he saw being exterminated. Such empathy might have endangered his psychological integrity, already thin. The physician's schoolmate, Otto, and the last snail in his garden, however, did trouble him. Had the physician not been able to relate to those two vignettes, he would have had no evidence of his reflective, moral self. He would have had to start to question his own morality and humanity, particularly during all those years after 1948, the year he was acquitted, from which point his life was no longer in any legal danger.

Observe what is being acknowledged in these few accounts: They are personal and say something about the perpetrators' feelings, yet they also acknowledge the humanity and emotionality of the victims. The cows and the last snail also represent the depersonalizing of people and the dehumanization of morality. The accounts give us a clue to the emotional and moral turmoil these persons have been living through.

Himmler himself may have been aware of how a paradoxical morality works. In his famous Posen address in 1943, he said:

The danger was very close: the path between two possible alternatives—to become tough and heartless, indifferent to the values
of human life, or to become soft and to deteriorate to a nervous
breakdown, this path between Scylla and Charybdis—is terribly
narrow . . . [we bear] the responsibility for a deed not an idea, and
will therefore take the secret with us into our graves. [Himmler,
1974 (1943), p. 169]

According to Himmler, there was no contradiction among the
perpetrators' atrocious behavior, morality, and love of their families,
even of some victims. The middle road that Himmler proposed,
maliciously but cleverly, would help the perpetrators maintain their
so-called integrity. We suggest they could maintain that "integrity"
during the postwar years only with the help of a paradoxical
morality.

Why, then, did we elicit only two accounts that support this kind
of morality? One could conclude with earlier theoreticians that the
potential confessors were open to listening, but there was nothing
to listen to. One could also conclude that they were reluctant to find
out about the perpetrators' paradoxical morality.

We know, from the therapeutic experience of Holocaust victims
and their children, that therapists were often part of their clients'
denial process and the accompanying emotional disturbances
(Danieli, 1980). There is evidence of a similar phenomenon in
Germany. We call this the "double-wall phenomenon" (Bar-On and
Charny, 1988). One wall was erected by the perpetrator, who was suppressing a conflict between survival and moral demands; another
was erected by the professionals in order to avoid being flooded
with emotions that they either could not handle themselves or
believed were impossible to work through.

We may have evidence of only one instance of a working-through
of this double-wall phenomenon. The report of the Jewish girl's eyes
came from a priest who was himself the child of a prominent perpetrator. Having worked through his own conflict of morality
concerning the atrocities committed by his father, and helped by his
new religious conviction, he was more open than other confessors
to accepting a suppressed conflict of morality in a perpetrator.

Maybe the professional confessors erected a wall because they
were afraid of not fulfilling their professional responsibility: A perpetrator who confessed would threaten the confessor who, in turn,
couldn't promise a positive solution. The confessors might have
been afraid of not being able to control the situation. *They might also
have been afraid that they were not so psychologically distant from the*

Holocaust victimizers. Maybe a paradoxical morality is simply a device used by many human beings, not only perpetrators.

An interesting illustration of the double-wall phenomenon is Nechama Tec's account (1986) of Polish rescuers of Jews during World War II. Tec couldn't pinpoint a specific education, socio-economic status, religious or political affiliation, and so forth to account for the humanistic act of rescuing. She found only psychosocial indicators: separateness, independence, previous moral commitment to helping needy family members. The rescuers mentioned these characteristics matter-of-factly and understated the risks they had taken, with almost no signs of a conflict. The rescuers played down their deeds in order to appear "normal," just as the perpetrators had tried to be "normal" family men. Could murderers *and* heroes in the extermination process have erected double walls, which helped create a reduction to normality in postwar European society? Could it be that society, too, didn't want to acknowledge its murderers as well as its heroes?

Obviously, children could not learn from their parents' silence and a reduction to normality at home whether a perpetrator-parent suffered pangs of conscience but had "succeeded" in suppressing a conflict concerning them. Nor could they know whether or not the parent's silence had been a strategy for distancing themselves and their children from the Holocaust, free of any feelings of shame or guilt. The parents' silence could be interpreted by the children in the following ways: Either the parents' moral selves had not functioned during the extermination process or later, or the parents had wished to protect the children from events experienced, about which they still felt ashamed or guilty (Boyce and Jensen, 1978). Perpetrators' children had few opportunities to discover which of these motives was valid, because they themselves tended to avoid open discussion with their parents. Coming to terms with a perpetrator-parent's past requires a certain strength and maturity. To look for signs of morality suppressed in one's father in the first place would require the child to confront conflicting aspects of the child's image of the father and the possibility that the beloved father, who raised the child, had killed other children at the same time (Haan, 1978; Kogan, 1982).

The group of fathers who committed suicide (6) are of interest to our discussion. One could, of course, attribute perpetrators' suicides to an acquiescence to moral demands, as two children proposed to us, but one shouldn't accept that interpretation at face value. Under the abnormal conditions of the Holocaust and the Nazi defeat, perpetrators could have committed suicide without any pangs of conscience and out of an inability to accept changing reality or out of loyalty to the Führer.

During the students' revolt in the sixties, some children approached their parents and accused them "for what they did, or did not do, during the war." But the children rarely tried to understand or listen in return and erected an even higher "wall" rather than cutting a "window" in it.

Three children reported that they had made more mature efforts to understand what their parents had actually experienced during the war, but they were turned away by the aged parents, who probably did not believe that their children could now make sense of and handle what was in their minds and souls. Possibly, they themselves couldn't.

After his soul-searching, the train driver in East Prussia wanted to communicate and to cut a window in his wall to try to make his child understand. The son, however, did not absorb any of the emotional and moral meanings in the information his father had disclosed and which he reported to me. During my entire evening with the son, I saw no sign that his father's story had affected him in any way. When I interviewed the man one year later, the memory was gone! He did not remember his father telling him about the incident or his telling me.

I learned something about the double wall between children and their perpetrator-parents from this coincidental exchange. Due to the son's conversation with me, it is possible that he asked his father questions that encouraged the father to take some of the load off his chest. It was the son, however, who could not absorb the meaning, possibly because his identification with his father was being threatened. How can we find out more about the paradoxical morality of a parent when a son perpetuates the father's silence, as well as his own paradoxical morality?

The story of the father whose daughter came to tell him she had found out about his past suggests that there was a wall penetrated by the daughter's belated acknowledgment of her father's atrocious activity 45 years earlier. The father, confronted by this sudden, moral acknowledgment, broke down emotionally.

The story of the religious railway worker is the only account of a witness-father who did not succeed in erecting a wall. The son was the one who had erected a wall that was, in turn, penetrated by a belated acknowledgment of the father's report.

In most cases, neither perpetrators nor their children showed strong emotional reactions to past events. The few exceptions suggest that the perpetrators' paradoxical morality influenced the development of a similar morality in their children. We found that the perpetrator-parents could not help their children develop healthy moral selves. Even if some perpetrators or their relatives had had the urge to disclose their conflicts to the children, the children might have blocked out such an urge. Were the children more "successful" than their parents at suppressing conflicts of morality? Did they have an opportunity to disclose to anyone their own inner conflicts or the conflicts regarding their perpetrator-parents? Because most children reported that the topic was also silenced in school, one wonders how they succeeded in working through the issue, if at all (Bar-On and Charny, 1988).

Conclusions

Our empirical evidence about the paradoxical conflict of morality in Holocaust perpetrators and their children is inconclusive. We learned about a few instances of ongoing, suppressed moral conflicts, which leaked out at different stages after the extermination process, but we still know little about the moral selves of most perpetrators and their children. The general silence indicates the possibility of the total destruction of moral functioning among most perpetrators.

The theory that some perpetrators had a suppressed inner conflict between their moral and existential selves sheds new and alarming light on our power to prevent or commit future genocide. Potential annihilators can feel quite safe 40 years after the Holocaust, because people can easily be drawn into an extermination process and then behave like normal human beings for the rest of their lives without even asking, Has an extermination taken place at all? What does my behavior say about my morality? Nor will their own or other children ask.

Our theory suggests also that *we cannot make a simple, clear-cut distinction between Holocaust perpetrators and the rest of society.* Each of us, daily, tries to feel moral and, at the same time, to block out excessive moral demands in favor of utilitarian or hedonistic ones (Nisan, 1986). By extensively suppressing our moral demands, we might not be able to resist being drawn into perpetrating activities, even when we do not identify with the motives that initiated them. We might not be able to prevent other genocides. Only if we acknowledge this problem can we establish criteria for identifying moral issues and expand our discussion of them: When is mercy killing merciful and when is it part of an extermination process? When is killing an act of self-defense, and therefore justifiable, and when is it the beginning of genocide?

We also need to develop a comprehensive theory of personality that will help us differentiate between perpetrators who were amoral in the first place, those whose moral selves "died" during the war, and those who lived with suppressed moral conflicts to the last day of their lives. In the absence of such criteria and such a theory, 40 years after the Holocaust, we can expect a pervasive pseudo-moralism, and more and more forgetting of what happened, as we move into the future without a real desire to learn from the past.

13

"GUILTY!"
THOUGHTS IN RELATION TO
MY OWN PAST
Letters to My Son

Gunnar von Schlippe

Preface

Suddenly the question is put to me: "Who were you in the Nazi time?" My son asks me—father, pastor, psychotherapist—and he asks as someone who meanwhile has become a psychotherapist himself.

Together in September of 1987 we had visited scenes from my past, both battlefields and prison camps. There, in Poland, we met the people who had saved my life, after having already suffered horribly themselves through the Nazi period. The encounter reopened the past—my own and that of our whole people. Guilt and shame, both things were there—but also something else, something new: I call it "presence."

Here, in letters to my son, I have partly reconstructed, partly continued our exchange from that time. This is my attempt to pursue his question to me. In the process, without realizing it, I myself gradually became the client, the one who wanted to break through some impasse, as unclear within me as a bygone dream. My son's question reached me at a particular place where we stood in Poland, before the remains of the very trenches I had helped to dig; his question touched me just as the man who saved my life was pointing out the spot where my comrades had been buried, and there again in Poznan, where it was my job to post the latest army bulletins in the news window in the market.

But this question goes still deeper and further back into the past,

209

into an experience of this time, so difficult to imagine now, whose shadows my son saw in me. He held me responsible for these shadows—or did it only seem that way to me? I had been involved, and even the dead had had something to do with me, as did many a one still living.

Who were you then? I heard this as the question of the extent of my own guilt, and I tried not to run away from it. I did not want to fail to meet guilt once more, just when it concerns me. I wanted to answer the question, "How could it happen?" In an excellent recent book, Stresemann's *How Could It Happen?* (1987), the question of guilt is taken up in a very objective and factual way. I wanted to consider it more in the light of my own personal experience.

Thus the following letters are a process of reflection that led me from thinking to feeling and from feeling to thinking again—no longer a thinking "about" something, but rather a kind of reflection within a field of experience.

First Letter

In the attempt to go further with the thoughts that you stimulated, I have gone down a strange path. I am seeking my own share of responsibility, and with it my guilt, and I have the fear that I might not find it, that I might miss it. It seems to me that you were right to ask me why I have never even touched on the subject of guilt. It may be that the experience of guilt is also an opportunity for an encounter with the self, and that this opportunity can be missed. It may even be that guilt is not an avoidable evil, but rather something that is a part of me, that may belong to me, that I can look at and must answer to, and bear.

Something bristles within me at these thoughts. I ask myself, Why do people protest so loudly when they are blamed? I recognize that in myself as well: I refuse to be blamed, and I know too how well I defend myself against reproach. Then I can always explain, justify, demonstrate precisely how I was not guilty at all, since things could not have been any different anyway. Thus I always experience myself as a person who is continually being "excused." "Excuse yourself"; I can hear myself saying that, to you, for example, when you had done something, or were guilty of something, or had hurt someone, or had neglected or forgotten to do something. The phrase is a familiar one from my childhood as well. Home, school, profession—

all have used it, to the point where I no longer believed myself capable of being guilty.

Behind this lies the ideal of a guilt-free world. That's how it should be. The ideal is for no one to be in anyone else's debt for anything. Thus the constant ritual of excuse and explanation. We were all of us excusable, after all, with the exception of the actual perpetrators. We, the Nazi generation, were only . . . victims, misled, ignorant, some perhaps blind dreamers, fellow travelers. And besides, things could not have been any different. Only in extreme cases can guilt be discerned; thus the continued effectiveness of the pseudo-Christian formula: "You must excuse yourself, since the explanation and the situation were what they were, and that's all there is to it." The sequence is automatic: after the accusation comes the excuse. In a society where guilt is not allowed to exist, the actual admission of guilt is life-threatening, insurmountable, and means ostracism, death. Anyone overcome by guilt so suddenly that he can find no excuse, no way out, is driven to desperate measures. To avoid this, we devise ever more refined excuses, and protest mightily when we are accused and the excuses fail to work. For even if we hope for mercy, this generally comes only after a ritual self-abasement. He who was guilty and received mercy is no longer entitled to speak up or to have a point of view: "Just hold your tongue! It's true you got out of it one more time, but just watch it. . . ."

I received my certificate of denazification* right away, immediately after my return from prison camp in Russia. After all, I was only 18 years old—what could I have done differently? I was not even in the Party. (My application had somehow gone astray; and yet I had submitted it all right, in the belief that it was the right thing to do since after all my older brother and even my beloved pastor, Prior T., were both members—naturally "just in order to avoid something even worse.")

As I write this, I note once more the underlying language of excuse: "Because," or "in order to." "I" didn't do anything; "because" did it. Because my brother, because my pastor, because "things" were that way. The "I" is renounced in favor of the excusing "because." It is replaced! Where "I" was, "because" shall be. And this is where the avoidance of guilt becomes so problematic. My "I" is replaced by something foreign, a "because," to which the "I" can now become subordinate. And there it is, our savior from guilt: Circumstances. ("We'd be so good, and not so low, but Circumstance won't have it

---

* See Glossary, here and wherever an asterisk appears. —Trans.

so"[1]) and brothers, pastors, conditions, destiny, parents ("That's just how I was raised"). Therefore it is not guilt itself, but rather the *excuse,* that annihilates the "I," annihilates me.

Certainly this formulation overstates the case. Real experience is generally different: I do seem to survive, along with my capacity for excusing myself; indeed, I am threatened when that does not work. I mean it on another level: insofar as my excuses serve to block or evade my own experience of guilt, then to that extent I also lose myself, by letting something other than my "I" stand in for me. With regard to your question to me, that means: all right, I too belonged to those who participated halfheartedly. I kept silent where one was supposed to keep silent, when it really was a matter of life and death; and the pride I took in my own objections and criticisms (which at times brought me close to arrest, cost me my leave, blocked my promotion) really does not count for much. I was obstinate without being really critical, uncooperative without actually putting sand in the machine of inhumanity.

For the older generation it was important to come back again and again to the liturgical mea culpa. I believe that if these words were really more than just a formula, they were in a better position to deal with guilt than we are, for whom the mea culpa are just words. My own guilt—and I do not mean the collective guilt but the guilt I experienced quite personally—was certainly more than the collective shame that crept over us when we began to learn about what had really happened, and more and more horrors kept coming out.

But then what use to us was the mea culpa? Was it a summons to chronic depression? What atonement could there be? I could not even feel my own serious wounds as a purifying punishment. But even under those conditions, I did perform "penitential exercises." Back then, in the face of probable death, I thought of my stern sergeant; in my mind I defended myself to him as to a court-martial, and said to myself: "I was forced to do what I did; I did not act irresponsibly when I stuck my head out of the foxhole." His judgment was so deep in my "I" that it forced me to search for a "because," an excuse, even at a time like that.

Sometimes I think that even our images of the Last Judgment could be a projection of this kind, because it is there that we expect to be presented with the cumulative accounts of our lives, which have not yet been added up. But excuses will be irrelevant then. How

---

1. A line from Brecht's ironical "Song of Circumstance" ("Über die Unsicherheit Menschlicher Verhältnisse"), in Brecht and Weill's *Threepenny Opera.* —Trans.

will we withstand this if we have learned only how to defend and excuse ourselves, when that no longer works—or better said, is no longer necessary? Indeed, according to biblical testimony, excuses are superfluous because God's way is totally different: He seeks not my "becauses"; He seeks me. But this would mean that Christian faith is something more like the possibility of turning to oneself (as Jochen Klepper once expressed it), of *metanoia*, leaving behind the alienating reaches of self-justification, of "because" and the like. This would be the experience of allowing myself to be engaged, of accepting guilt, of answering "Here!" when guilt calls my name. By this I am thinking not so much of punishment or expiation (that is, a legalistic response), but rather something more like a real encounter with the source of the guilt. Encounter is something different from balancing the books, liquidating the debt, forgiving, settling accounts, "quick, get rid of it." There has to be something else, when it comes to guilt, besides acquittal or erasure, through excuses or pointing the finger in another direction.

Quick forgiveness prevents the encounter with guilt, and hence actually achieves nothing—any more than do over-psychologized, tranquilizing formulas like "Everything is okay," which I hear not just from gurus but from many a psychologist as well. To make my actions and my being irrelevant by saying that everything is acceptable or okay is a pseudo-remedy. I lose my bearings. To be sure, understanding and acceptance are offered, which I see as good and important; but at the same time, this amorphous position becomes a hiding place from the encounter with guilt. Once again we slip away from it, without ever looking it in the face. The relief that I feel obscures the fact that I have lost touch with an important part of my being.

But then how do I arrive at this encounter with guilt, this acceptance, this "coming to myself," this repentance? (By repentance I understand not just contrition, but rather a place where I become visible to myself; for me it contains a dynamic, even a creative element, more felt than thought out.) Repentance, the encounter with guilt, is then possible only if I can leave fear behind. As long as I am controlled by fear, the encounter will not take place. However, one cannot get beyond the fear by simply redefining the guilt as something without consequences—which is to say, by guaranteeing that it will come without punishment. To get beyond the fear must mean something like a new paradigm for self-recognition, in which I can discover that the encounter with myself in my guilt is more important than the advantages of denial. The previous paradigm, the preexisting "excuse mentality," which forces us to present our lives as guilt-free, can never form the basis for a new experience of relationship to guilt. Indeed, it must react with fear whenever such a new relationship threatens to emerge—which is not to say it cannot also express itself in a sort of *salto mortale* into pathological forms of self-blame, self-accusations, and self-reproaches, themselves a form of escape which serves to prevent any new acceptance of guilt. And then it often happens, in my experience, that someone else feels obliged to take over the excusing function. In therapeutic relationships it may even be experienced as offensive if the therapist fails to take up the expected rituals of excusing, pacifying, and explaining until everything is all right again.

Repentance, encounter with guilt, are a kind of breakthrough beyond this old pattern. I can accept and love myself as guilty, since I am not required to separate myself from my guilt. It belongs to me. I think I can also find a biblical basis for this. Not so much in Paul, whose way of defining the relationship to God does not always seem helpful to me for an encounter with the experience of guilt. Since guilt is held to be total, automatically inherent, it can no longer be experienced as something to be discovered—or at most only in extreme cases. This excess of hopelessness in the face of guilt can reduce the whole question to empty platitudes: "We are all sinners." That can lead to an avoidance of guilt just as much as other forms of repression. Encounter can only take place on the concrete level.

Here it occurs to me once again how difficult it is, in looking back on the Nazi past, to break through from the generalized "We were all at fault," to the concrete "mea culpa." The dull, shadowy sensation of guilt in the face of that time does not become differentiated for me until I think of a particular situation—for example, hand-to-hand combat (of which more later), or other specific instances where I kept silent instead of speaking out. Indeed, a part of the excuse ritual is this dissolving of the specific into generalities.

In stories about Jesus, the encounter with guilt becomes more clearly accessible for me. The adulteress encounters her guilt in the very fact that she is not punished but rather is given the possibility of seeing herself anew, as guilty without judgment. Peter, after his own encounter with guilt, is given the exhortation, "Tend my sheep!" Guilt is no longer seen as alienating, but rather is treated as an experience which can reveal new possibilities (as for example in the parable of the prodigal son). This kind of forgiveness is not something that comes down from on high, but rather something that takes an individual's experience of guilt and makes it into an occasion for changing the relationship of that individual to everyone concerned. "Mea culpa" is no longer a depressive chant of self-recrimination, but a concrete offer of relationship to oneself, to other human beings, to one's community, to nature, to God, and it extends to everyone concerned. The story of Jesus tells us that God is also involved when we encounter our guilt. For this reason I believe that our nation too can change, if we the older generation face our own guilt. Then the new generation need no longer deny its own, and can be open to change.

Second Letter

You ask me why I write *about* the problem of guilt, but not how I myself have experienced it. My reflections strike you as abstract, theoretical; I remain too much the thinker who philosophizes about guilt, without ever reaching the feeling. As I reread my letter, I find this partly true. I notice that something in me has become confused. For one thing, I feel responsible for what was; for another, I feel responsible for what has happened and continues to happen. But I do not yet know within myself why it is that I feel this way.

I experience this not so much as something that weighs on me, but more as something that is part of me. It is as though I had awakened from some dark dream, where I was persuaded that I was just an onlooker in life, only to find on awakening that I myself had taken part. I feel ashamed not to have discovered this sooner.

When I speak of shame, I mean the disappointment of discovering that I and others have behaved in a way not true to ourselves. I have failed to live up to certain rules, which were given me along with my humanity, and which I knew. I feel shame, moreover, not only for myself but for others as well—for my people, my generation. Something in me is ashamed that despite my family, despite my Christian education, I could behave like a puppet on a string, standing at attention, lying down on command (at least most of the time). Something in me is ashamed that I submitted to common thugs ("boors," as we called these Nazi bullies in our family).

It is painful to hear myself saying "Jawohl," and I feel pain and shame to find that I believed not in my own nature, but in the slogans of those in power; a part of me really believed in them. In order to support that belief, I even doubted myself, since I did not correspond to the ideal of "German youth." I experience it as an embarrassment—and not as guilt—that I betrayed myself and lost my dignity in moments of danger. I have this feeling with regard to others as well, to whom I felt connected. I felt ashamed of my countrymen, not just because they were capable of all the horrors in the Nazi period that we learned of later, but also for their shameless fawning to the occupation powers, their snatching up of cigarette butts in front of foreign soldiers, their bowing and scraping and selling of themselves for small advantages. I felt shame for the Christians and found it embarrassing, the way they eyed the CARE packages. When I was given a necktie from some American donation and was told I must write a thank-you letter to the donor, at first I refused, because it seemed so stupid. Then, however, I was informed I would have no share in future donations—and I gave in! And felt ashamed. I felt ashamed, but it was not a feeling of guilt.

The feeling of guilt itself actually remained quite faint in me, because I had such difficulty in conceiving it concretely, nor am I so conscientious as to feel guilty all that easily. Even when I challenge the phrase "I knew nothing about it"—after all, one did hear or see something, which one would not or could not integrate—still I do not get to that feeling of guilt. Back then as well I found no access to feelings of guilt—at least in this regard—but rather to feelings of shame. And yet there was something there which pointed to a deeper moral disturbance. I know that feeling, so difficult to shake off, which requires one to stay at the superficial level. One tries to get rid of it, or attach it to some harmless side issue. Luther spoke of the "baby sins," which were within the bounds of admissibility and seemed quite trivial to others (while giving a good impression of a strict conscience), but actually were the expression of a deeper guilt which one would not or could not face.

Only gradually did I realize that my strong political activism, beginning right after my return from captivity, had something to do with all this. I had found something like my own kind of "reparations." But then I must in some way have felt guilty. I was there from the beginning when Gustav Heinemann* founded the Emergency Committee for Peace, and I followed him in founding the German People's Party. I helped organize the first Easter Marches and came to a confrontation with my church and the Baltic Citizens' Union when I joined the German Peace party (DFU) under Renate Riemeck.* And yet all these activities did not suffice to unmask underlying feelings of guilt. I could sense it only indirectly, by way of my need to make reparations. When I began to learn later on, in psychoanalysis, that my career choice of theology was related to these feelings as well (even if other motivations developed in the course of practice), I saw that I had not even been aware of how deeply the whole experience had affected me. Of course, I then had the "advantage" of being able to find a concrete basis in my own memories of the horrors of war: hand-to-hand combat, captivity, the countless comrades I saw dying. But I knew myself that it was not the actual experiences that were at issue (not even having to kill in close combat), but rather a much more ineffable sense of guilt. I recalled the voice of a fellow soldier, who lay dying beside me, saying, "Comrade, I am in the throes of death," and how I was more taken by the odd phrase than with the man himself, and so failed him as a human being. I recalled a moment in battle when I experienced something like battle lust or combat fever. Those were the moments where guilt became tangible to me. I suspect that it is not the bad deed in itself that gives rise to a feeling of guilt, but rather that there is something that lies behind the behavior that makes any reparation impossible. That seems to require some other answer, which we alone cannot give ourselves. Here I was helped by Luther's words: "For where there is forgiveness of sin, there is life and joy."

But that came later. First, after my return, I sought something like a strong inner experience, an experience of depth. I found the Anthroposophists. It was a fascinating lesson for me (and from it I understand the many young people who succumb to the various promises of esoteric religions); nevertheless, something stirring deep within me was not touched. It was all sublimely above the level of that which was plaguing me so mysteriously. I tried to reach those lofty levels, but something about it all never rang true for me. I even gave the Catholics a try, but I was never at home with their way of dealing with guilt through ritual. Luther was a key to my question, but the doors which he opened led to paths where he could only partly accompany me. There was still a great deal of useless mental furniture in the way, and a great housecleaning was needed, in a historical moment in which not only I was caught up, and where I floundered—in the words of Kurt Scharf*—"between impotence and omnipotence." All this offered little of the peace promised as the result of resolving guilt. I do not mean the quiet that comes from being finished with it; perhaps something more like the stone which has broken a hole in the meaningless silence, through which feelings can come streaming out. These feelings will then not hurt us, but will perhaps regain a language based intimately on love.

It disturbs me that we still have not found this language, after so long a time. All too quickly we find guilty parties who can be held responsible, sometimes in the place of others. Behind this lies a compulsory ethic, which sings the journalist's well-crafted ritual song of accusation (naturally from a position of unassailability). Here, too, guilt is sought darkly, without hope; the world is divided into guilty and innocent. It is the search of the righteous with the beam in their eye for the mote in the eye of others. But acceptance, in my experience, depends on a common ground. Only this makes a reconciliation with the past possible. Whoever denies the common ground, by standing among the righteous, cannot participate in coming to grips with guilt and cannot be open to understanding. The righteousness remains there as a wall, which many do not recognize as their own.

Three weeks ago, as we visited the scenes of long ago in Poland, found the old trenches, the old pick with which I hacked at the frozen ground, and as we faced the ruins of the past—our own wounds and scars and those of others—there was no more talk of guilt between the Poles and us. We stood on common ground. What had happened? To me it does not seem as though I had "mastered" anything, but rather that something happened to us, as we let the past into our being together in the present. We laughed and cried together, were fully present together, yet were only there at all because of the past. It was the Poles themselves who allowed us to be fully present there. You experienced it the same way, as if you had lived through both past and present along with us. The fitting answer to guilt seems to me to be that we take it into the present, with love and laughter and tears, and not shut it out. That is like a gift. There is no more need for excuses, because guilt itself no longer separates us.

It was something like the way I read the story of Zacchaeus (Luke 19). Here the guilt is neither imposed nor revealed, but rather unloaded, in a liberating way, into and through the present encounter. In the whole story there is no tortured feeling of penitent confession, because there is no judgment here, only encounter. The guilt is there, but how is it really experienced by Zacchaeus? As forgiven? I do not really know if I can characterize it that way; it is rather experienced as "transformed," as a chance of approaching life afresh. Zacchaeus himself thinks in terms of reparation; and yet to me that does not seem the central thing. Something had already been changed within him, something that had previously made it impossible for him to be the man that he could be, once he included his own guilt. Inasmuch as Jesus accepted him, he too was able to accept himself, as sinning and guilty. This is like an acceptance of his human right to guilt and error.

Since error and guilt have been forbidden to us by the threat of punishment, both have become covert, bottled up, and thus deadly. In today's complex systems that much seems obvious to me. If we had learned early on that to err is human, and to become guilty a human right, then maybe we might have done penance more easily. Perhaps what is required is the encounter with people so accepting that they also embrace us in our error and our guilt.

My own faith—surely not guided by Nazi propaganda alone— that Hitler could not err, that *he* at least could not be guilty, made me blind to the critical consciousness that is given us as humans, as a constant corrective to our error and our guilt. This superstition is paralyzing and gives rise to myths both political and religious. I see that today as well, when I encounter the expectation from members of the congregation that I can rule on right and wrong. And likewise in therapy: the competent advice of an expert! I note the embarrassing credulousness toward fascinating "enlightened beings" or other charismatics, with their supposedly guilt-free and infallible authority—which is to say inhumanity (which they call "super-humanness"). They beam forth the radiance of superior beings.

The human right to error and guilt might help us not only to deal more carefully and critically with the myths and idols that are offered to us, but perhaps to become more loving as well. We might then be more loving toward those who are "caught in the act," thereby enabling them to accept themselves, to do penance, and not to think they have to take refuge in ever more elaborate rationalizations.

I wish to be allowed to make mistakes and to be "of good cheer" in my guilt (as Luther once put it), yet not to let either error or guilt take root to the point of destroying me. Unconfessed error and unaccepted guilt will have further effects: political, moral, religious, indeed even somatic. That seems demonstrable to me. The problem remains, naturally, of whether I can afford that admission. The encounter with accepting human beings is rare; the fear of consequences is well-founded (could I have written all this 45 years ago?). Under fascism it was hardly possible for its dependents—and not just those of a young age—to have the liberty of discovering guilt and error in themselves and others, without thereby being destroyed. Perhaps at that time we did not even realize this in the first place. Only a few of those encounters in which and through which I am able to realize my guilt will be healing; others will leave only ruin in their wake, since only a few people succeed in breaking through to their own humanity.

Third Letter

To me it seems that your question about the meaning of
Auschwitz and the whole breakdown of civilization in the Third
Reich lies on a different level from my attempt in my previous letters
to grasp guilt—personally, psychologically, theologically; but it does
throw into relief the weaknesses and limitation of my approach. I
note how I abandon the sure ground of my own thinking, feeling,
and experience in the face of your question. I understand how to cat-
egorize my own experiences and their analogues in the experiences
of others, how to analyze psychological processes, how to point out
pathological structures; your question, however—or at least an
important aspect of the question—goes beyond all that. This break
in civilization, with its rational-technological calculus of inhumanity, seems to me to be another paradigm of experience entirely,
for which I can find few analogies in my own experience. If I
nonetheless do try, it is because I would like to understand to what
extent I myself am involved—rather than taking the position of the
"detached judge," which I find inappropriate to the whole theme of
guilt.

In my "bag of analogies" I find two experiences which I will
use—fearfully—to approach the subject. One experience familiar to
me is the "wish for purification," the desire to get rid of everything
evil, disturbing, restrictive of life. The less I can come to terms with
something within myself, the more I try to solve it on the outside.
I detected this wish in myself early on, with regard to my difficult
situation in our so-harmonious family. The real problem first became
clear to me after I saw Giraudoux's *The Madwoman of Chaillot*. I
sensed that his solution (the bad were lured with gold into the sewers
and then locked up there, while the good marched forth brandishing
gladiolas) also contained this kind of basic eschatological yearning
for a final purification from all evil. At the same time, however, this
seemed inhuman to me. Salvation was only possible here through
the destruction of evil (compare the advice of the servants in Jesus'
parable about plucking out the weeds in Matthew 13:25). But what
is "evil?" How convenient to decide according to the view of the
moment (Jews, Christians, Communists, etc.), and thereby set in
motion a mythologically based purification mania. Is Auschwitz the
result of just such a purification mania, attached in this case to
specific racial concepts, which identified the bad, the ones guilty of
all the evil, as those who came from a particular "inferior race," or
those who were "degenerates"?

That homosexuals and the insane became caught up in the machinery of extermination—does that not follow from the mythic image, of "natural, healthy, pure human beings"? The attempt to locate evil as something clearly exterior to ourselves became inhuman. Auschwitz, and all that the name stands for, is the result of a grandiose, mythic-eschatological, and projective purification wish, or so it seems to me. But then how could it take on such dimensions?

As for the second experience, this concerns a familiar concept in psychology (though certainly without reaching the fateful dimensions of the case of Auschwitz itself): feelings of inferiority, caused by or associated with blocked aggression, will lead to depression. In a word, this describes the condition of our people after the First World War. The attempt to solve unaddressed internal problems by means of outward aggression, power, and victory celebrations had failed. The aggression brought not victory, but disaster. Weakness, internal chaos, partisan quarrels, and the inability to come to terms with the new reality—along with the unemployment—strengthened the wish for "salvation" from the depressive paralysis. The depression sought release in the repetition compulsion to the rhythm of the old three-beat measure: inferiority (feelings of impotence), aggression (without success), depression (and back to the beginning). This meant not only tragedy and an unhappy choice of means, but guilt as well. No one wished to heed the warning voices, because that would have meant facing the real situation and giving up the means of rising again, which was the aggression itself.

This then is the other experience with which I would like to approach the subject. It is the depression of the loser, who remains stuck in his grandiosity and his aggressivity. As the history of the 1920s shows, the depressive symptoms, if not dealt with, must find compensation in manic activity. "Movement" and "revolution" then offer themselves as the antidote to depression. "The new day," "the new man" became the slogans of this longing for salvation, which associated itself with the "will to power." (Much has been written about this, not just in regard to the First World War. The same thing surely applies to processes in church history right up to the present "movements," which aim at a "renewal" of a church ever more reduced to depression and not surprisingly speak of a theology of "strength and power.")

I was offended, yet also inwardly stirred, as I read in 1943 where Hitler began one of the chapters of *Mein Kampf* with the biblical citation (Isaiah 9:2): "the people that walked in darkness have seen a great light." That was what he meant and what he imagined as a cure for the depression of his "*Volk*." At the time, however, few understood that this light was only the repetition of a manic defense, which itself required violence and victory. The only chance to fulfill this aggressive drive seemed to lie in escalating it (the mania of grandiosity), in the use of totalitarian means and technically improved weapons. "Greater Germany,"* "military build-up," "show of force," all the way to "total war"—these were the steps of that escalation. As long as the need to escalate persists, the aggressive depression has not been overcome. Thus I find it not unreasonable to fear that the atomic arsenal will lead to a new escalation in this armed competition, so long as the underlying psychic factors have not changed, which is to say, so long as the symptomatology of manic depression has not been left behind.

This escalation, this exaggeration which Hitler required for "salvation," complemented the exaggerated denigration of the others, the enemy. They were declared to be subhumans, vermin, and thus their extermination was held to be legitimate. Such an idea can only live through the destruction of others. The idea itself justifies the means. I know this urge to escalate and the power of unconsummated aggression, even if only in my fantasies. I know the wish for total victory, joyfully achieved, in which the evil and the inferior will always draw the short straw (even if out of loving kindness they are not wiped out). It is comforting.

With Hitler this was more radical, more thoroughgoing. At the same time, it seems to me that this whole process would depend on a complete personality split,[2] and thus in practice could be only partially carried out. Functionaries who were gregarious family types could carry out their destructive functions, which after all were "in the service of the people," and at the same time conduct themselves with normal feelings, even sentimentality, in other areas. Thus the criminalizing effect on them of all this could remain virtually imperceptible to them.

One of the most shocking things to me is how little remorse and insight could be seen in the subsequent trials of Nazi criminals. The personality split prevents an integrative recognition. We know this from the hysterical persecution of witches in its day, from the Crusades, from the extermination of the unbelievers (and not only

---

2. I am thinking here of a personality split in which two processes run along side by side: the ideological dream image, formed out of grandiose wishes for power, purity, and salvation, lost more and more of its connection with reality, with the possible, with the traditional frame of values. This latter, however, continued untouched, at least in part, in the private domain. Only gradually did this realm become criminalized as well; for a time the old human processes appeared to continue undisturbed.

under Khomeni). Fear and the idealization of obedience, already present in the Prussian tradition of our people, created the mass conditions that first made something like Auschwitz possible.

If I then ask concretely where the fault lies, I would answer first of all that this mechanism was never successfully interrupted, but only escalated repeatedly. With this, certain aspects of this guilt complex become comprehensible for me: (1) we could have recognized this pathological process from history, including the history of our own people; (2) we allowed ourselves to be paralyzed by fear and obedience; and (3) we must have known that to live at the cost of others' lives can never be our right, as it was declared to be.

Not to see what is there to be seen, is guilt: stupidity too is a moral quality. I do not say that there are no circumstances which limit insight, but I will not deny that this too is guilt, objectively speaking. This limitation of vision, however, seems to me to be a consequence of guilt as well—an insane consequence, to the point of running completely amok in the desperate depression of the last years of the war. But this too could be reframed for us in ideological terms: in the context of our preconceived notions, any critical voice seemed like treason. Guilt and innocence became twisted into a mad tangle, which for many people still clouds the question of the resistance fighters of the July 20 conspiracy.* Are good intentions good enough? Is being fair already something like being innocent?

Tears flowed down my cheeks as we prisoners of war were dragged through Poznan in triumphal procession, spat upon by the population, and beaten by the victors. We had to pass by a great billboard on which was written (in Russian and Polish): "We (the Russians) have saved European culture." On it was the figure of a man with broken chains and another with a swastika on his armband, lying on the ground. Beside the billboard stood Russian and Mongolian troops with camels and tents. It seemed to me like a mockery: *these* were the ones, of all people, who were supposed to have saved European culture! I thought of the mocking inscription on Jesus' cross (INRI—Jesus of Nazareth, King of the Jews), and considered us to be the children of Calvary. Not until much later did I understand how true the billboard actually was. But the thought of Calvary (without the dawn of Easter) was revealing of my state of mind at the time. I did regard myself as a sacrifice to evil powers, come to crucify us who had meant only good. The negative, destructive results of our war did not strike me as grounds for guilt at the time and as for the information we were given in prison, I could only understand it as outrageous enemy propaganda. I could not recognize my own blindness and guilt until I encountered this reality in the context of a human experience which had personal meaning for me.

Later, after my return, Gustav Heinemann and Hermann Ehlers,* with whom I worked for a time, helped greatly in this process of recognition. Guilt can never be merely asserted, but rather must be made comprehensible, so that one can confront it. This was not possible for us at that time because of the inextricable tangle of interpretations and feelings in which we found ourselves. Thus it was that only the military and societal collapse and the encounter with a different human experience could enable us to have some insight into the circumstances of our guilt. It was astonishing to me that the fanatics could "swing around" and settle into new ideologies much more quickly; the others took somewhat longer.

There were some among the Nazis as well who really underwent an inner transformation which seemed genuine to me. As a student I knew of one such case, in which by degrees I comprehended that the guilty person had not made a new commitment to "Christian ideology" out of opportunism, but rather had had an experience of an encounter in which he was accepted without punitive contempt. Thus he was not forced back down into depression (because he was guilty), which in turn could have led to renewed aggression (if not against others, then against himself, as autoaggression or suicide).

Perhaps that was something like forgiveness, which is the offer of a new way of looking at things, a change of heart and mind. This dissolves the inner compulsion in guilt, which otherwise comes out either cripplingly or aggressively. It does not dissolve the guilt itself, but rather makes it recognizable at last, and thereby offers at the same time something like a new beginning. By that I do not mean "renewal." To me that suggests too strongly the risk of repetition of the same structure, only with different means—as is well known in psychotherapy (e.g., in symptom substitution). A new beginning takes place within the old life conditions, but with a changed conception of reality. The human being and his limitations in constructing and mastering life have not changed; he can only learn to approach them in a different way from before. It is this learning process, which grows out of the encounter with guilt, that is important to me. It is not a matter of punishment, though I can see that punishment does have a place in the process of finding one's way in the old world with its laws. It is rather a matter of support in learning to live with guilt and with the pain of unfulfilled dreams.

It may seem strange, but something like this is how I understood the political and economic help offered to us by the Americans as well. In spite of everything, it made something like autonomy and self-respect possible. Naturally, love for one's neighbor was not the primary consideration at work here; political and economic factors were no doubt more telling. For them it was simply self-interest to act that way and not to put the Morgenthau Plan* into effect, with its emphasis on punishment. Thus they could gain allies and support a market, which was also in their own self-interest.

Sometimes it seems to me that a "pragmatic" or "rationally based" forgiveness is not only a political position, but also a biblical one. Jesus repeatedly advises (e.g., Luke 16:9) that you should make friends with the help of the gains of Mammon, and create allies for yourself by canceling debts, so that in your time of need they will take you into their huts. That is "pragmatic" and "rational." Here the cycle of depression and revenge is broken. In the end one gains more respect, gratitude, and reliability in this way than from the submissiveness of the slave, whose freedom one will have to fear ("Woe to the people whose king was a servant"; Proverbs 30:22).[3] The need for relieving or lessening the injury to one's own feelings of self-worth, through repression or projective transference, is removed, and thereby a positive relation to reality, suffering, and struggle is made possible. That would be something on the order of the "presence" I spoke of in my first letter to you. Whether this can be better learned through considerations of political or religious self-interest seems to me at the moment only a question of means, not of principles. In any case, forgiveness is a hermeneutical theme and thus a relational process. It must be credible and understandable in the behavior of other people through whom I can encounter my guilt. I cannot be aware of every aspect of my guilt and forgiveness in every moment, under all conditions. The importance of my situation, and the context for my insight into guilt and my acceptance of it must not be underestimated. (Here lies a problem that particularly concerns me in the church, with its largely ineffectual approach to guilt.) Forgiveness would have to be in some way a dissolution of the repetition dynamic of guilt.

In view of the horror of the Nazi past, in which we as contemporaries took an active or passive part, it seems to me of practical importance to create learning supports for this process of rethinking.

If our guilt lies in the fact that we exaggerated and repeated themes from the value systems of our own history, then we must learn a cautious attitude about the dynamics of escalation, whether under the name of progress, maximization of profit, growth, or "Star

---

3. This is an approximate rendering of Luther's version of the proverb. The King James, which is more familiar to English readers, is somewhat different. —Trans.

Wars." Neither in economics, nor defense, nor welfare ideology can quantitative growth have a positive quality in and of itself. There is such a thing as pathological growth (even cancer is a kind of cellular egotism, in which cells can pass on only profiteering and no longer cooperation). There is growth which plunders the planet, out of here-and-now egotism, and which leads to narcissistic exhaustion (with or without heart attack). The study of our history should lead us less in the direction of self-affirmation and more in the direction of a critical attitude toward growth.

If our guilt lies in the fact that we let ourselves be captured by anxiety and an obedience ethic raised to mythic proportions, then we must cultivate an attitude that values protest over obedience. We should develop a new feeling for nonconformism and regard anxiety not as a given destiny, but rather as a challenge, to trace it back to its sources. This seems to me to be a question not only of pedagogy, but of psychotherapy as well.

If our guilt lies in the fact that we saw it as our right to live at the expense of others, then for me that means not just the end of colonialism of every kind, but also a more dignified and helpful intercourse with the so-called Third World, which can no longer defend itself against the exploitation of men and nature, so long as it is dependent on us. Beyond that, there should also be an exposure of the latent contempt for minorities in general (foreigners, homosexuals, and others). They become all too quickly the targets for projection of unresolved frustrations and anxieties (e.g., unemployment: "and we have so many foreign workers").

Perhaps one of our greatest sins in fascist times was our inattention to these deadly forces, which sometimes offer themselves in friendly or unthreatening guise to us today as a momentary crutch. To unmask them is our task today, lest a new breakdown of civilization be our lot. That such a breakdown is not impossible is proven for me not only by Auschwitz, but also by the conduct of nations all around us (to name them is not necessary), and it is proven, as well, through the encounter with our own inner world, since illness is never on the outside alone.

TRANSLATOR'S AFTERWORD

This book is filled with the meaning of historical events in personal lives and with the meaning of personal lives in historical events. All of these essays tell about what it cost in the long run to be silent about the events of the Third Reich and the Second World War, especially in private family settings, but also in public settings. These essays also tell how difficult it often is simply to talk. All the authors speak of how hard it has been, and still is, for Germans to talk openly about the Nazi past and about their family's role within it. And they also speak of how hard it has been for the children of the perpetrators or of the bystanders, people born during or after the war who did not directly experience the Nazi times, *not* to be told about the past. In our western culture as a whole we had learned, over the past two hundred years, to use silence as a way of coping with dirt, sin, and death. And in our own time a *collective silence* about the Nazi past permeated Germany up until fairly recently. Sometimes this silence was broken. These essays tell of how it was broken in psychotherapeutic settings. When that happened the listeners were allowed to see intimate parts of their common tragedy and gained insight into how the sins of the fathers and mothers of the Third Reich had come to be visited upon some of their children. I believe, however, that there exists a whole spectrum of ways of dealing with the pains and silences visited upon the descendants of Third Reich parents. Some descendants, unlike the people in this book, did not suffer inner pain because of their parents' or grandparents' activities during the Hitler years. Thus what we hear in this volume are probably only a part of the spectrum of post-war voices.

The people we hear in this book speak about a time when there were no voices. But these essays are not concerned with the generation of the parents and grandparents of contemporary German adults nor with the immensity of horror on all levels of life which they endured: the devastating bombings; the massive troop movements; the starving millions of civilians fleeing before advancing Russian troops; war and destruction and death, here and now; ghastly things seen and heard by one's own eyes and ears, sometimes atrocities inflicted by one's own hands; the destruction of the source of all one's youthful pride and hopes. These were the immediate experiences of the parents and grandparents of the voices we hear in this book. Thus a first source of the collective silence was the individual experience of terrible things coupled with a collective sense of shame and guilt.

The experience of terror and horror can influence us in ways those of us without such experience can scarcely imagine. The psychogenic blindness of some of the Cambodian widows—women who since watching their tortured, bleeding, screaming husbands being thrown alive into the consuming flames have been unable to see at all—tells us how profound is the human need to avoid truth which cannot possibly be permitted to enter consciousness (*New York Times Magazine,* June 23, 1991). The collective silence and denial of the Nazi perpetrators and bystanders are psychologically parallel to the blindness of the victimized Cambodian widows. In these pages people do not speak, perhaps some actually were unable to speak, about things they perhaps could scarcely bear to remember. It is in this vein that Irene Anhalt describes the vivid case of her father.

Many varied responses to the horrors of the times led to a widely shared German choice to ignore and be silent about the recent war and the Nazi past, and to hurry ahead with rebuilding the country after the "zero hour," the capitulation in May of 1945. My own friend Ursula Seemann who was imprisoned for several years by the Nazis for listening to the BBC, was advised by well-meaning acquaintances after the war not to speak of her wartime past, lest she and others be compromised or embarrassed.

In contrast to the post-war silence, the later voices in these essays *do* do justice to the crippling silence experienced by the *children* of those who had failed (or failed even to try) to prevent atrocities or had shared in their perpetration. And these voices do do justice to the "healing power of truth-telling" as Judith Lewis Herman calls it (*New York Times Book Review,* Jan. 10, 1993).

These stories reflect one of the choices given us because we can speak: the choice of not speaking. It has recently become increasingly evident in psychotherapeutic circles that the choice of *not* speaking, the choice of silence, is frequently made in extremely painful or shaming personal circumstances, such as in cases of incest or abuse. The German postwar collective silence was surely in many cases a means of fending off the resurfacing of intolerably shameful and painful memories. And, further, the wish to face these topics was in short supply.

In our own present situation in the West, however, our silences are usually silences in the private realm where only two or three or a small number of people are being silent about sins or crimes within the personal or family group. The collective silence, from which this book takes its name, refers to the silence of almost an entire population for almost half a century about personal experiences of public disasters. In this book Sammy Speier eloquently spells out the reaches of this apparent dichotomy between "public" and "private."

In the United States our situation has remained simpler than the German experience. Although each one of us confronts moral and religious choices every day, and although we have fought many wars, as a nation we have not fought a war on our own shores since the Civil War, more than four generations ago. Wars or revolutions at home change private life into public life for everyone. As a national community we have seldom been forced to experience and explore the confusions between private and public life. Nevertheless the Vietnam War forced a segment of our population into such experience and exploration.

Most of the experiences described in this book were those of people living in western Germany. Although there has been little information about the work of the few psychotherapists in eastern Germany, evidence to date reveals similar attempts to be silent about or to deny or reject or shift the blame for the events of the Nazi regime; in the East the process of denial has been supported by the notion that Nazism was solely the responsibility of western Germany, whereas East Germans had fought on the side of the Russians and Poles *against* Nazi Germany. As more is discovered and written about the parallel events, deeds, and feelings that have occurred in eastern Germany in the years since World War II, we may find additional similarities as well as disparities between the experiences in the two parts of Germany. (see Barbara Heimannsberg's remarks on this topic in her article in this volume.) The present volume, however, is essentially concerned with experiences of western Germans.

A second root of the collective silence results from the fanaticism accorded the Third Reich by its followers. Such fanaticism may arise in part out of childhood pain. Nevertheless Ervin Staub (1989, p. 31) asserts that "fanatical devotion to an ideology has more *direct* influence on the actions of perpetrators than childhood experience or psychopathology." Describing such "devotion," Staub quotes Tom Segev: "joining the SS was to become part of an elite, an aristocracy, a religious order, a secret society, a gang, an army, and a family all at the same time" (1989, p. 130). Waltraud Silke Behrendt speaks of these same sentiments in this book when she describes the patient who told of the "warm stall" of the comradeship he had known and for which he fearfully longed. Another example is to be found in this volume in Helm Stierlin's description of the Nazi father of the Mehnert family, who "continued to speak proudly of the time when he followed the flag of the Führer to defend the German fatherland."

In Nazi Germany, as is to be expected amidst such fanaticism, devotion to the cause was coupled with a silence about anything which might in any way detract from its apparent perfection, even one's own personal failings. In the present volume, Gunnar von Schlippe reports how he and his fellow soldiers were punished if they so much as admitted out loud to error or guilt. Thus silence was promulgated as an official policy. He goes on to say that he now feels an active repentance would be easier if he had learned early in life that it is human to err and that to be guilty is a human right. In this book Heidi Salm shows how keeping silence was cultivated as a high virtue in the SS during the Hitler years. The silence which was deemed a virtue in the elite ranks of the military must have been both symptom and cause of its subsequent extensive use in the generation as a whole. You will recall that in this book Margarete Hecker tells how the murder of Uta's great-grandfather by her grand-uncle was kept secret in her family for a generation. Assuredly both public and private silence formed the roots of the collective silence.

In this silent and fanatical world, fear and the drive to obey permeated German life. The traditional German virtue of obedience to authority was reinforced in Nazi Germany by fear of reprisal. The combination became an almost irresistible force supporting Nazi rule. For most, being obedient to another was esteemed more highly than being true to oneself. Many of the therapists and patients in this volume speak of how they wish they could have been more outspoken, less obedient, less silent during the Nazi years. Their voices tell us how difficult that was.

How can human beings be healed from having kept silent for so long about such dreadful matters? This volume clearly shows that individual healing from such circumstances and events can happen through psychotherapy. This means finally coming to talk extensively and honestly with another person about the matters that lay behind one's silence. It is in talking together that the healing from extensive silence can occur. Thus healing from a prolonged silence will take place more readily in an interactive rather than in an analytical therapy.

The root process of psychotherapy is putting experiences into feeling words. Without emotion, words lead to understanding more readily than they do to healing. Words spoken with feeling to another person help us to allow the heat of painful past experiences to cool within us so that we can, at last, let the painful experience become simply a fact of our past, rather than a force absorbing our energy in our present life.

So it is natural that people at first became able to tell their therapists about their Nazi pains. This process of talking and telling began perhaps about 1980, as the children of wartime and of the post-war era reached their thirties and forties and sought therapy (or were encouraged to seek it). Thus in the therapeutic settings of the early '80s the collective silence could for the first time begin to be broken in real depth.

But over the long run, this seems not to have been enough. In many places people began meeting in groups. Our talking takes on an additional, enriching dimension when we can speak openly among a group of our peers about things that have hurt us, maybe hurt all of us. Thus we may hunger to meet with others who shared similar insults as we.

We already know of many groups which meet to deal with the Nazi legacy in its various forms. In 1981, a self-help group began in Holland, made up of Dutch persons whose parents had collaborated with the Nazis. In Boston a group of children of survivors of the Holocaust has been meeting regularly for many years. In Germany itself as early as 1987, Wolfgang Bornebusch and the Jewish-American therapist Isaac Zieman brought together a three-generational group of 20 people, including two Jews, to deal with these memories; this meeting is described in the present volume. In 1988, a group of 8 of the perpetrators' children whom Bar-On interviewed began to meet as a group. This led, in June of 1992, to a meeting of Holocaust survivors together with the children of perpetrators. In this book, Irene Wielpütz tells about how a group of her own contemporaries became central in helping to heal her from the Holocaust. In the spring of 1992 Bornebusch and Zieman joined again in putting on a week-long workshop in New York City for 12 Germans and 12 Jews. At the Harvard Medical Education Center in Boston, Ilona Kuphal, the daughter of an SS officer, and Mona Weissmark, the daughter of Holocaust survivors, held a conference in September, 1992 for the children of survivors and the children of Nazis. Presumably similar inner needs led people to all of these groups. And surely many more groups of which we are unaware have begun to meet in Germany and elsewhere. As more talking and sharing occurs people will gradually become able to let the past become simple fact, past no longer driven by emotion. Some groups may then go out of existence because they are no longer needed, others may continue as they address other issues, and some may turn into action groups addressing public issues.

As some sort of personal mastery of the past is achieved, many people are eager to share their feelings and experiences with others, even with those from "the other side." That such meetings and endeavors are possible bodes some cheer as we confront a world fearfully divided by ethnic and other strife. Certainly the meetings described here offer some insight into dealing with the residue of intergroup conflict.

There is however an important factor to be noticed: the groups described here are all made up of people removed from the disasters by at least one generation, by thirty or forty years. And also the groups are made up of people who chose to participate in them. It seems absurd to think that immediate participants in horrendous events could or would choose to meet in a group with their victims or murderers to "work through" what they had perpetrated or suffered. Even so the groups described here point in a new direction which must be pursued.

Massing wrote at the end of her article: "Human misery in the form of neurotic symptoms—as the expression of a powerful, indeed *healthy contradiction*—will lead us inevitably, let us hope, to a *completely integrated vision* of individual and cultural suffering at last."

We hope and trust that this work makes a contribution to such an "integrated vision" of suffering.

— *Cynthia Oudejans Harris*
HAMPTON, CONNECTICUT
APRIL, 1993

GLOSSARY

Aktion "Sühnezeichen." Church-based program in post-war Germany focusing on repentance and reparations, in part through volunteer work in Israel.

Anschluss. The annexation of Austria by Germany in March 1938. After the war Austria was treated by the Allies as one of the countries invaded and conquered by the Nazis, and not as a member of the defeated Axis nations. At the time, however, the Nazis had wide political support in Austria, and the Anschluss was accomplished with much public celebration and without significant resistance. The question of Austria's role and responsibility as a nation in the Holocaust, never really publicly debated or resolved, was reopened by the candidacy and election of Kurt Waldheim to the presidency of the country in 1986.

Aryan Certificate. Nazi legislation from April, 1933 restricting Jewish access to the civil service, universities, the professions, and so forth raised the legal question of an official definition of Jewishness, as well as the identification of individuals as "Aryan" or otherwise. The solution was the *Ariernachweis,* or Aryan Certificate, which attested to the individual's "Aryan identity." A "full Jew" was legally defined as a person having at least three fully Jewish grandparents. A "half Jew," or "Mischling first degree," was a person having two Jewish grandparents; and a "quarter Jew," or "Mischling second degree" had one. Each category had somewhat different rights and restrictions, and these differences themselves changed over time. Obviously the arithmetic could become more complicated in cases involving grandparents who were themselves products of mixed marriages, and much legal process was given over to the question of the exact status of individuals, especially among the "Mischlinge," whose number was estimated to be in the hundreds of thousands in 1933. Cases involving a change of classification (sometimes through a claim of illegitimate ["Aryan"] paternity, or some alteration of documents) or any exception from marriage and other restrictions, were personally ruled on by Hitler himself.

BDM. League of German Girls; see Hitler Youth.

CDU. Christian Democratic Union, the conservative/centrist governing party (in coalition with the CSU and at times the Free Democratic Party) in West Germany throughout most of the post-war period.

CSU. Christian Social Union, the Bavarian counterpart of the CDU, heavily identified with Catholic politics and generally considered somewhat to the right of its national coalition partner, the Christian Democrats.

Denazification. The postwar policy of attempting to remove Nazi influence

---

Note: Where not otherwise cited, references are to Gutman, *Encyclopedia of the Holocaust,* 1990.

and exclude former Nazis from public life. Under a 1946 regulation of the Allied Control Council, former Nazis were to be classified into five categories, ranging from "major offenders" to "persons exonerated" (including "followers" born after 1918, who were granted an automatic "youth amnesty" in the absence of specific charges). Possible penalties included detention in a labor camp, fines, loss of pension rights, and restriction from voting or holding public office. In all, nearly four million Germans were processed in the Western zones under denazification regulations, with some one million receiving punishments of varying degrees of severity. "Paragraph 131" refers to related restrictions on military pensions and survivors' benefits for certain offenders and their families.

Ehlers, Hermann. Political and church leader, CDU member, President of the Bundestag.

Einsatzgruppen. Task forces of mobile killing units operating in German-occupied territories during World War II.

Freisler, Roland. Judge and president of the "people's court" which conducted the mock trials of the resistance fighters of the July 20, 1944, conspiracy to assassinate Hitler.

Führer. The word "Führer" in German simply means "leader," or "driver," from "führen," to steer or lead. A "Führerschein" in German is a driver's license. In English (and many other languages) the word now exists as a common noun, meaning "dictatorial leader," or "tyrant," generally used mockingly or sardonically. In Nazi Germany it was illegal to use the word, except in compounds, other than as Hitler's title (and note here Richard Picker's discussion of how the Nazis "stole" German words). Since the war, the word is again in common use as an ordinary noun, but with a sort of double life, since it can also refer to Hitler or to any tyrant in the English sense, and these overtones are easily evoked. Thus a streetcar conductor (a Führer), if he is stern or overbearing, might be addressed by fractious youths as "Herr Führer," in a tone clearly implying derision yet not technically impudent, since that really is his title. "Führerin" is the feminine form of the same word.

Generalgouvernement. General Government for the Occupied Areas of Poland. Established in October, 1939 to administer occupied Poland, including nearly two million Jews, who were relocated and ghettoized, with the survivors ultimately deported to camps.

Greater Germany (Grossdeutschland). Meaning all the German-speaking or "German national" regions of Central Europe. During the struggle for German unification in the 19th century, Bismarck had opted for a "Kleindeutschland" solution—i.e., a German state that left out German-speaking areas in Austro-Hungary, Switzerland, Italy, present-day Poland, and so forth. Hitler sought to reverse this policy and unify all "German nationals" in one German state.

Heinemann, Gustav. Social Democrat political leader, founder of the liberal German People's Party, whose program was the reunification of Germany as a neutral demilitarized state. Minister of the Interior in Adenauer's first post-war cabinet; resigned in protest over Adenauer's rearmament policy. Later President of West Germany, 1969 to 1974.

Hereditary Health Code. A body of laws enacted from 1933 on, with the aim of protecting "pure Aryan" racial stock and selecting out (through sterilization or, later, euthanasia) individuals suffering from various physical, mental, or emotional handicaps. These laws included the Law for Prevention of Hereditary Disease, the Nuremberg Law for Protection of German Blood and Honor, and the policies of the euthanasia program (some of them illegal even by the standards of the times). The goal was a nation of "pure Germans," in Hitler's words, "as hard as steel, as strong and pliant as leather, and as fast as greyhounds" (Gutman, 1990, p. 41). See also "Racial Hygiene."

Historians' Debate. The academic debate, which has erupted into the popular press in Germany, over the question of whether the Judeocide is basically comparable or noncomparable with other horrors and genocides in history. The implications of the question for Germany's identity and national self-concept are both obvious and powerful.

Hitler Youth (Hitlerjugend). The Nazi youth movement. The counterpart for girls was the League of German Girls (BDM). Taking children from the ages of 10 to 19, both branches concentrated on the inculcation of Nazi ideology and the training of future Nazi leaders and citizens.

"Horst Wessel Lied." Horst Wessel, an SA member, was the author, in 1929, of a pro-Nazi poem which appeared in Goebbels' newspaper, *Der Angriff* (The Attack). In 1930 Wessel was killed, in a private quarrel, by a Communist. The Nazis then accorded Wessel the status of a political martyr, and the poem, set to music, became the official Nazi anthem.

"International Conspiracy." See "Jewish World Conspiracy."

"Jewish World Conspiracy." According to Nazi dogma, Germany did not lose World War I on the battlefield, but rather was betrayed into surrender by Communists and left-wing labor unions, who themselves were orchestrated by a "Jewish World Conspiracy," thought to include, somewhat incongruously, both international bankers and the international Communist Party. This same union of anti-German forces, supposedly under Jewish coordination, was perceived as orchestrating opposition to the Nazi movement and then to the German war effort.

July 20, 1944. See Stauffenberg Conspiracy.

Kristallnacht. Literally "Crystal Night," known in English as "Night of Broken Glass," November 9–10, 1938, the first mass, officially sponsored pogrom in Nazi Germany and Austria (staged on the 15th anniversary of Hitler's abortive "Beer-Hall Putsch" in Munich, November 8–9, 1923). Led by the SA, crowds attacked Jewish stores, homes, and synagogues, burning and looting the buildings and attacking individual Jews. The official number of Jews killed was given as 91; in addition, some 30,000 Jews were arrested. The explicit goal of the pogrom, as of Nazi policy in general up to the outbreak of the war, was to intimidate and coerce Jews into emigrating; indeed some 140,000 Jews did leave Germany in the period from 1938 to 1941, before mass deportations began.

Lanz von Liebenfels, Adolf. "The man who gave Hitler his ideas" (v. Daim, Wilfried, *Der Man, der Hitler die Ideen gab*. Vienna: 1985). At one time a Cistercian monk, Lanz left the order at a young age to devote himself to the mission of protecting the "Aryan race" from subordination by other, "inferior races," especially Jews. His racist periodical *Ostara* (the name of a Germanic goddess of spring) was read by Hitler in Vienna in the years before World War I, and directly influenced many of the racist ideas in *Mein Kampf,* as well as later Nazi policy. It was Lanz's idea, for example, that the Jews were evolutionarily inferior and closer to apes than were Aryans. Thus Lanz was a major figure in the transition from traditional, religiously based anti-Semitism to a much more virulent, pseudo-scientific anti-Semitism based on "racial hygiene."

League of German Girls (BDM). See Hitler Youth.

Lebensbornheimen. The Lebensborn organization ("Wellspring of Life"), an offshoot of the SS, promoted the adoption of "Aryan" children by SS families and the active breeding of "racially pure" babies for the future of the Reich. The *Heimen,* or homes, were orphanages specifically designed for the raising and training of the offspring of these arranged unions.

Lenz, Fritz. German biologist and geneticist, a leader in the attempt to put political eugenics on a scientific basis. In 1923 Lenz was appointed to the first university chair in "racial hygiene," at the University of Munich. Under the Nazi regime, he held a similar position in Berlin. After the war, he disavowed his racist views and continued as professor of genetics in Göttingen until his retirement in 1955.

Morgenthau Plan. Proposal to return Germany to a permanently agrarian, pre-industrial condition after the war. The author of the plan was Secretary of the Treasury under Roosevelt.

Mother's Cross. An award given to mothers in the Nazi era for service to the state. A part of the general militarization of society, the award was meant to recognize and support the traditional, conservative view of a home-centered role for women. Women's role was to serve the military state by raising sons who would be good soldiers and Party members.

NAPOLA. Acronym for the National Political Education Institute, founded in 1933 by the SS and the Education Ministry to train future military and civil service leaders, but soon taken over entirely by the SS. By 1938 there were 21 such schools, each with about 100 students, ranging in age from 10 to 18.

National Work Corps. The public works administration of the Nazi regime.

"Old Fighter." An early Nazi, from the days before the Party took power.

Organization Todt. Nazi administration for large-scale military and armaments construction work; named for its founder, Dr. Fritz Todt. After Todt's death in a plane crash in 1942, his offices, by now including the ministry for armaments and munitions, were taken over by Albert Speer.

Paragraph 131. See Denazification.

Pimpfe. Literally "cub;" the youngest group in the Hitler Youth.

"Racial hygiene." The pseudo-scientific doctrine of "racial purity," which lay behind the Nazi policies aimed at establishment and promotion of

"pure Aryan stock," and the elimination of hereditary defects and other conditions. See also Hereditary Health Code and Aryan Certificate.

Reichskristallnacht. See Kristallnacht.

Riemeck, Renate. One of the founders of the DFU, the German Peace Party, which opposed Adenauer's plans for rearmament of West Germany in alliance with NATO.

Röhm Putsch. See SA.

SA. Sturmabteilung, storm troopers, also known as the "Brownshirts," in imitation of Mussolini's Blackshirts. Because of its semi-autonomous nature, the SA was always both a tool and a problem for Hitler, who used the threat and reality of street violence to intimidate his political enemies, yet portrayed himself as the man who could protect the state, the military, and the propertied classes from this freelance army. This tension came to a climax on June 30, 1934, the night of the so-called Röhm Putsch, when Hitler ordered and personally supervised the murder of Ernst Röhm and other leaders of the SA. Thus Hitler reassured the army, in the early days of the Nazi regime, that left-wing or socialist elements of the Nazi movement would not be allowed to threaten the interests of the military and economic establishment.

Scharf, Kurt. Protestant theologian, leader of pastoral resistance to Nazism.

Schumacher, Kurt. Incarcerated in concentration camps for twelve years, Schumacher survived and emerged to become a leader in the Social Democratic Party after the war.

SD. Sicherheitsdienst, security service. As a division of the SS, the SD was the intelligence service of the Nazi party. The relationship between the SD and the Gestapo was always somewhat unclear, but both were under the command of Himmler, who was himself directly under Hitler. Since the SD was generally charged with identifying enemies of the state, and since Jews by definition were considered enemies of the state, the SD became directly involved in implementation of the Judeocide.

SS. Schutzstaffel, protection squad, also known as the "Blackshirts." Originally drawn from the ranks of the SA, the SS was founded in 1923 as a personal bodyguard for Hitler. By 1925, the SS numbered some 200 and was regarded in the Party as a particularly loyal and "racially pure" elite (members and their wives were required to demonstrate "Aryan purity" back to at least the year 1700). Under Himmler, the SS established and ran the first concentration camps, beginning in 1933. By 1936 the SS was amalgamated with the Gestapo, the secret police, which in turn controlled the political police of the various German states. After the outbreak of World War II, the SS grew enormously, to 165,000 by 1941 and to 800,000 by the end of the war. Its function in wartime was both as a security force against unrest at home and as "pacification" troops in the occupied East, generally following in the wake of the frontline troops. The SS was thus given general charge of the "final solution" in occupied Eastern Europe, both through mass killings by firing squad and through the extermination camps.

Stauffenberg Conspiracy. July 20, 1944, the date of the most dramatic of the many failed attempts on Hitler's life. As part of a long-standing and highly organized plan for assassinating Hitler, taking over the government and army, and ending the war, Colonel Claus von Stauffenberg succeeded in smuggling a bomb into supreme headquarters. The bomb went off as scheduled, but through a fluke Hitler survived the explosion. In retaliation the Nazis summarily murdered some thousands of friends, relatives, and possible sympathizers of members of the conspiracy.

Valhalla. A hall of honor built in the 1830s by King Ludwig I of Bavaria. The hall held busts and statues of various notable Germans and was prized by the Nazis for its glorification of German culture.

Volksschädlich. Literally, "damaging to the race," anti-social; a Nazi term for persons or actions considered to be harmful to the "Aryan" community.

Volkssturm. Roughly, "people's army"; the army reserve made up mostly of overage or otherwise unfit men. Originally a civil defense unit, the Volkssturm, along with older units of the Hitler Youth, became drawn into actual fighting as Allied troops reached and invaded Germany itself.

Weimar Republic. The German republic (1919–1933) established after World War I. Its constitution was drawn up in the small city of Weimar, home of Goethe and thus the symbolic seat of liberal German culture.

"Zero Hour." The new beginning after World War II. The term carries overtones of a greater or lesser degree of unwillingness to look into personal or institutional history before that date.

REFERENCES

Amendt, G. (1986). *Der neue Klapperstorch* [The new stork]. Herbstein: März.

Arendt, H. (1977). *Eichmann in Jerusalem: A report of the banality of evil.* (rev. ed.) New York: Viking Penguin.

Bar-On, D. (1986). *The pantomime stick. Conversations with parents and their children after the Holocaust.* Tel Aviv: Merav.

Bar-On, D. (1989). *Legacy of silence: Encounters with children of the Third Reich.* Cambridge, MA: Harvard University Press.

Bar-On, D. (1990, March). Die Kinder der Holocaust-Täter und ihre Suche nach moralischer Identität. [The children of perpetrators of the holocaust and their search for a moral identity]. *Integrative Therapie.*

Bar-On, D., & Charny, I. W. (1988). Children of perpetrators of the Holocaust: How did they create a moral self? *Psychology, 1*(1), 29–38.

Binion, R. (1976). *Hitler among the Germans.* New York: Elsevier.

Blasi, A. (1983). Bridging moral cognition and action: A theoretical view. *Development Review, 3,* 178–210.

Boszormenyi-Nagy, I., & Krasner, B. R. (1986). *Between give and take: A clinical guide to contextual therapy.* New York: Brunner/Mazel.

Boszormenyi-Nagy, I., & Spark, G. M. (1973). *Invisible loyalties: Reciprocity in intergenerational family therapy.* New York: HarperCollins.

Boyce, W. D., & Jensen, L. C. (1978). *Moral reasoning: A psychological-philosophical integration.* Lincoln: University of Nebraska Press.

Bromberger, B., Mausbach, H., & Thanna, K. D. (1985). *Medizin, Faschismus, und Widerstand* [Medicine, facism, and resistance]. Köln: Pahl-Rugenstein.

Buber, M. (1965). *Nachlese.* Heidelberg: Lambert Schneider. (English trans., *A believing humanism: My testament 1902–1965.* New York: Simon & Schuster, 1967).

Buber, M. (1984) *Das dialogische Prinzip* [The dialogical principle]. Heidelberg: Lambert Schneider.

Bühler, C., & Allen, M. (1974). *Einführung in die humanistische Psychologie* [Introduction to humanistic psychology]. Stuttgart: Klett-Cotta.

Charny, I. W. (1982). *How can we commit the unthinkable: Genocide the human cancer.* Boulder, CO: Westview.

Charny, I. W. (1986). Genocide and mass destruction: Doing harm to other as a missing dimension in psychopathology. *Psychiatry, 49*(2), 144–157.

Cremerius, J. (1979). Gibt es zwei psychosomatische Techniken? [Are there two psychosomatic techniques?]. *Psyche, 33,* 577–599.

Cremerius, J. (1983). Sandor Ferenczis Bedeutung für Theorie und Therapie der Psychoanalyse [The significance of Sandor Ferenczi for psychoanalytic theory and therapy]. *Psyche, 37,* 988–1015.

Cremerius, J. (1984). Die psychoanalytische Abstinenzregel [The psychoanalytic rule of abstinence]. *Psyche, 38,* 769–800.

Danieli, Y. (1980). Countertransference in the treatment and study of Nazi Holocaust survivors and their children. *Victimology, 5,* 3–4.

Davidson, S. (1980). The denial effects of massive psychic trauma in families of Holocaust survivors. *Journal of Marital and Family Therapy, 1,* 11–21.

Diner, D. (1986). Negative Symbiose: Deutche und Juden nach Auschwitz [Negative symbiosis: Germans and Jews after Auschwitz]. *Babylon, 1,* 9–20.

Diner, D. (Ed.). (1987). *Ist der Nationalsozialismus Geschichte? Zu Historisierung und Historikerstreit* [Has National Socialism become history? Toward making the historians' dispute into history]. Frankfurt am Main.

Dressen, W. (1988). Die Identität der Deutschen. Von der Sehnsucht nach Normalität [The identity of Germans: Concerning the longing for normality]. *Niemanland, 6,* 88.

Ekman, G., & Lundberg, U. (1971). Emotional reaction to past and future events as a function of temporal distance. *Acta Psychologica, 35,* 430–441.

Erdheim, M. (1983). Über das Lügen und die Unaufrichtigkeit des Psychoanalytikers [Concerning the lies and insincerity of the psychoanalyst]. In H. M. Lohmann (Ed.), *Das Unbehagen in der Psychoanalyse* [Psychoanalysis and its discontents]. Frankfurt: Qumran.

Erikson, E. H. (1950). *Childhood and society.* New York: Norton.

Erikson, E. H. (1968). *Identity, youth and crisis.* New York: Norton.

Focke, H., & Reimer, U. (1984). *Alltag unterm Hakenkreuz* [Daily life under the swastika]. Rheinbek: Rowolt.

Freud, S. (1930). Das Unbehagen in der Kultur [Civilization and its discontents]. In *Gesammelte Werke* [Collected works] (Vol. 14, p. 419ff).

Friedman, M. (1987). *Der heilende Dialog in der Psychotherapie* [Healing dialogue in psychotherapy]. Köln: Edition Humanistische Psychologie.

Füssel, S. (1983). Bücherverbrennung und bibliothekslenkung im Nationalsozialismus [Book burning and the administration of libraries during National Socialism]. In *Göttingen untem Hakenkreuz* [Göttingen under the swastika]. (pp. 95–104). Göttingen: Stadt Göttingen Kulturdezernat.

Gilbert, G. M. (1963). *The mentality of SS murderous robots* (Vol. 6). Jerusalem: Yad Vashem Studies.

Giordano, R. (1987). *Die zweite Schuld oder von der Last, Deutscher zu sein* [The second guilt, or the burden of being a German]. Hamburg: Rasch und Röhrig.

Grubrich-Simitis, I. (1979). Extremtraumatisierung als kumulatives Trauma [Extreme traumatization as cumulative trauma]. *Psyche, 33,* 991–1023.

Grubrich-Simitis, I. (1984). Nachkommen der Holocaust-Generation in der Psychoanalyse [Descendants of the Holocaust generation in psychoanalysis]. *Psyche, 38,* 1–28.

Gutman, I. (Ed.). (1990). *Encyclopedia of the Holocaust.* New York: Macmillan.

Haan, N. (1978). Two moralities in action contexts: Relationship to thought, ego regulation, and development. *Journal of Personality and Social Psychology, 36,* 286–305.

Habermas, J. (1986, July 11). Eine Art Schadensabwicklung. Die apologetischen Tendenzen in der deutschen Zeitgeschichtsschreibung [Finalizing the damages: Apologetic tendencies in the writing of contemporary history]. *Die Zeit.*

Habermas, J. (1986, November 7). Vom öffentlichen gebrauch der Historie [The public use of history]. *Die Zeit.*

Haffner, S. (1978). *Anmerkungen zu Hitler.* München: Kindler. (English trans., *The meaning of Hitler.* Trans. by E. Osers. New York: Macmillan, 1979.)

Halbwachs, M. (1985). *Das Kollektive Gedächtnis.* Frankfurt: Fischer. (English trans., *The collective memory.* Trans. from the French by F. J. Ditter, Jr., and V. Y. Ditter. New York: HarperCollins, 1980.)

Hardtmann, G. (1989). "They looked as they were always described to us. . . ." concerning perversion of education. In H. F. Rathenow & N. H. Weber (Eds.), Erziehung nach Auschwitz [Education after Auschwitz] (pp. 45–63). Pfaffenweiler.

Harris, M. B., Benson, S. M., & Hall, C. (1975). The effects of confessions on altruism. *Journal of Social Psychology, 96,* 187–192.

Hartmann, D. D. (1984). Compliance and oblivion: The absence of sympathy in Germany for victims of the Holocaust. In I. W. Charny (Ed.), *Towards the understanding and prevention of genocide* (pp. 199–203). Boulder, CO: Westview.

Hecker, M. (1983). Die deutsche Nachkriegsfamilie. Lernerfahrungen in einem Familientherapieseminar auf dem Hintergrund der eigenen Familiengeschichte [The German family after the war: Learning experiences in a family therapy seminar against the background of one's own family]. In E. J. Brunner (Ed.), *Eine ganz alltägliche Familie* [Just an ordinary family]. München: Kösel.

Heer, F. (1968). *Der Glaube des Adolf Hitler* [Hitler's religious beliefs]. Munich: Bechtle.

Helbig, L. (1982). *Und sie werden nicht mehr frei, ihr ganzes Leben! Eine kleinbürgeriche Kindheit und Jugend im "Dritten Reich"* [And they will never be free again their whole life long! A lower-class childhood and youth in the "Third Reich"]. Basel: Beltz, Weinheim.

Herbst, P. G. (1976). Totalitarian logics: The quest for certainty. In *Alternatives to hierarchies* (pp. 69–83). Lieden: Nifhoff.

Himmler, H. (1974). Posen address. In B. F. Smith & A. F. Peterson (Eds.), *H. Himmler: Secret Talks* (p. 169). Berlin. (Original speech given October, 1943).

Keilson, H. (1983). Wohin die Sprache nicht reicht [Where speech cannot enter]. *Psyche, 38,* 915–926.

Kepner, J. (1992). *Healing tasks for survivors.* Cleveland: Gestalt Institute Press.

Klein, H. (1986). Der Holocaust, seine Folgen und Bewältigungsmechanismen [The Holocaust, its results and the mechanisms of overcoming it]. In V. Faust (Ed.), *Angst—Furcht—Panik* [Fear—Terror—Panic]. (pp. 157–162). Stuttgart: Hippokrates.

Kegan, R. (1982). *The evolving self.* Cambridge, MA: Harvard University Press.

Kogan, E. (1950). *The theory and practice of hell: The German concentration camps and the system behind them.* New York: Farrar, Straus & Giroux.

Kogan, E. (1946). *Der SS-Staat: Das System der Deutscher Konzentrationslager* [The system of the German concentration camps.]

Kohlberg, L. (1969). Stage and sequence: The cognitive-developmental approach to socialization. In D. A. Guslin (Ed.), *Handbook of socialization: Theory and research.* Chicago: Rand-McNally.

Lerner, M. J. (1970). The desire for justice and reactions to victims. In J. Macaulay & L. Berkowitz (Eds.), *Altruism and helping behavior.* New York: Academic Press.

Lifton, R. J. (1986). *The Nazi doctors. Medical killing and the psychology of genocide.* New York: Basic Books.

Lockot, R. (1985). *Erinnern, Durcharbeiten* [Remembering, working through]. Frankfurt: Fischer.

Lockowandt, O. (1984). Die Erkenntnisquellen und Methoden der humanistischen Psychologie [The sources and methods of humanistic psychology]. In H. Petzold (Ed.), *Wege zum Menschen. Methoden und Persönlichkeiten moderner Psychotherapie* [Paths to the human being: Methods and personalities of modern psychotherapy]. (Vol. 1). S. Paderborn: Jungfermann.

Lohmann, H. M. (Ed.) (1983). *Das Unbehagen in der Psychoanalyse* [Psychoanalysis and its discontents]. Frankfurt: Qumran.

Mann, H. (1918). *Der Untertan* [The vassal]. Vienna: Wolff.

Massing, A., & Beushausen, U. (1986). *"Bis ins dritte und vierte Glied." Auswirkungen des Nationalsozialismus in den Familien* ["Unto the third and fourth generation": Effects of National Socialism in families]. *Psychosozial, 1,* 27–42.

McGoldrick, M., & Gerson, R. (1985). *Genograms in family assessment.* New York: Norton.

Meyer's Lexikon (1939). (Vol. 7). Leipzig: Bibliographisches Institut.

Miller, A. (1983). *Am anfang war erziehung.* Frankfurt: Suhrkamp. (English trans., *For your own good: Hidden cruelty in child-rearing and the roots of violence.* Trans. by H. and H. Hannum. New York: Farrar, Straus & Giroux, 1983.)

Milgram, S. (1975). *Obedience to authority.* New York: HarperCollins.

Mitscherlich, A. (1963). *Auf dem Weg zur vaterlosen Gesellschaft.* München: Piper. (English trans., *Society without the father.* New York: Harcourt Brace Jovanovich, 1969.)

Mitscherlich, A., & Mitscherlich, M. (1967). *Die Unfähigkeit zu trauern* [The inability to mourn]. München: Piper.

Mitscherlich, A., & Mitscherlich, M. (1970). *Eine deutsche Art zu lieben* [A German way of loving]. München: Piper.

Mitscherlich-Nielsen, M. (1978). *Das Ende der Vorbilder* [There are no models anymore]. München: S. Fischer.

Mitscherlich-Nielsen, M. (1979). Die Notwendigkeit zu trauern [The necessity of grieving]. *Psyche, 33,* 981–990.

Mitscherlich-Nielsen, M. (1981). Die Vergangenheit in der Gegenwart [The past in the present]. *Psyche, 35,* 611–615.

Montessori, M. M. (1987). *Children of the* [Dutch] *National Socialist Movement: Second Generation.* In *Children of the War.* Essays derived from a series of lectures, organized January–April, 1986 by the RIAGG Center/Old–West Amsterdam and South/New–West Amsterdam in collaboration with the Foundation ICODO in Utrecht (pp. 45–57). Utrecht–Amsterdam.

Nerin, W. F. (1986). *Family reconstruction: Long days' journey into light.* New York: Norton.

Nietzsche, F. (1883). *Thus spake Zarathustra.* Leipzig: E. W. Fritzsch.

Nietzsche, F. (1973). *Beyond good and evil.* London: Penguin. (Original work published 1886).

Nisan, M. (1986). Moral balance—a model for moral decisions. In W. Edelstein & G. Nunner-Winkler (Eds.), *Zur Bestimmung der Moral* [On the determination of morality]. (pp. 347–376). Frankfurt am Main: Suhrkamp.

NS-erbe: Das Thema der Nachkommen [National Socialist heritage: The theme of the descendants]. (1987, November 6). *Der Spiegel*, pp. 74–80.

Parin, P. (1978). *Der Widerspruch im Subjekt* [The contradiction in the subject]. Frankfurt: Syndikat/EVA.

Parin, P. (1983). *Der ängstliche Deutsche. Kleinbürger ohne Selbst-Bewusstsein* [The anxious German: Lower-class people without self-confidence]. In *Die Seele und die Politik* [The soul and politics]. A *Psychology Today* special volume published by the editors of *Psychology Today.* Basel: Beltz, Weinheim.

Parin, P. (1984). *Anpassung oder Widerstand* [Adjustment or resistance]. *Psyche, 38,* 627–635.

Parin, P., & Parin-Matthèy, G. (1982). Das obligat unglückliche Verhältnis der Psychoanalytiker zur Macht [The necessarily unfortunate relationship of the psychoanalyst to power]. In H. M. Lohmann (1983). *Das Unbehagen in der Psychoanalyze* [Psychoanalysis and its discontents]. Frankfurt: Qumran.

Pehle, W. H. (Ed.). (1990). *Der historische Ort des Nationalsozialismus. Annäherungen* [The location of National Socialism in history: Attempts]. Frankfurt am Main.

Petzold, H. (Ed.). (1985). *Leiblichkeit* [Bodiliness]. Paderborn: Jungfermann.

Peukert, D., & Reulecke, J. (Eds.). (1981). *Die Reihen fast geschlossen. Beiträge zur Geschichte des Alltags unterm Nationalsozialismus* [The ranks closed: Contributions to the history of daily life under National Socialism]. Wuppertal: Hammer.

Piaget, J. (1926). *The language and thought of the child.* New York: Routledge & Kegan Paul.

Psychoanalyse unter Hitler—Dokumentation einer Kontroverse [Psychoanalysis under Hitler—the documentation of a controversy]. Published by the editors of the journal *Psyche,* Frankfurt am Main, April 1984.

Rosenfeld, H. (1984). Narzissmus und Aggression [Narcissism and aggression]. In *Protokolle zur Arbeitstsagung der DPV vom 21.–24. 11,* 65–84.

Rosenkötter, L. (1979). Vergangenheitsbewältigung in Psychoanalysen [Overcoming the past in psychoanalyses]. *Psyche, 33,* 1024–1038.

Rosenkötter, L. (1981). Die Idealbildung in der Generationsfolge [The formation of ideals in the sequence of generations]. *Psyche 7*(35), 593–599.

Segev, T. (1989). *Soldiers of evil: The commandants of the Nazi concentration camps.* New York: McGraw-Hill.

Senfft, H. (1990). *Ein Blick hinter die Fassaden des "Historikerstreits"* [A glimpse behind the facade of the historians dispute]. Hamburg: Hamburger Stiftung für Socialgeschichte des Zwanzigsten Jahrhunderts.

Sereny, G. (1974). *Into that darkness: From mercy-killing to mass murder.* New York: McGraw-Hill.

Sichrovsky, P. (1985). *Wir wissen nicht was morgen wird, wir wissen wohl, was gestern war. Junge Juden in Deutschland und Österreich.* Köln: Kiepenheuer & Witsch. (English trans., *Strangers in their own land: Young Jews in Germany and Austria today.* New York: Basic Books, 1986.)

Sichrovsky, P. (1987). *Schuldig Geboren. Kinder aus Nazifamilien.* Köln: Kiepenheuer & Witsch. (English trans., *Born guilty: Children of Nazi families.* Trans. by J. Steinberg. New York: Basic Books, 1988.)

Sigal, J. et al. (1971, Nov. 28–Dec. 4). *Some second-generation effects of survival of the Nazi persecution.* Paper presented at the World Congress of Psychiatry, Mexico City.

Simenauer, E. (1982). Die zweite Generation—Danach. Die Wiederkehr der Verfolgermentalität in Psychoanalysen [The second generation—afterward: The return of the persecution mentality in psychoanalyses]. In *Die Wiederkehr von Krieg und Verfolgung in Psychoanalysen* [The return of war and persecution in psychoanalyses]. [Contributions to the Conference of the Central European Psychoanalytic Organizations in Bamberg, March 30 to April 4].

Simon, F. B., & Stierlin, H., (1984). *Die Sprache der Familientherapie. Ein Vokabular* [The language of family therapy: A vocabulary]. Stuttgart: Klett-Cotta.

Spence, D. P. (1983). The paradox of denial. In S. Breznitz (Ed.), *The denial of stress* (pp. 103–123). Madison, CT: International Universities Press.

Sperling, E., Massing, A., Georgi, J., Reich, G., and Wöbbe-Mönks, E. (1982). *Die Mehrgenerationen-Familientherapie* [Family therapy with multiple generations]. Göttingen: Vandenhoeck & Ruprecht.

Staub, E. (1989). *The roots of evil: The origins of genocide and other group violence.* Cambridge: Cambridge University Press.

Stierlin, H. (1975). *Adolf Hitler—Familienperspektiven.* Frankfurt am Main: Suhrkamp. (English tran., *Adolf Hitler: A family perspective.* New York: Psychohistory Press, 1976.)

Stierlin, H. (1978). *Delegation und Familie* [Delegation and family]. Frankfurt am Main: Suhrkamp.

Stierlin, H. (1980). *Eltern und Kinder. Das Drama von Trennung und Versöhnung.* Frankfurt am Main: Suhrkamp. (English trans., *Separating parents and adolescents: Individuation in the family.* New York: Jason Aronson, 1981.)

Stone, L. (1981). Notes on the noninterpretive elements in the psychoanalytic situation and process. *Journal of the American Psychoanalytic Association, 29,* 89–118.

Stresemann, W. (1987). *Wie konnte das geschehen?* [How could that happen?]. Berlin: Allstein.

Stürmer, M. (1986, May) *Suche nach der verlorenen Erinnerung* [Searching for the lost memory]. *Das Parlament,* pp. 17–24.

Tec, N. (1986). *When light pierced the darkness: Christian rescue of Jews in Nazi-occupied Poland.* New York: Oxford University Press.

Tournier, M. (1972). *The ogre.* (B. Bray, Trans.). Garden City, New York: Doubleday.

Vogel, F. (1974). Der Mensch und die moderne Genetik [Man and modern genetics]. In *Meyers Enzyklopädisches Lexikon* (Vol. 10, pp. 40–54), Mannheim: Bibliographische Institut.

Vogt, R. (1986). *Psychoanalyse unter Hitler—Psychoanalyse heute* [Psychoanalysis under Hitler: Psychoanalysis today]. *Psyche, 40,* 435–440.

Wangh, M. (1985). Die Herrschaft des Thanatos [The rule of Thanatos]. In *Zur Psychoanalyse der nuklearen Drohung* [On the psychoanalysis of the nuclear threat]. Göttingen: Vandenhoeck & Ruprecht.

Westernhagen, D. von (1987). *Die Kinder der Täter. Das Dritte Reich und die Generation danach* [The children of the perpetrators: The Third Reich and the subsequent generation]. München: Kösel.

Westernhagen, D. von (1988). Die Kinder der Täter. Deutsche Geschichte als Familiendrama: Selbstzweifel, Zwiespältigkeit, Hass und Schuldgefühle [The children of the perpetrators. German history as family drama: Self-doubt, deception, hate, and feelings of guilt]. *Die Zeit, 14,* 17–20.

White, H. (1991). *Metahistory. Die historische Einbildungskraft im 19. Jahrhundert in Europa.* [Metahistory: The historical imagination in nineteenth century Europe]. Frankfurt am Main.

Wiesenthal, S. (1976). *The sunflower: With a symposium.* Jerusalem: Schocken.

Wolff, C. (1979). *Kindheitsmuster* [Model of childhood]. Darmstadt: Luchterhand.

Zimbardo, P. G., with Banks, W. C., Haney, C., & Jaffe, D. (1973, April 8). The mind is a formidable jailer: A Pirandellian prison. *The New York Times Magazine,* p. 36.

INDEX

O

Obedience: ethic of, 150, 223, 226,
230; and National Socialist
complex, 122–123; necessity for,
167
Odysseus, 40
Old Fighters, 76–77, 79
Organisation Todt, 91
Parents: confronting Nazism of,
49–60; remembering by, 150–151;
role of, in Nazi past, 148–151; tasks
of, 146–148. *See also* Fathers;
Women
Patience, lack of, 113
Patients: National Socialist complex
for, 120–129; silence of, 27–29
Paul, 214
Perls, F. S., 13, 21
Perpetrators: aspects of morality of,
195–208; background on, 195–196;
children of, 169–170; conclusions
on, 207–208; confronting history
of, 49–60; discussion of, 201–207;
fathers as, 31–48; findings on, 198–
201; method of studying, 196–198
Perseus, xvii
Personality split, and guilt, 222–223
Peter, 214
Peukert, D., 97, 105, 107–108
Piaget, J., 144
Picker, R., xxiii, 11
Prisoner of war: experiences of,
223–224; father as, 140; perpetrator as, 35–39, 43; shooting of,
200
Projection: and evil, xv–xvi; and guilt,
212–213; and Nazi past, 167
Psychic illness: and history, 63, 69;
and National Socialist complex,
124–129; and Nazi past, 175–176;
among widows, 228
Psychotherapy: boundaries in, 14, 15,
137; and ethics, 133–136, 169;
healing from, 230–231; and nazi
past, 11–29, 103–106; and storytelling xvii
Purification, wish for, 220

R

Racial hygiene, in worldview, 97, 100,
101, 103–105, 106, 107
Racism, in worldview, 101–103, 107
Realist, and idealist, 129
Reality: fear of, 172; issue of, in psy-
choanalysis, 61–72; mistrust of,
138–139; unbearable, 65, 68, 70
Reich, W., 13
Reimer, U., 97, 98
Remembering: and healing, 166, 169;
by parents, 150–151; work of,
163–170
Reparations, work of, 159, 216–217
Repentance, and guilt, 213–214
Repetition compulsion: and depres-
sion, 221–222, 223, 224; and
reality, 62
Repression: extreme, 180; impact of,
88–89, 90–91
Resignation, and National Socialist
complex, 132
Responsibility: confronting, 50; con-
necting with, 170; and moral con-
flict, 202–203; and National
Socialist complex, 126–128;
reducing, 150, 167; and values, 21
Reulecke, J., 97, 105, 107–108
Reunification: experiencing, 7–8,
190, 191; and national identity,
163–170
Riemeck, R., 216
Robert's family, 99–101
Rohm, E., 149
Rosenfeld, H., 68
Rosenkötter, L., 64, 104
SA (*Sturmabteilung,* storm troopers):
grandfather in, 102; and Nazi past,
22, 48, 58–59
Salm, H., xiii–xiv, 49, 230
Satir, V., 56n, 73, 183–184
Scharf, K., 217
Schiller, J., 13, 42
Schleyer, 160
Schlippe, G. von, xxvi, 209, 230
Schmidt, C. J., xviii, xxv, 3
Schumacher, K., 127